My Sister, the Cat

1

story & art
senko

Contents

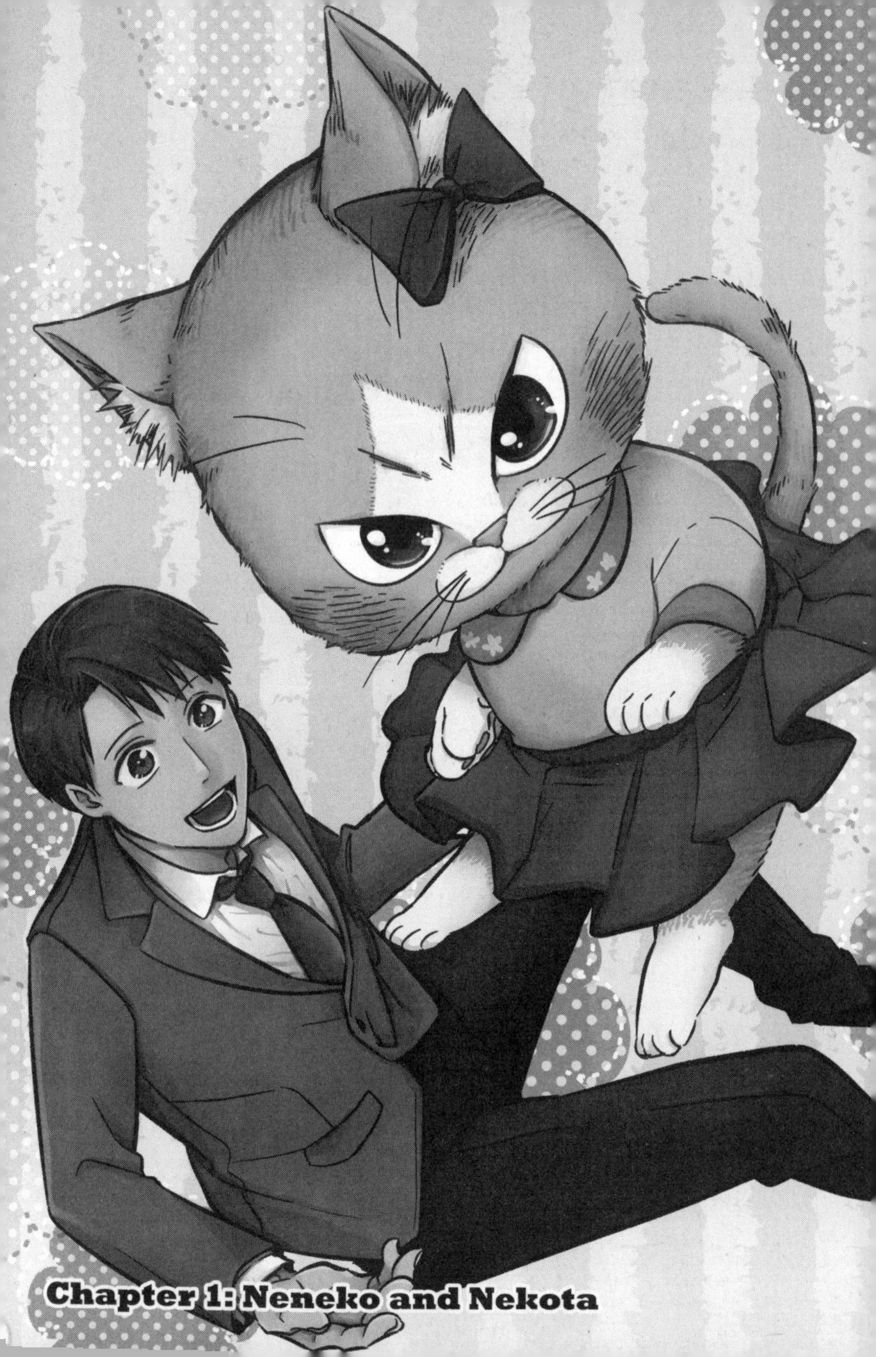
Chapter 1: Neneko and Nekota

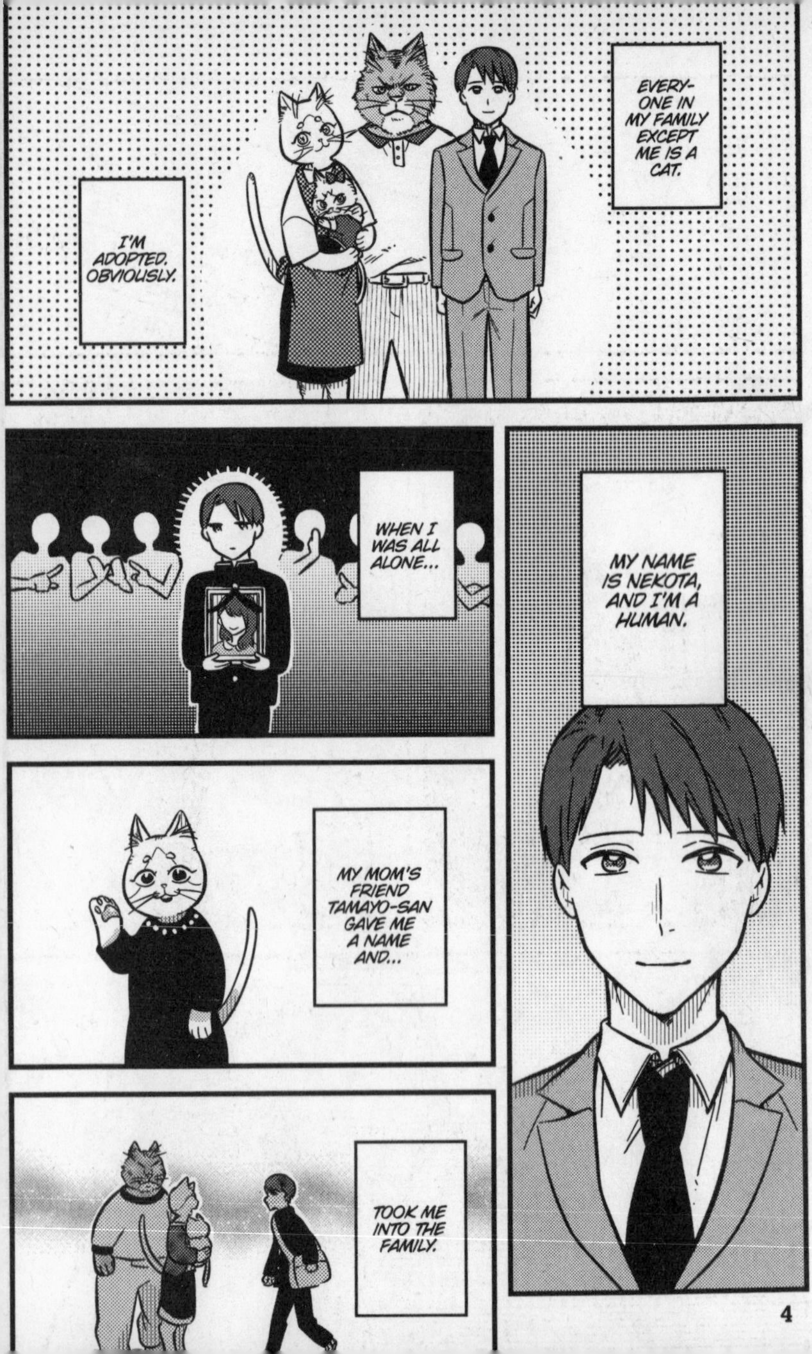
EVERY-ONE IN MY FAMILY EXCEPT ME IS A CAT.
I'M ADOPTED. OBVIOUSLY.
MY NAME IS NEKOTA, AND I'M A HUMAN.
WHEN I WAS ALL ALONE...
MY MOM'S FRIEND TAMAYO-SAN GAVE ME A NAME AND...
TOOK ME INTO THE FAMILY.

SIGH...

MIDTERM EXAMS		
SUBJECT	CONTEMPORARY WRITINGS	ANCIENT WRITINGS
	90 POINTS	

I NEED TO STUDY MORE.

MY SCORES FELL.

I'M HOME!

KA-CLACK

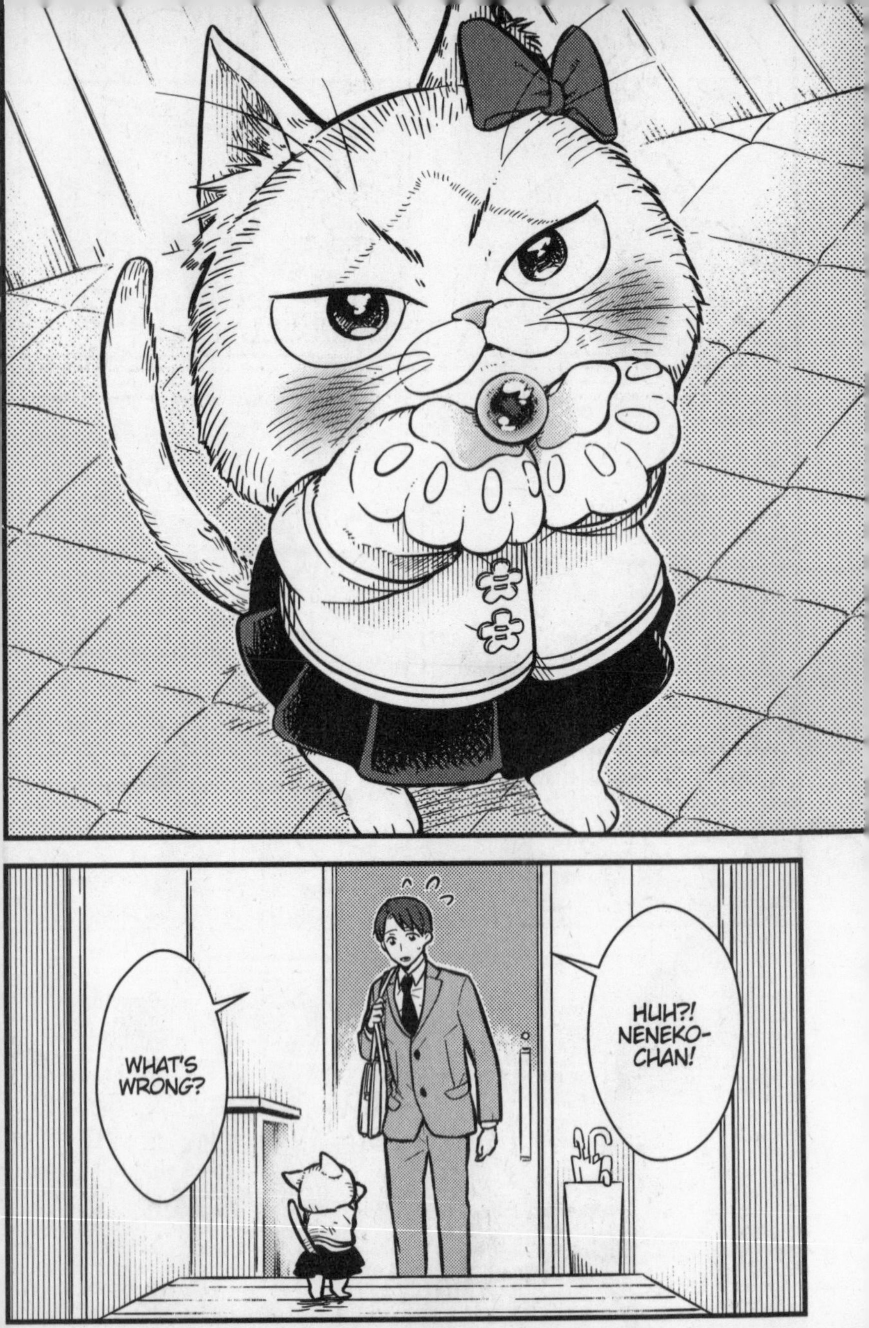
HUH?! NENEKO-CHAN!
WHAT'S WRONG?

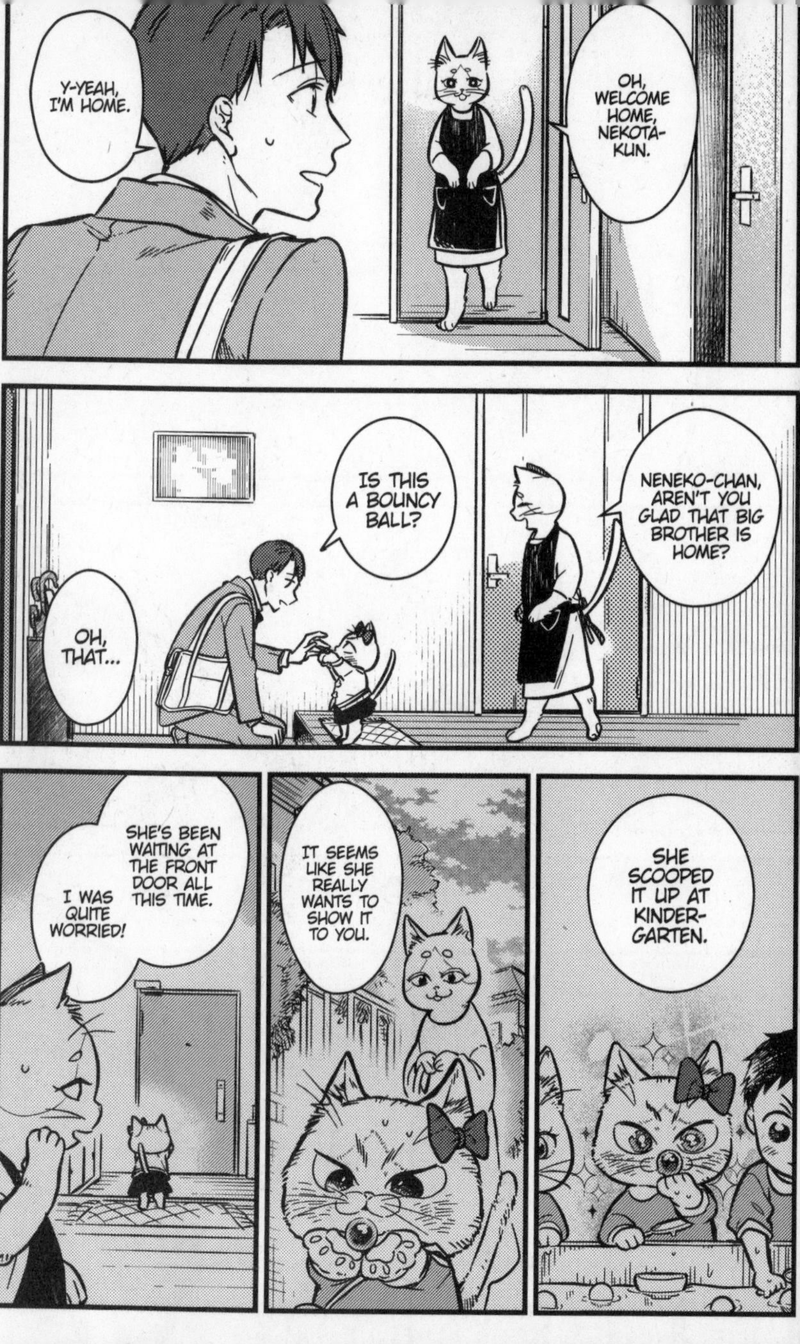
OH, WELCOME HOME, NEKOTA-KUN.
Y-YEAH, I'M HOME.
NENEKO-CHAN, AREN'T YOU GLAD THAT BIG BROTHER IS HOME?
IS THIS A BOUNCY BALL?
OH, THAT...
SHE SCOOPED IT UP AT KINDER-GARTEN.
IT SEEMS LIKE SHE REALLY WANTS TO SHOW IT TO YOU.
SHE'S BEEN WAITING AT THE FRONT DOOR ALL THIS TIME.
I WAS QUITE WORRIED!

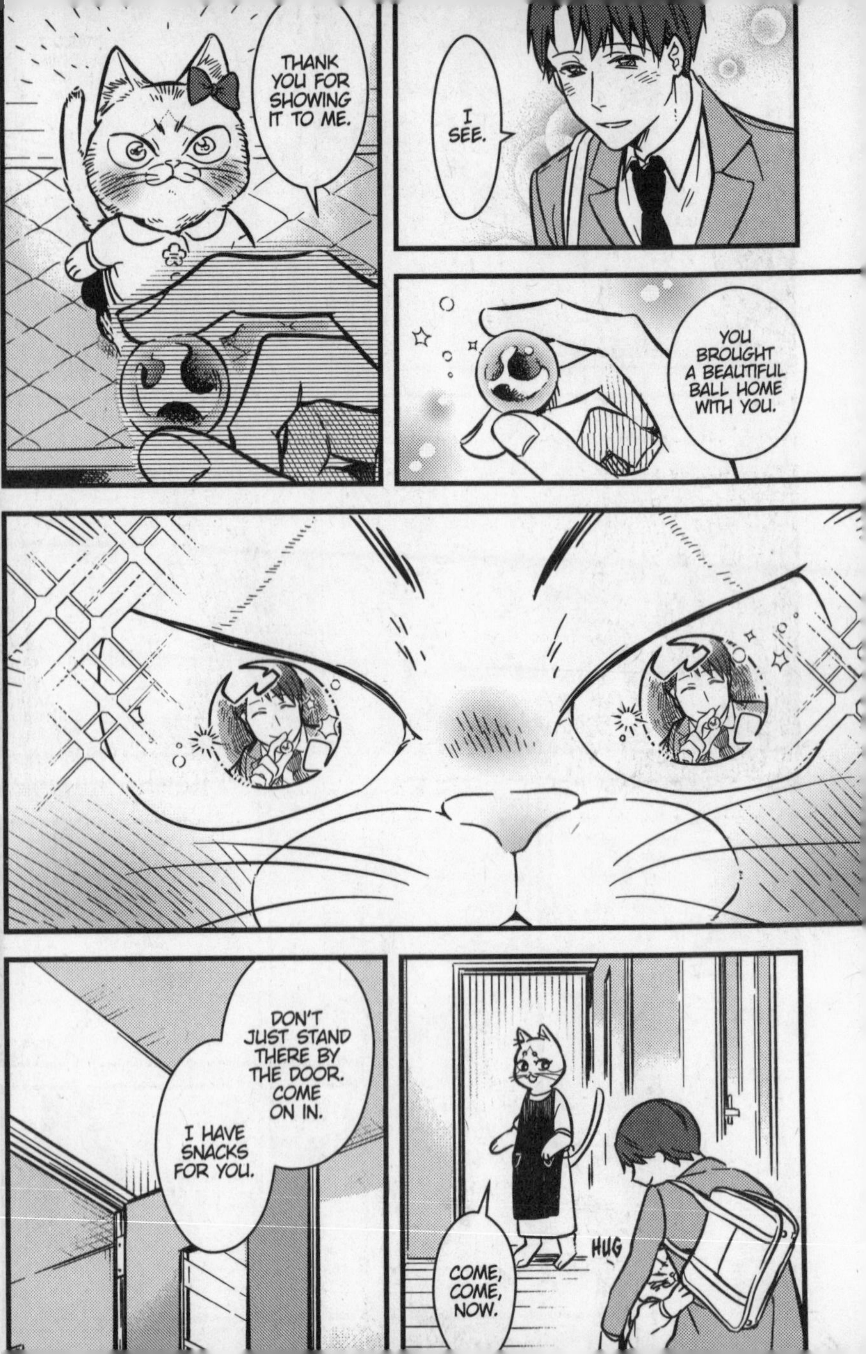
I SEE.
YOU BROUGHT A BEAUTIFUL BALL HOME WITH YOU.
THANK YOU FOR SHOWING IT TO ME.
COME, COME, NOW.
HUG
DON'T JUST STAND THERE BY THE DOOR. COME ON IN.
I HAVE SNACKS FOR YOU.

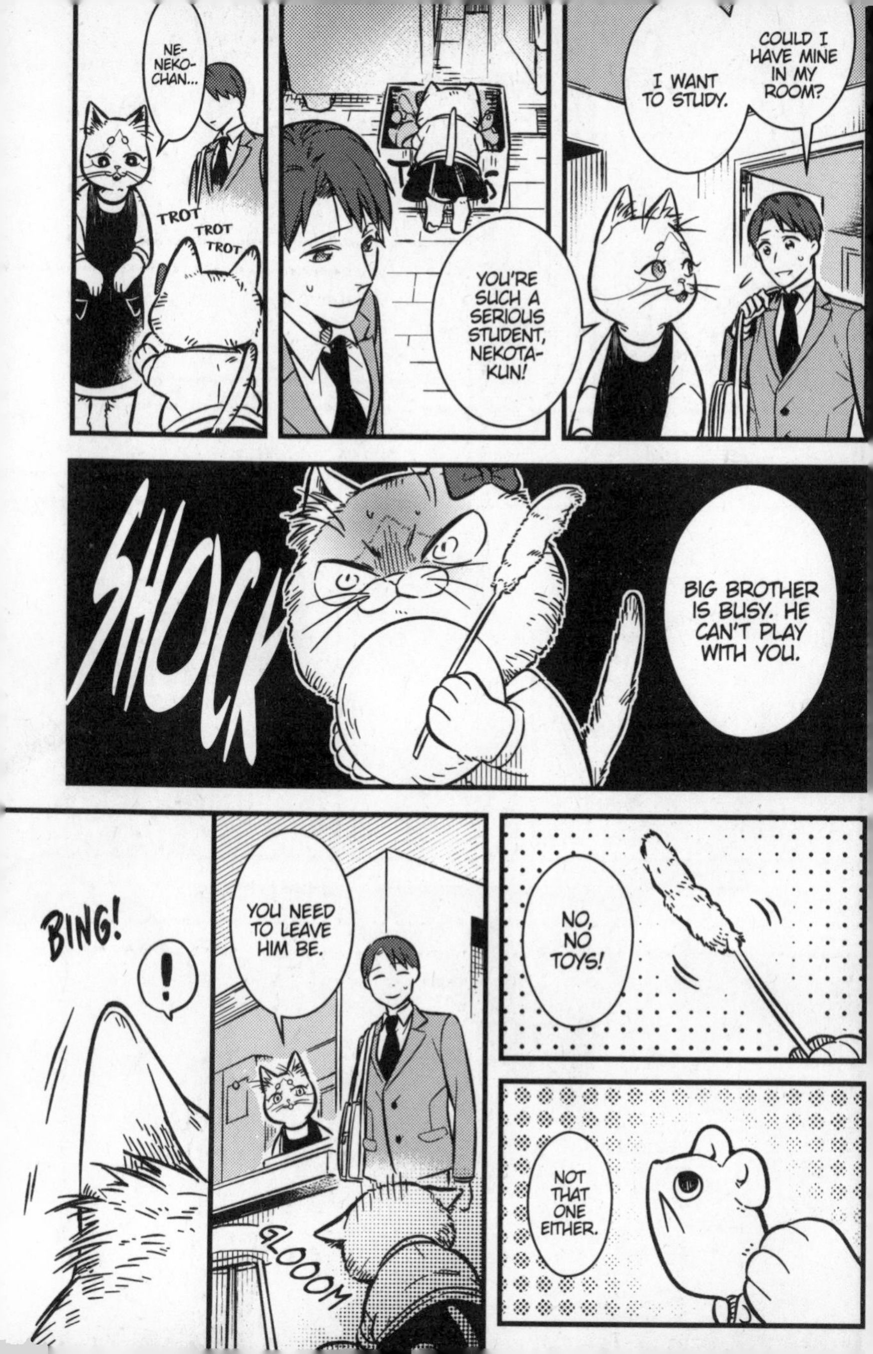
COULD I HAVE MINE IN MY ROOM?
I WANT TO STUDY.
YOU'RE SUCH A SERIOUS STUDENT, NEKOTA-KUN!
NE-NEKO-CHAN...
TROT TROT TROT
BIG BROTHER IS BUSY. HE CAN'T PLAY WITH YOU.
SHOCK
NO, NO TOYS!
NOT THAT ONE EITHER.
YOU NEED TO LEAVE HIM BE.
GLOOOM
BING!
!

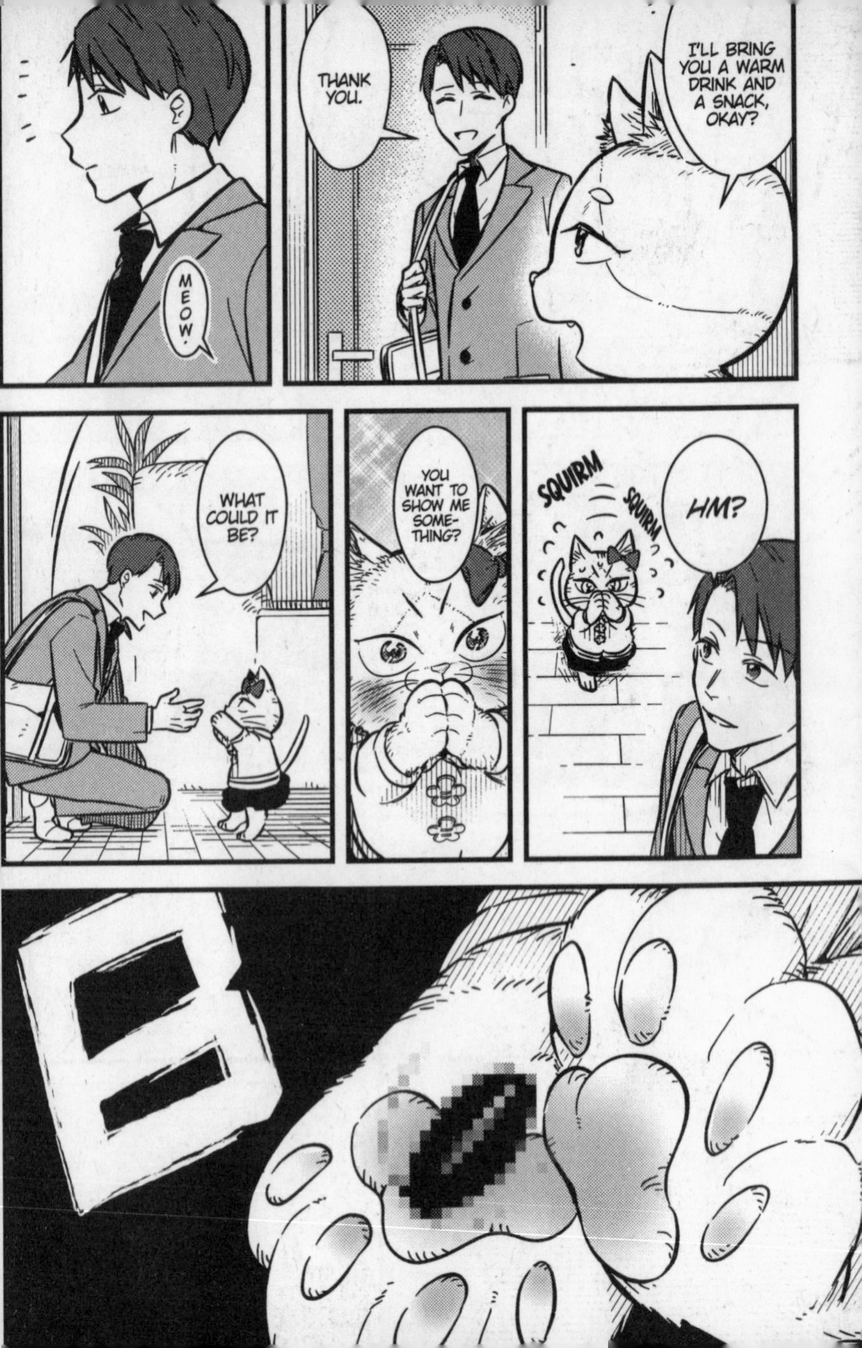
I'LL BRING YOU A WARM DRINK AND A SNACK, OKAY?
THANK YOU.
MEOW.
HM?
SQUIRM
SQUIRM
YOU WANT TO SHOW ME SOME-THING?
WHAT COULD IT BE?

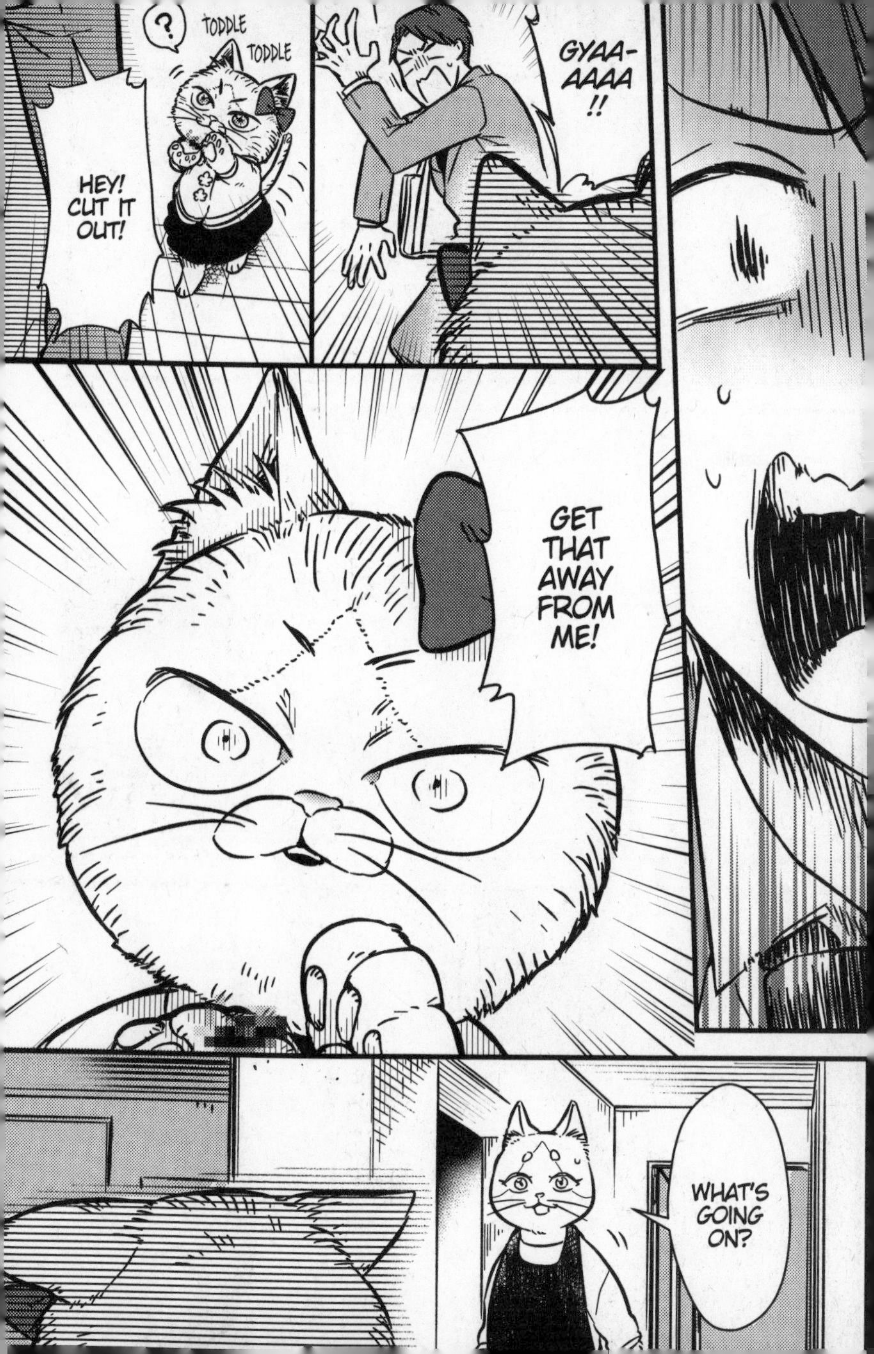
GYAA-AAAA !!
TODDLE TODDLE
?
HEY! CUT IT OUT!
GET THAT AWAY FROM ME!
WHAT'S GOING ON?

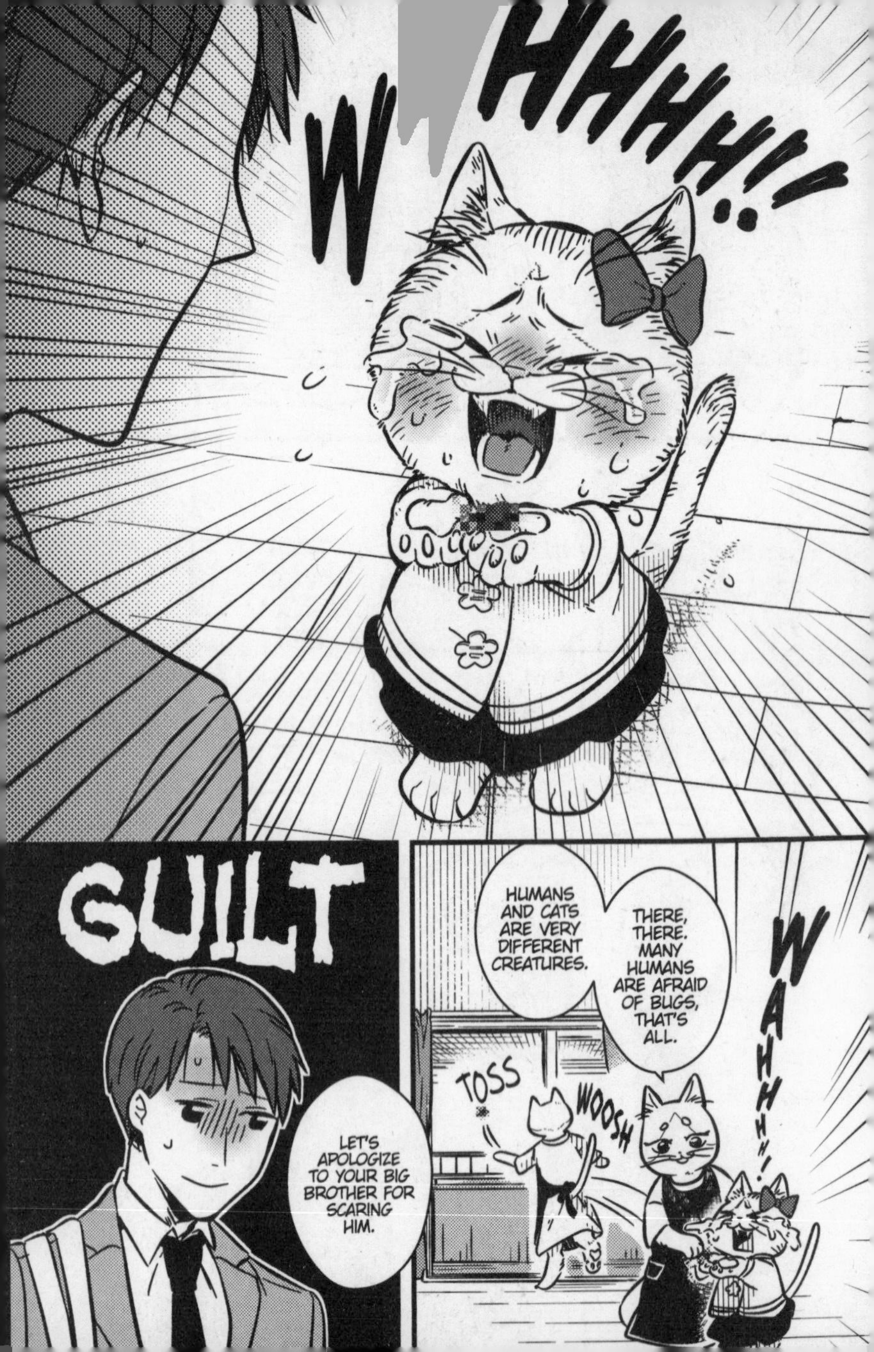
WHHHHH!!
WAHHHH!
THERE, THERE. MANY HUMANS ARE AFRAID OF BUGS, THAT'S ALL.
HUMANS AND CATS ARE VERY DIFFERENT CREATURES.
WOOSH
TOSS
GUILT
LET'S APOLOGIZE TO YOUR BIG BROTHER FOR SCARING HIM.

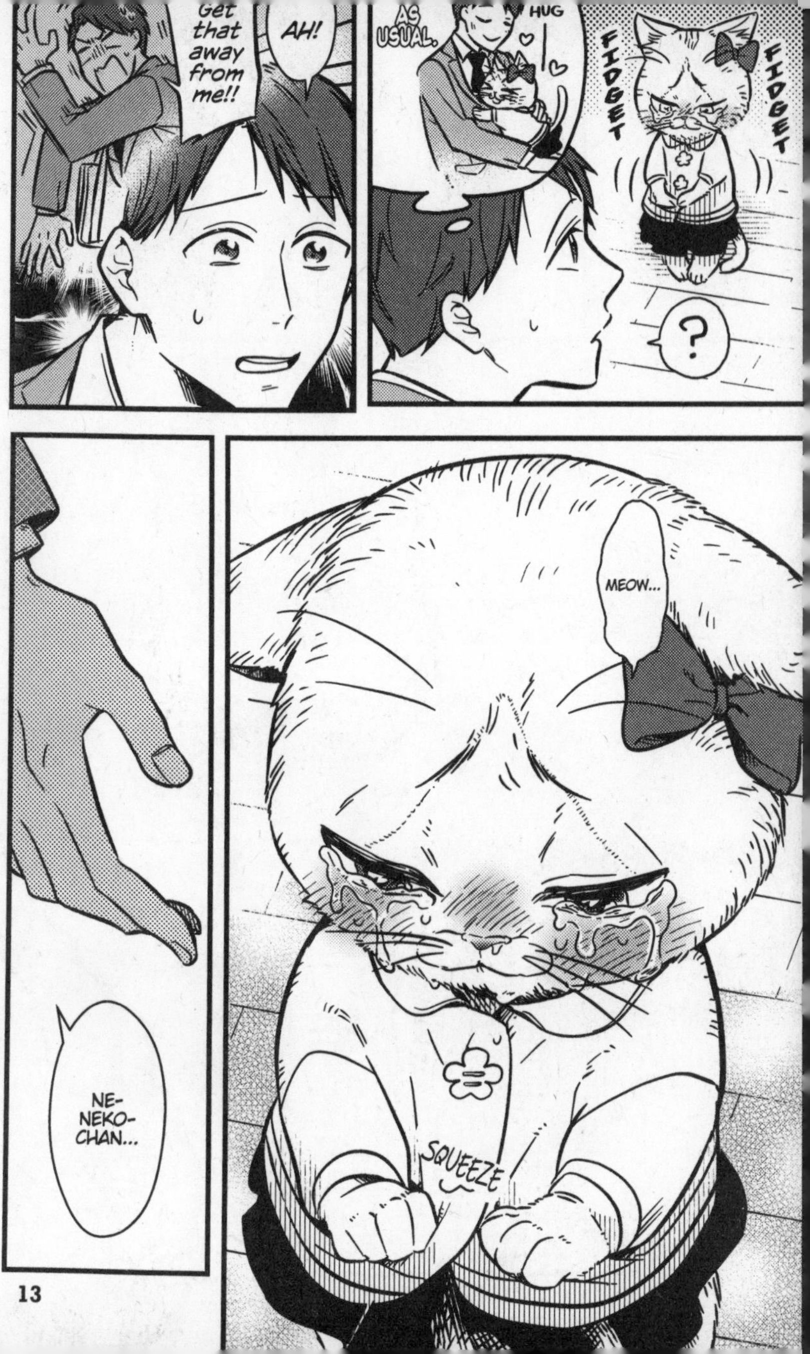
FIDGET
FIDGET
HUG
AS USUAL.
?
AH!
Get that away from me!!
MEOW...
SQUEEZE
NE-NEKO-CHAN...

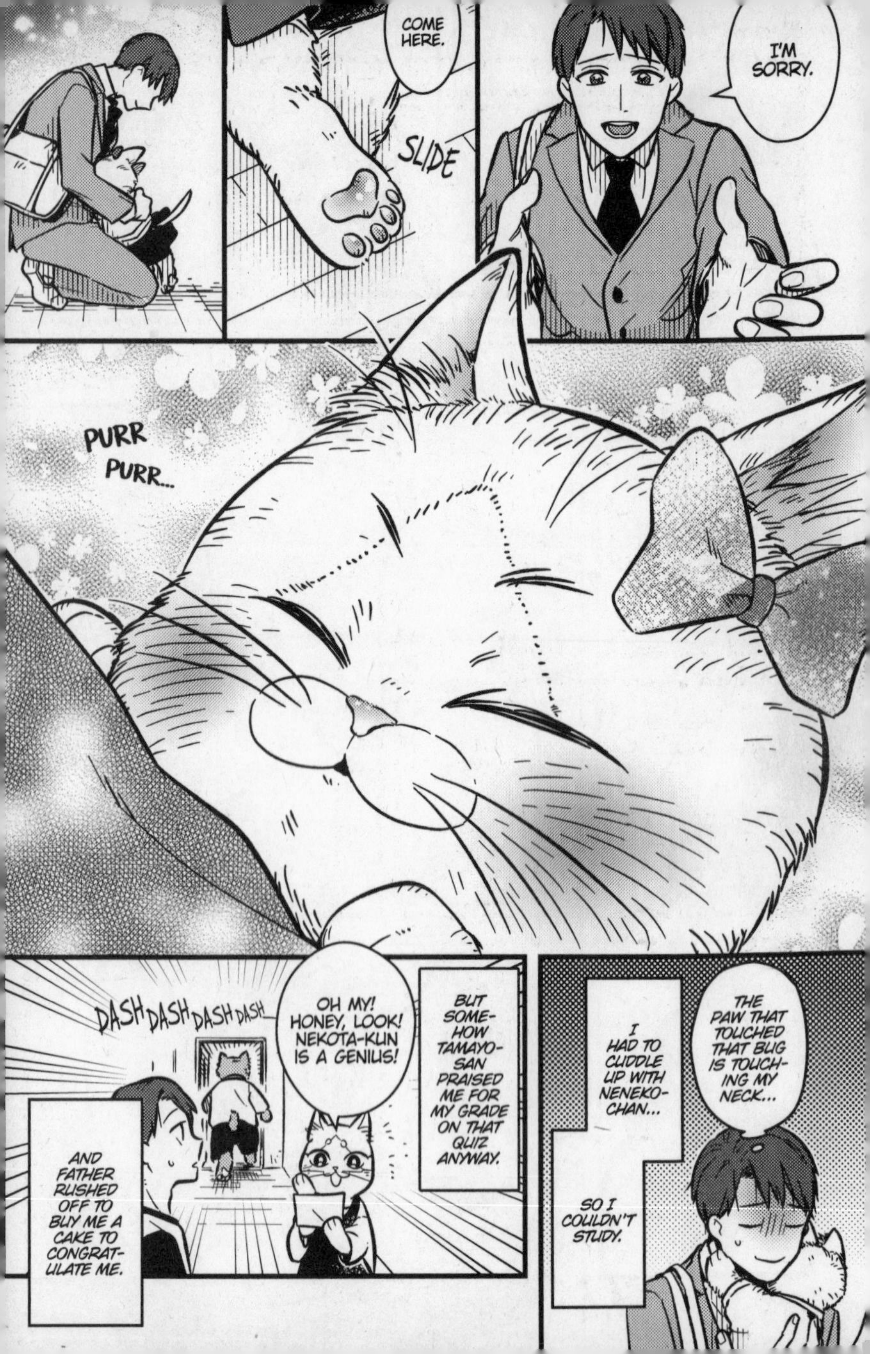
I'M SORRY.
COME HERE.
SLIDE
PURR PURR...
THE PAW THAT TOUCHED THAT BUG IS TOUCHING MY NECK...
I HAD TO CUDDLE UP WITH NENEKO-CHAN...
SO I COULDN'T STUDY.
BUT SOMEHOW TAMAYO-SAN PRAISED ME FOR MY GRADE ON THAT QUIZ ANYWAY.
OH MY! HONEY, LOOK! NEKOTA-KUN IS A GENIUS!
DASH DASH DASH DASH
AND FATHER RUSHED OFF TO BUY ME A CAKE TO CONGRATULATE ME.

Extra 1

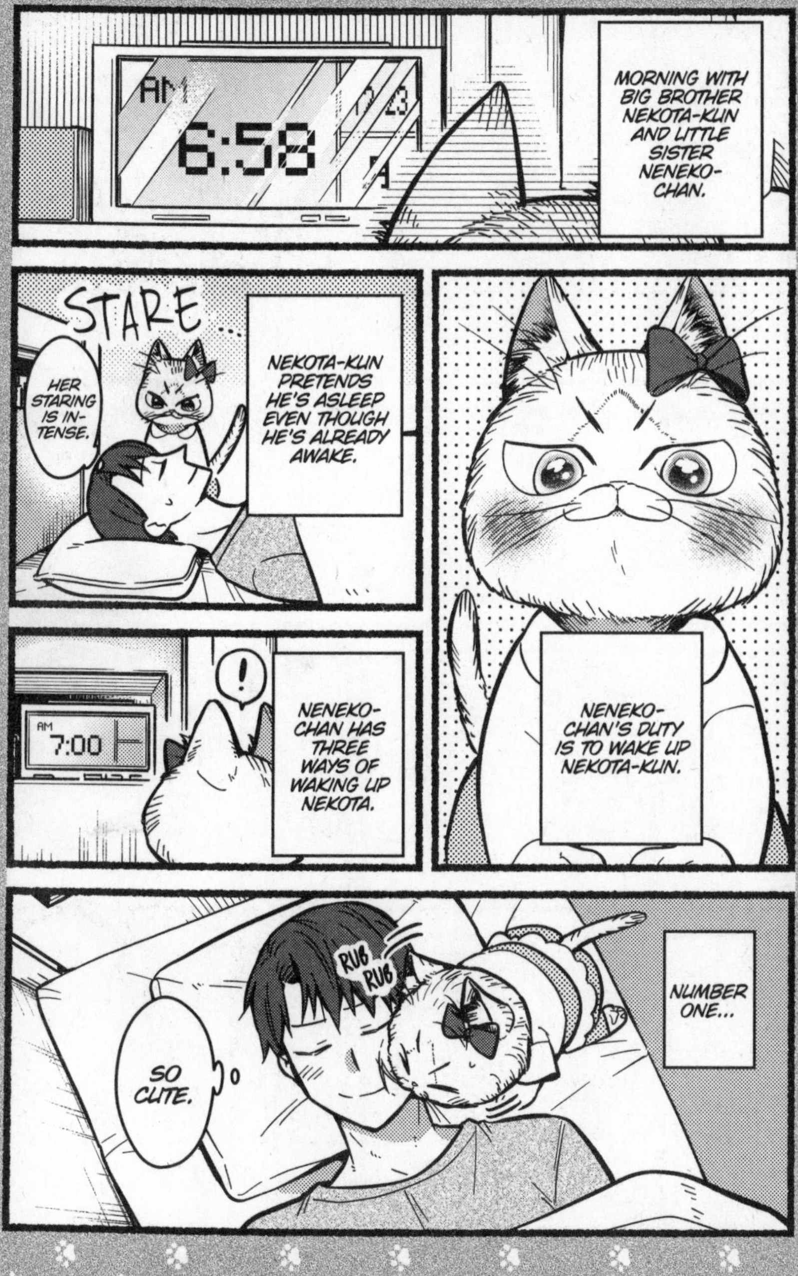
AM
6:58
MORNING WITH BIG BROTHER NEKOTA-KUN AND LITTLE SISTER NENEKO-CHAN.
NENEKO-CHAN'S DUTY IS TO WAKE UP NEKOTA-KUN.
NEKOTA-KUN PRETENDS HE'S ASLEEP EVEN THOUGH HE'S ALREADY AWAKE.
STARE
HER STARING IS IN-TENSE.
NENEKO-CHAN HAS THREE WAYS OF WAKING UP NEKOTA.
!
AM
7:00
NUMBER ONE...
RUB RUB
SO CUTE.

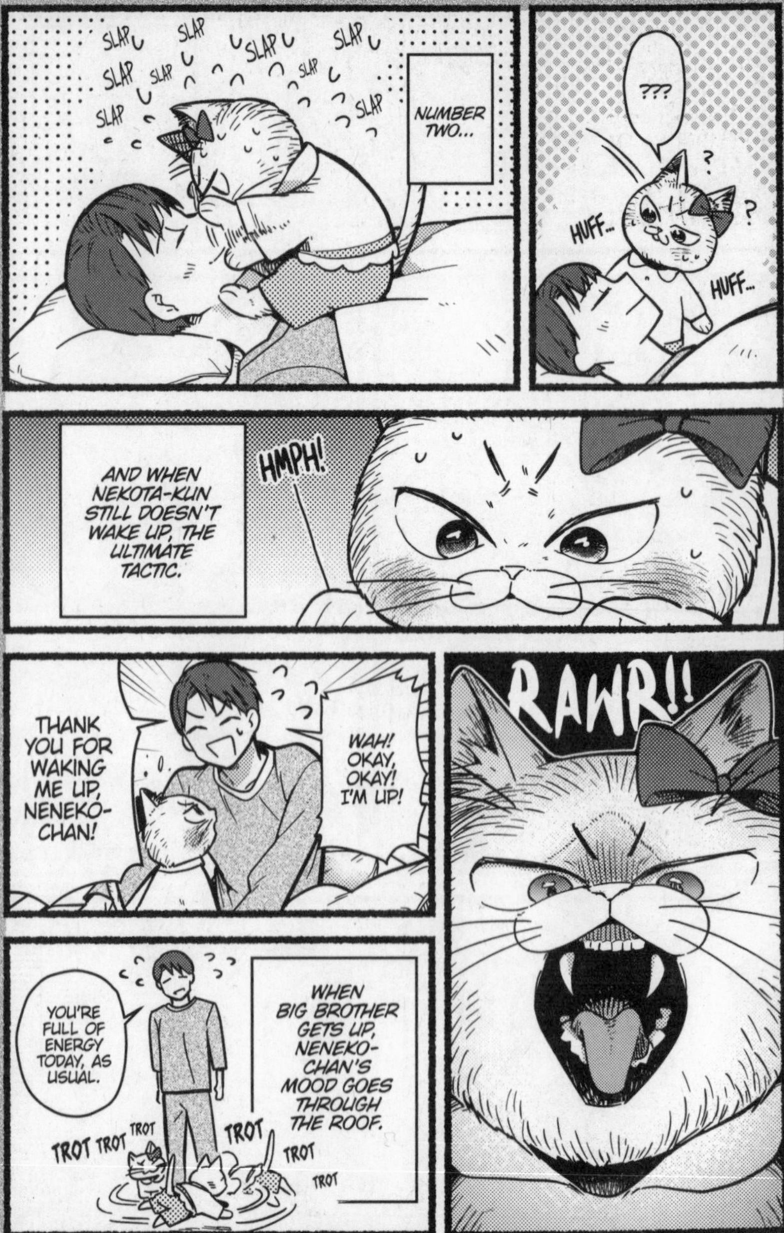
???
?
?
HUFF...
HUFF...
NUMBER TWO...
SLAP
SLAP
SLAP
SLAP
SLAP
SLAP
SLAP
SLAP
SLAP
AND WHEN NEKOTA-KUN STILL DOESN'T WAKE UP, THE ULTIMATE TACTIC.
HMPH!
RAWR!!
WAH! OKAY, OKAY! I'M UP!
THANK YOU FOR WAKING ME UP, NENEKO-CHAN!
WHEN BIG BROTHER GETS UP, NENEKO-CHAN'S MOOD GOES THROUGH THE ROOF.
YOU'RE FULL OF ENERGY TODAY, AS USUAL.
TROT
TROT
TROT
TROT
TROT
TROT
TROT

Chapter 2: Neneko and the Video Call

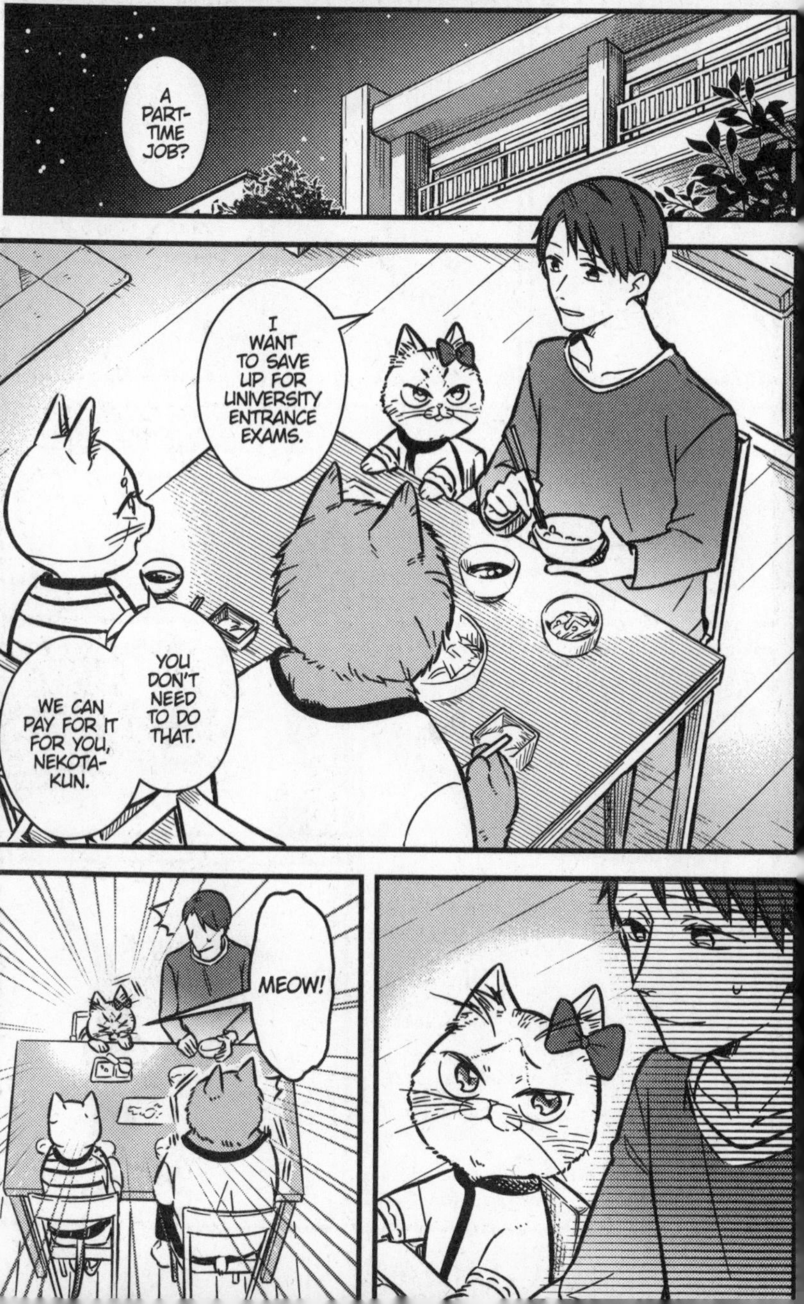
A PART-TIME JOB?
I WANT TO SAVE UP FOR UNIVERSITY ENTRANCE EXAMS.
YOU DON'T NEED TO DO THAT.
WE CAN PAY FOR IT FOR YOU, NEKOTA-KUN.
MEOW!

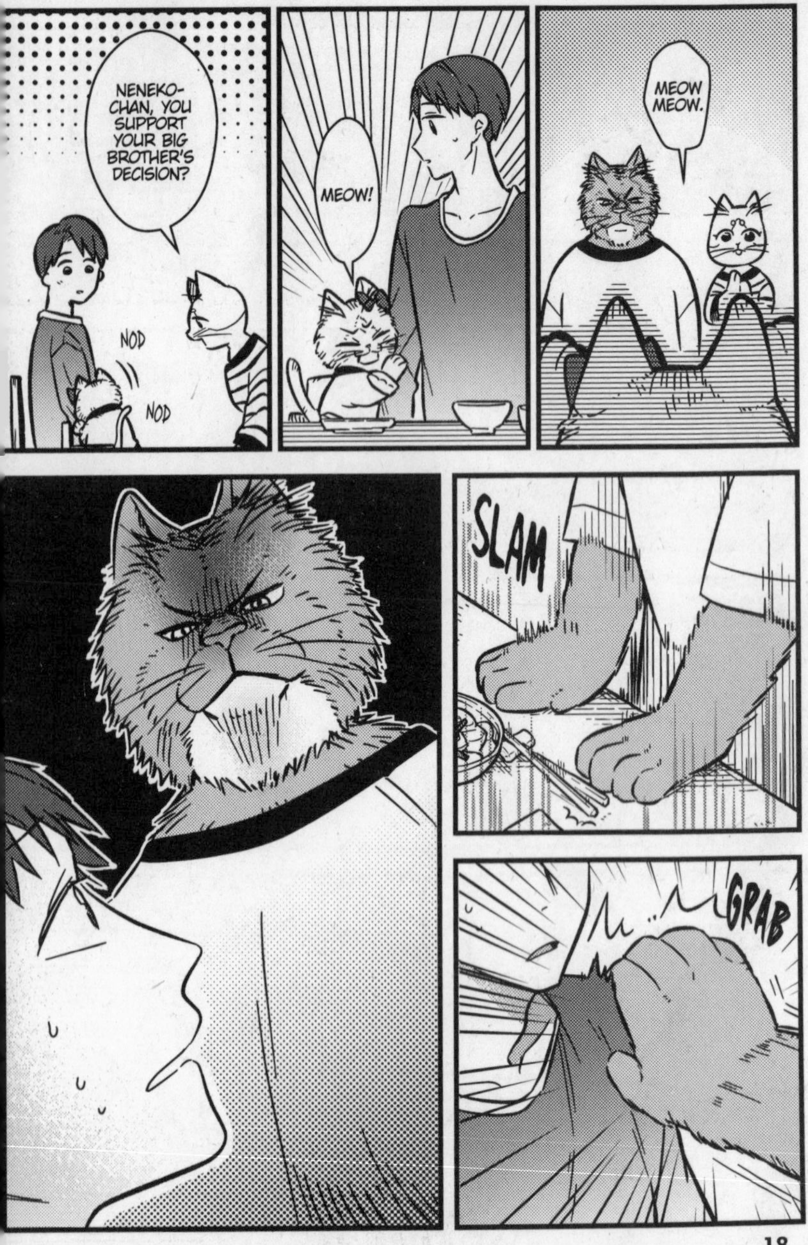
MEOW MEOW.
MEOW!
NENEKO-CHAN, YOU SUPPORT YOUR BIG BROTHER'S DECISION?
NOD
NOD
SLAM
GRAB

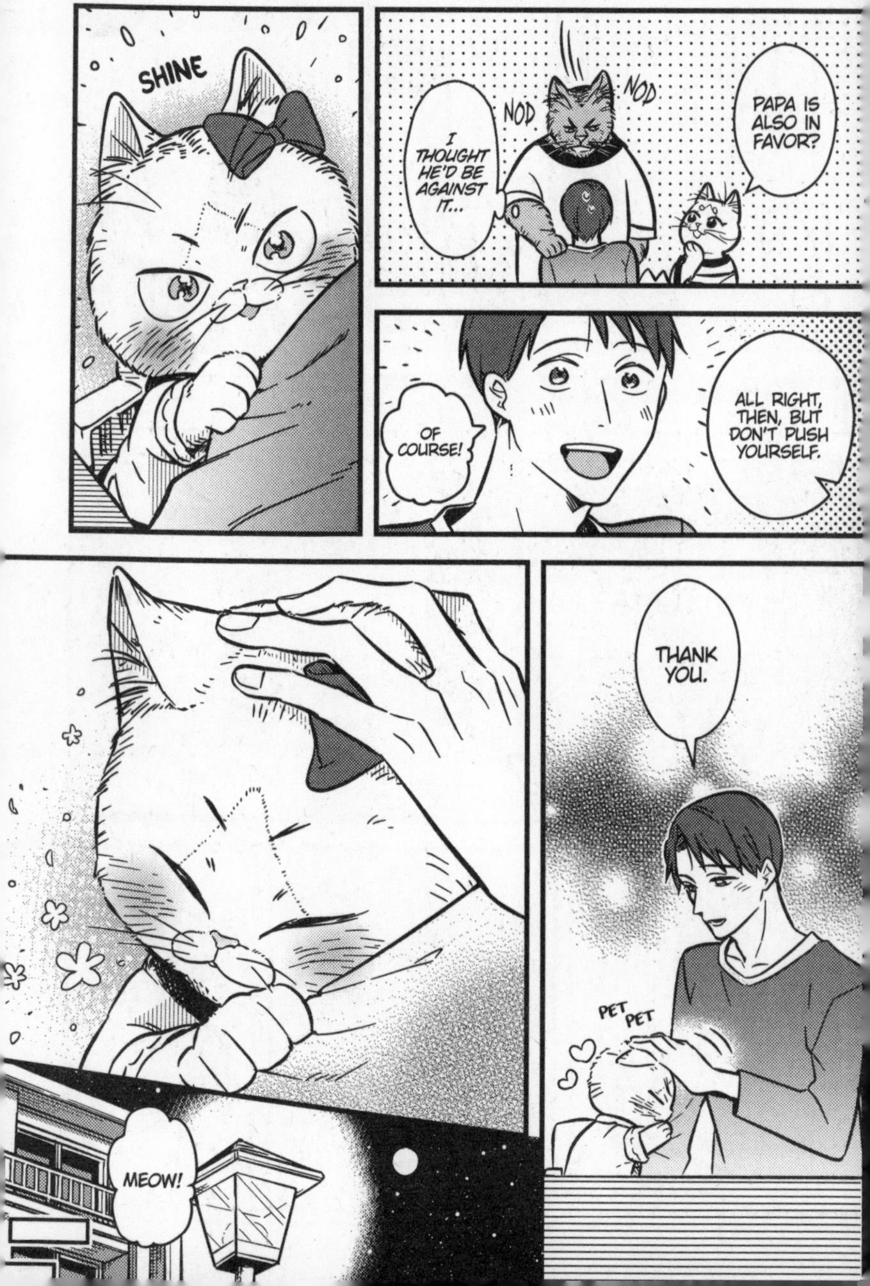
PAPA IS ALSO IN FAVOR?
NOD
NOD
I THOUGHT HE'D BE AGAINST IT...
ALL RIGHT, THEN, BUT DON'T PUSH YOURSELF.
OF COURSE!
SHINE
THANK YOU.
PET PET
MEOW!

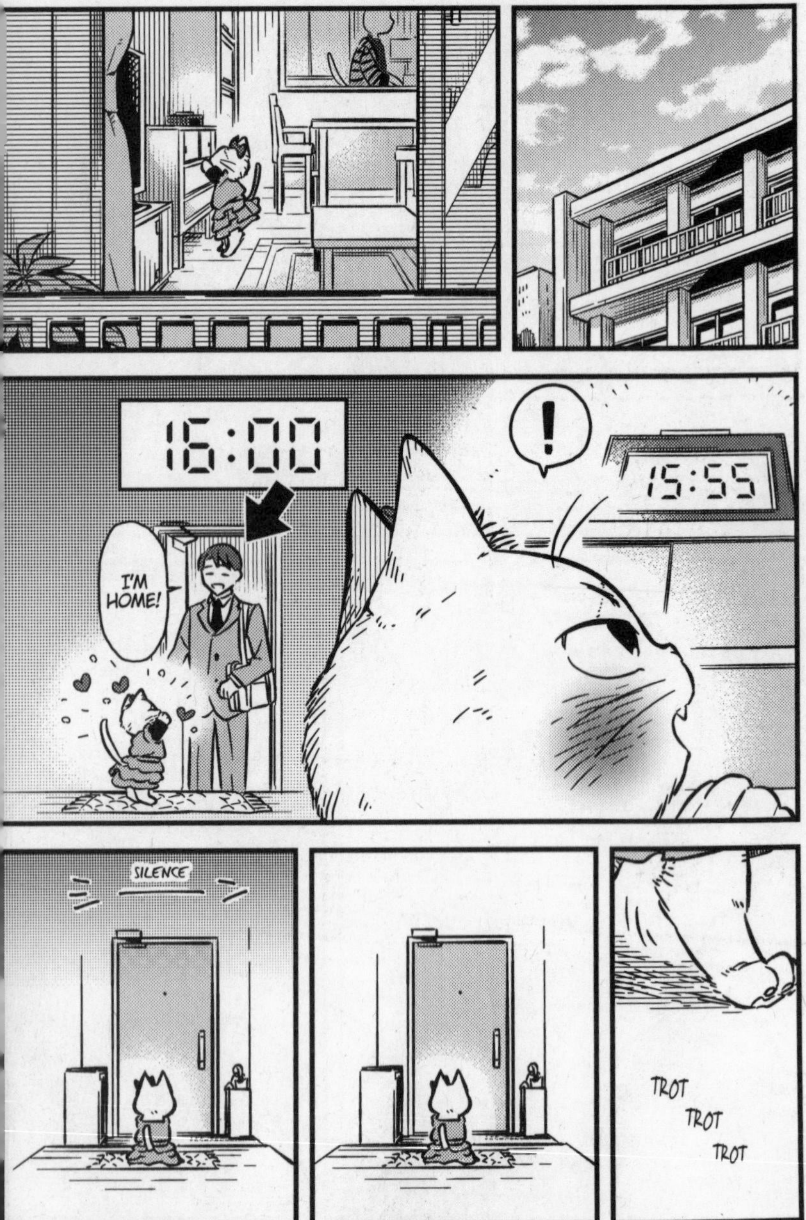
!
15:55
16:00
I'M HOME!
TROT
TROT
TROT
SILENCE

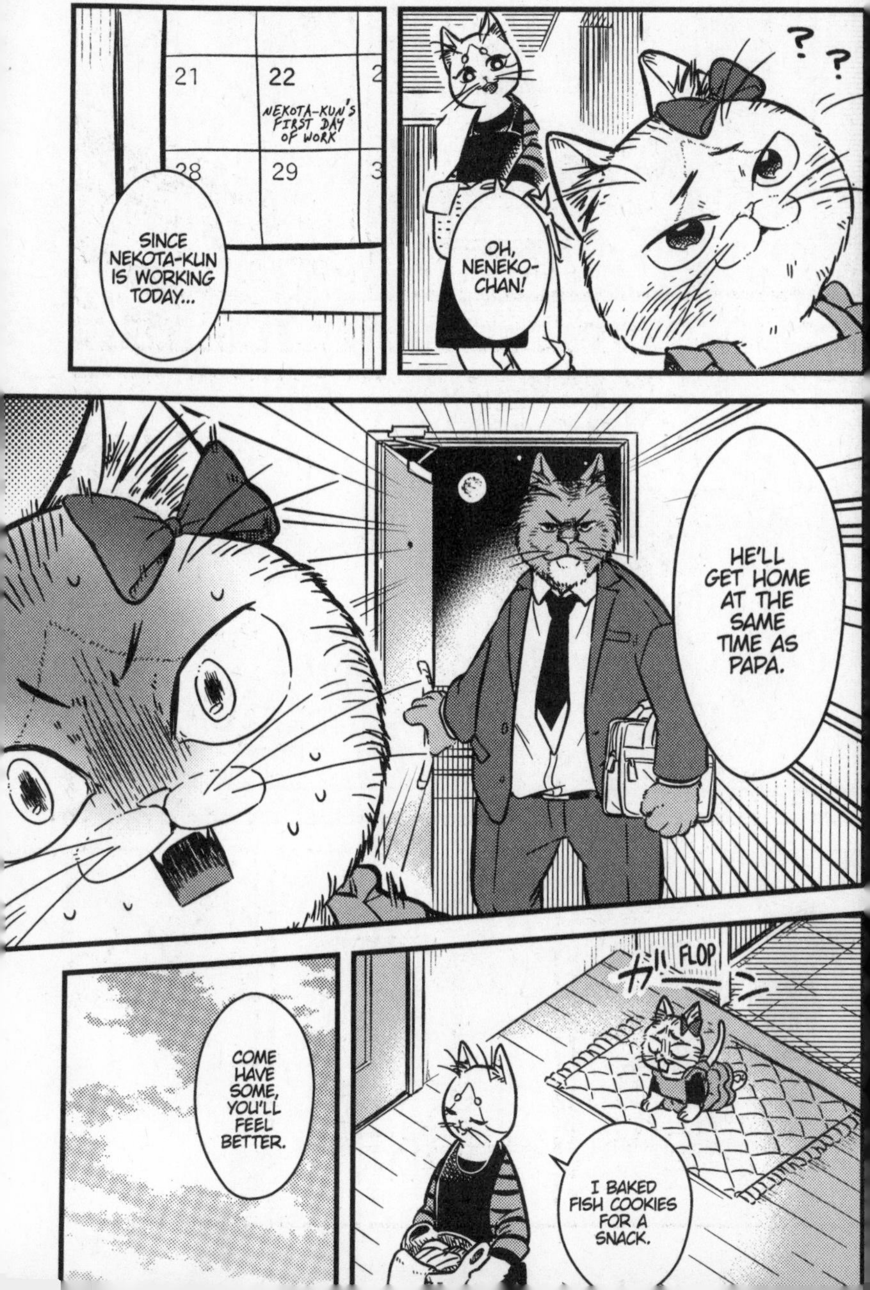
? ?
OH, NENEKO-CHAN!
21
22
NEKOTA-KUN'S FIRST DAY OF WORK
28
29
SINCE NEKOTA-KUN IS WORKING TODAY...
HE'LL GET HOME AT THE SAME TIME AS PAPA.
FLOP
I BAKED FISH COOKIES FOR A SNACK.
COME HAVE SOME, YOU'LL FEEL BETTER.

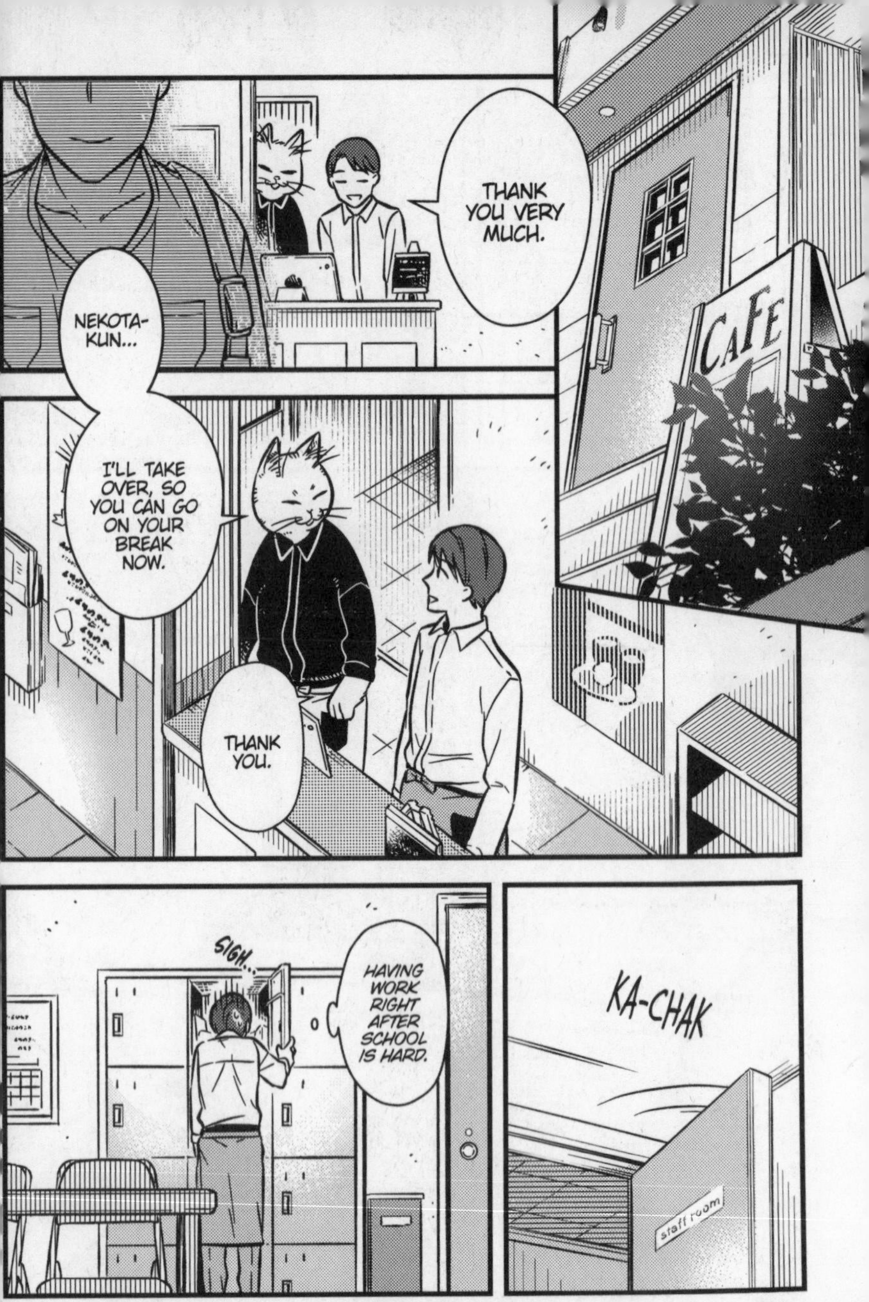
CaFe
THANK YOU VERY MUCH.
NEKOTA-KUN...
I'LL TAKE OVER, SO YOU CAN GO ON YOUR BREAK NOW.
THANK YOU.
KA-CHAK
staff room
SIGH...
HAVING WORK RIGHT AFTER SCHOOL IS HARD.

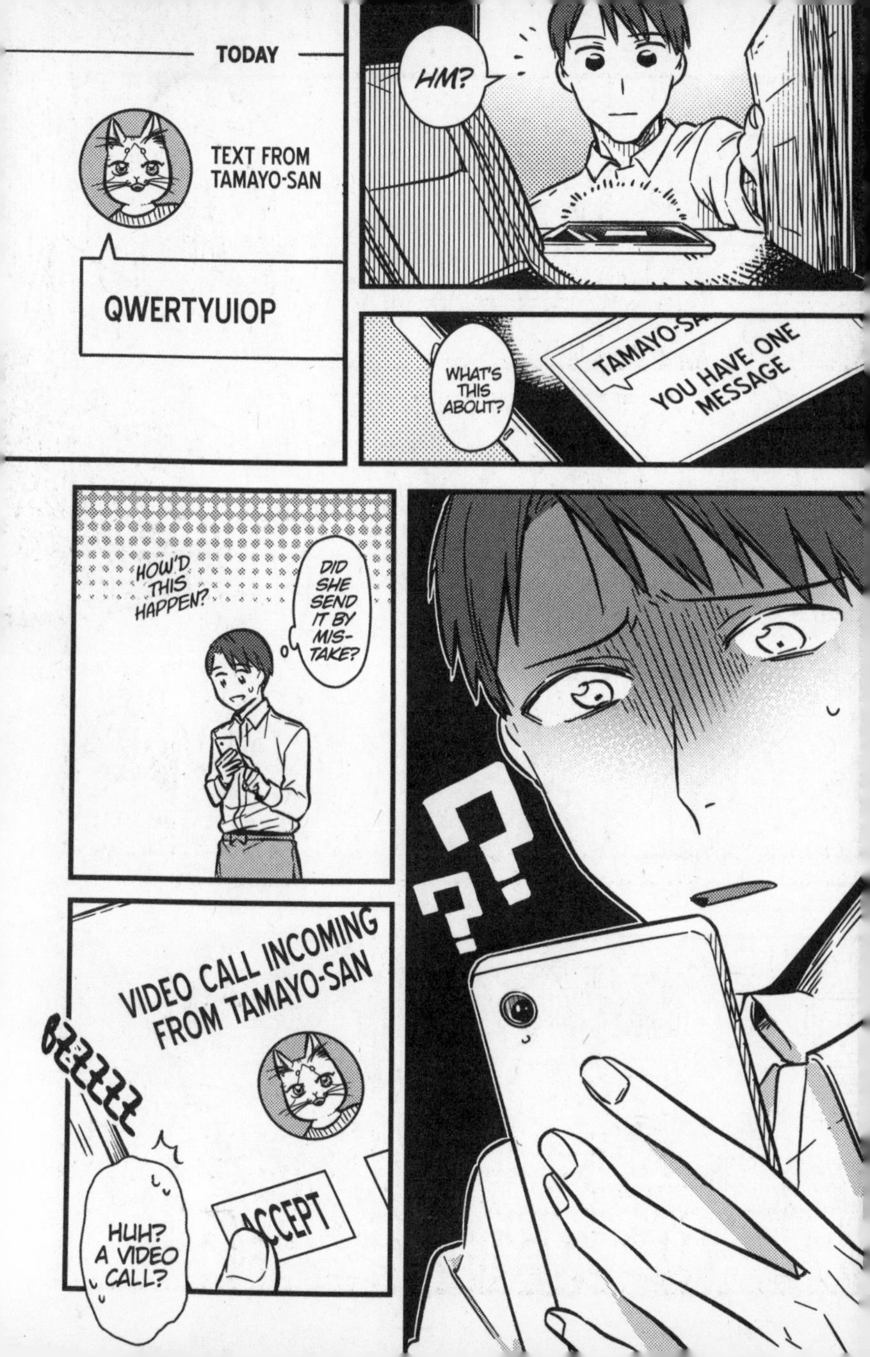
HM?
WHAT'S THIS ABOUT?
TAMAYO-SAN
YOU HAVE ONE MESSAGE
TODAY
TEXT FROM TAMAYO-SAN
QWERTYUIOP
DID SHE SEND IT BY MIS-TAKE?
HOW'D THIS HAPPEN?
VIDEO CALL INCOMING FROM TAMAYO-SAN
BZZZZZ
ACCEPT
HUH? A VIDEO CALL?

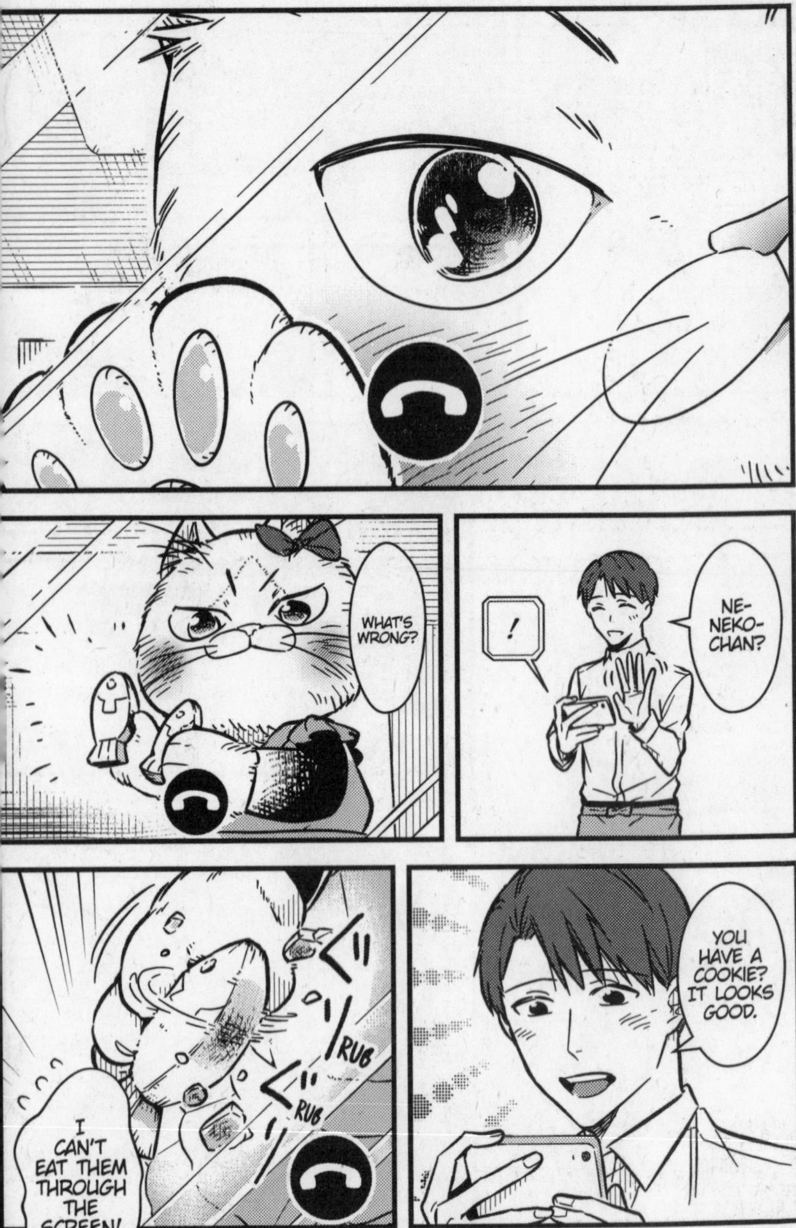
NE-NEKO-CHAN?
!
WHAT'S WRONG?
YOU HAVE A COOKIE? IT LOOKS GOOD.
RUB
RUB
I CAN'T EAT THEM THROUGH THE SCREEN!

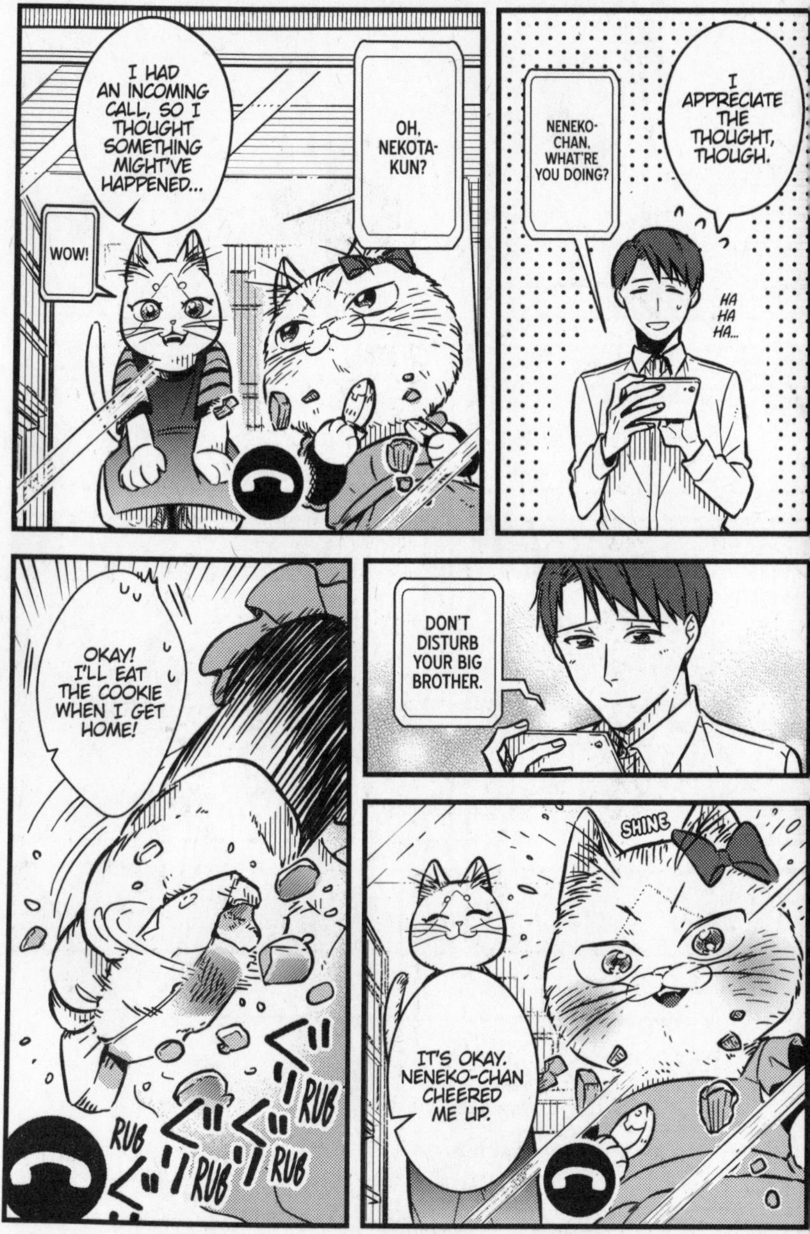
I APPRECIATE THE THOUGHT, THOUGH.
NENEKO-CHAN, WHAT'RE YOU DOING?
HA HA HA...
OH, NEKOTA-KUN?
I HAD AN INCOMING CALL, SO I THOUGHT SOMETHING MIGHT'VE HAPPENED...
WOW!
DON'T DISTURB YOUR BIG BROTHER.
SHINE
IT'S OKAY. NENEKO-CHAN CHEERED ME UP.
OKAY! I'LL EAT THE COOKIE WHEN I GET HOME!
RUB
RUB
RUB
RUB

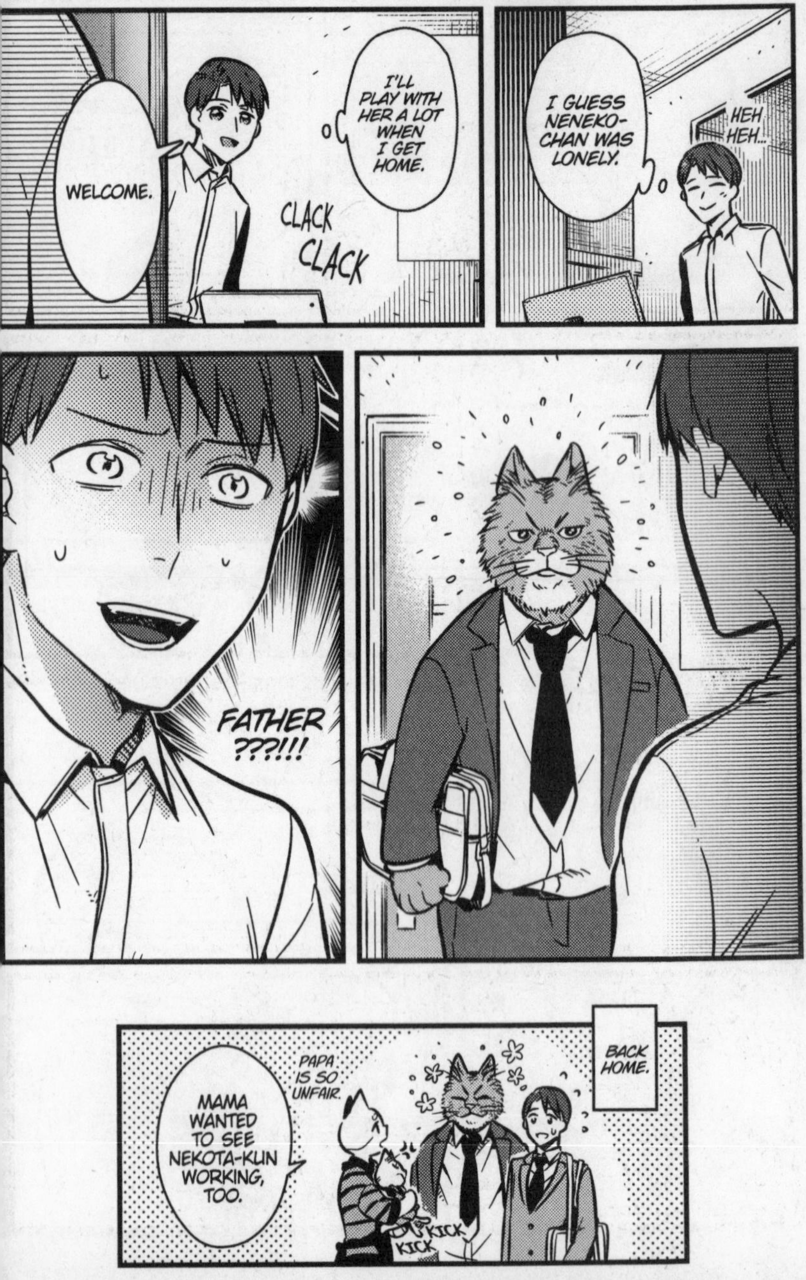
I GUESS NENEKO-CHAN WAS LONELY.
HEH HEH...
I'LL PLAY WITH HER A LOT WHEN I GET HOME.
CLACK CLACK
WELCOME.
FATHER ???!!!
BACK HOME.
PAPA IS SO UNFAIR.
MAMA WANTED TO SEE NEKOTA-KUN WORKING, TOO.
KICK KICK

Extra 2

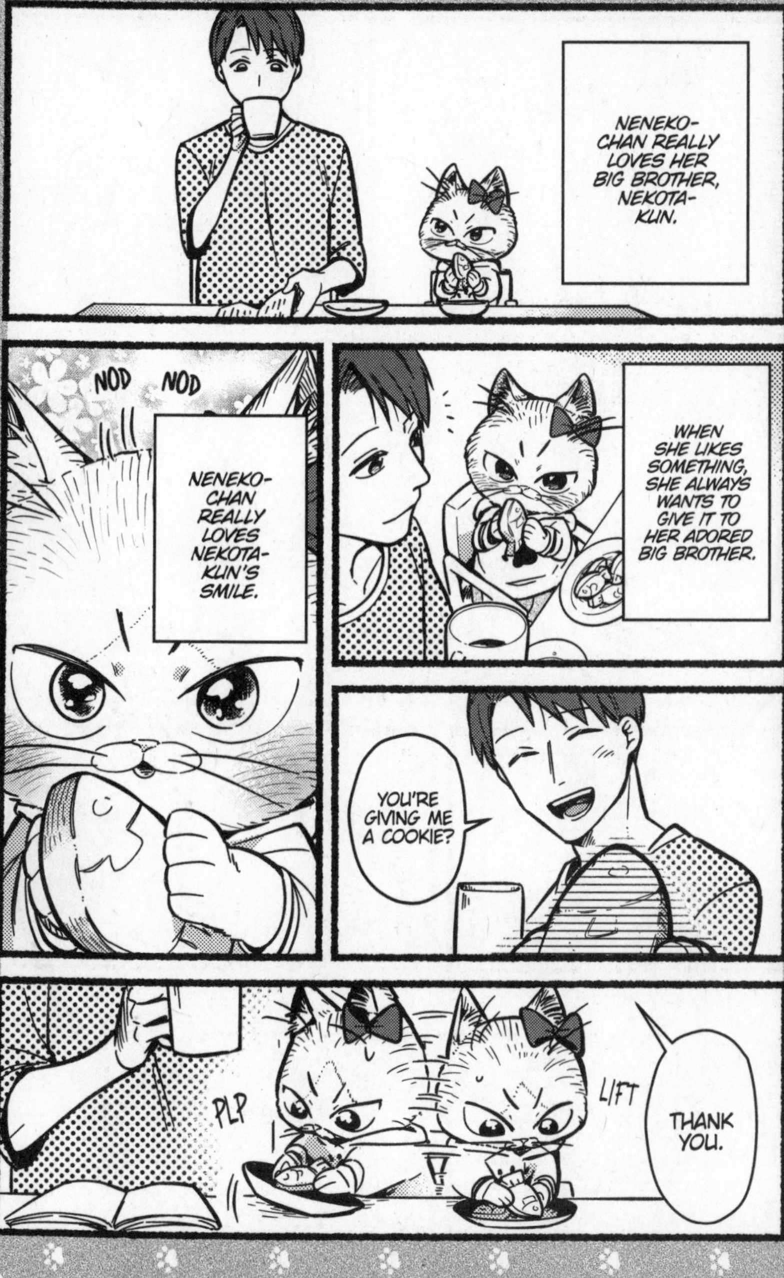
NENEKO-CHAN REALLY LOVES HER BIG BROTHER, NEKOTA-KUN.
WHEN SHE LIKES SOMETHING, SHE ALWAYS WANTS TO GIVE IT TO HER ADORED BIG BROTHER.
YOU'RE GIVING ME A COOKIE?
NOD
NOD
NENEKO-CHAN REALLY LOVES NEKOTA-KUN'S SMILE.
THANK YOU.
LIFT
PLP

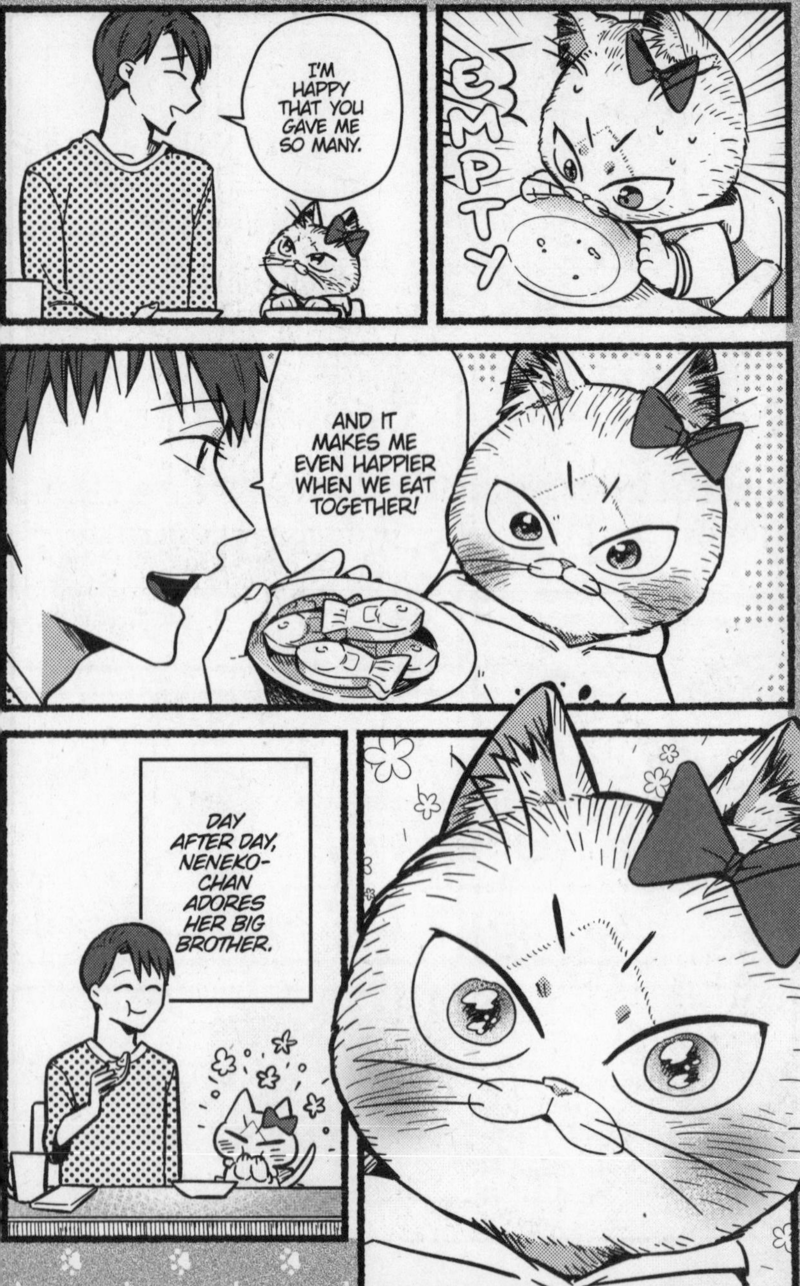
EMPTY
I'M HAPPY THAT YOU GAVE ME SO MANY.
AND IT MAKES ME EVEN HAPPIER WHEN WE EAT TOGETHER!
DAY AFTER DAY, NENEKO-CHAN ADORES HER BIG BROTHER.

Chapter 3: Neneko and the Drawing

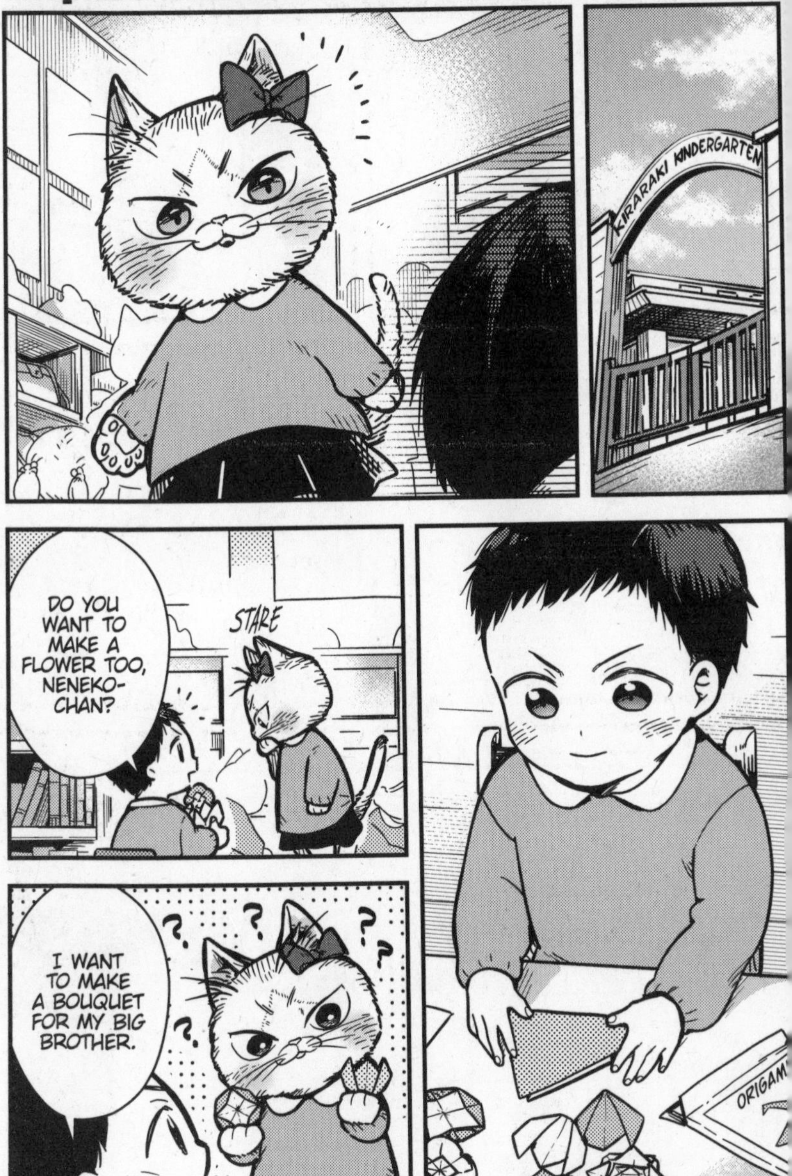
KIRARAKI KINDERGARTEN
STARE
DO YOU WANT TO MAKE A FLOWER TOO, NENEKO-CHAN?
I WANT TO MAKE A BOUQUET FOR MY BIG BROTHER.

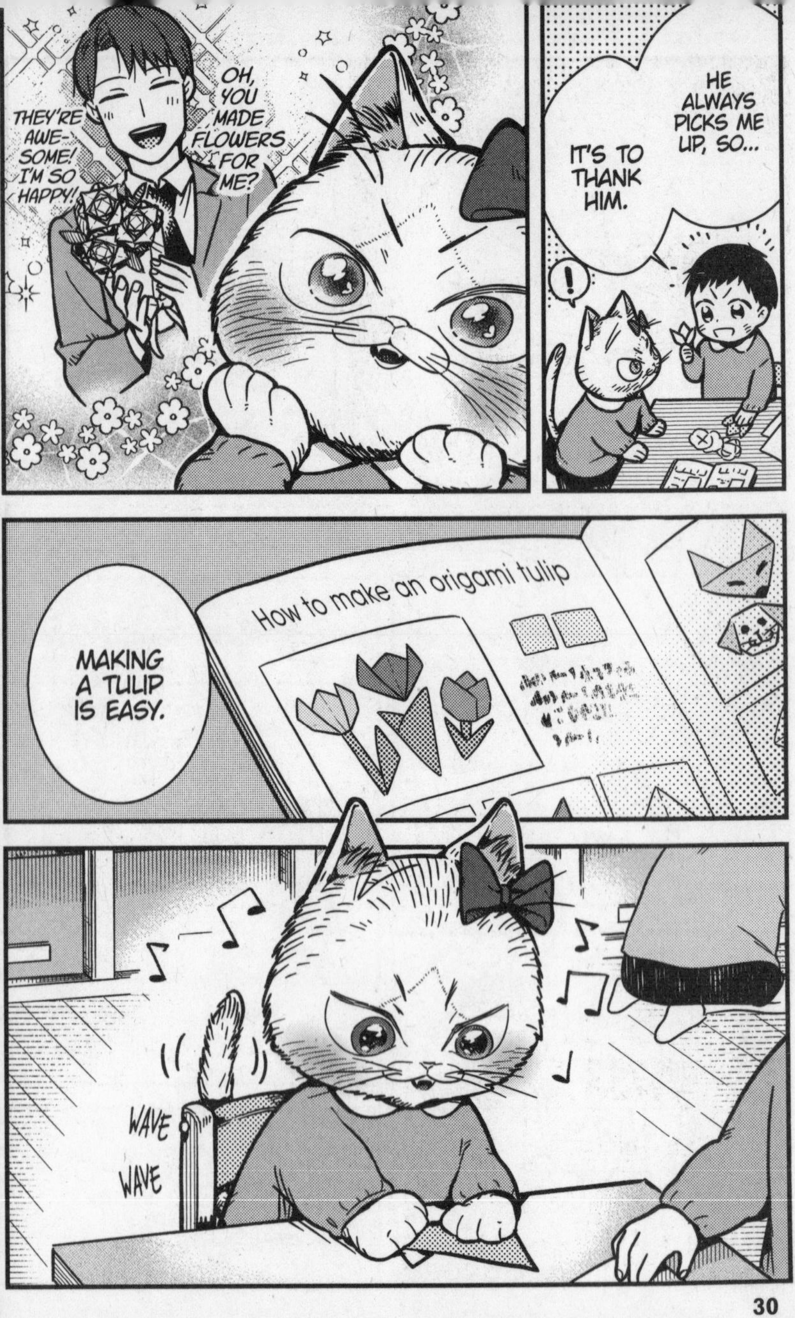
HE ALWAYS PICKS ME UP, SO...
IT'S TO THANK HIM.
!
OH, YOU MADE FLOWERS FOR ME?
THEY'RE AWE-SOME! I'M SO HAPPY!
How to make an origami tulip
MAKING A TULIP IS EASY.
WAVE
WAVE

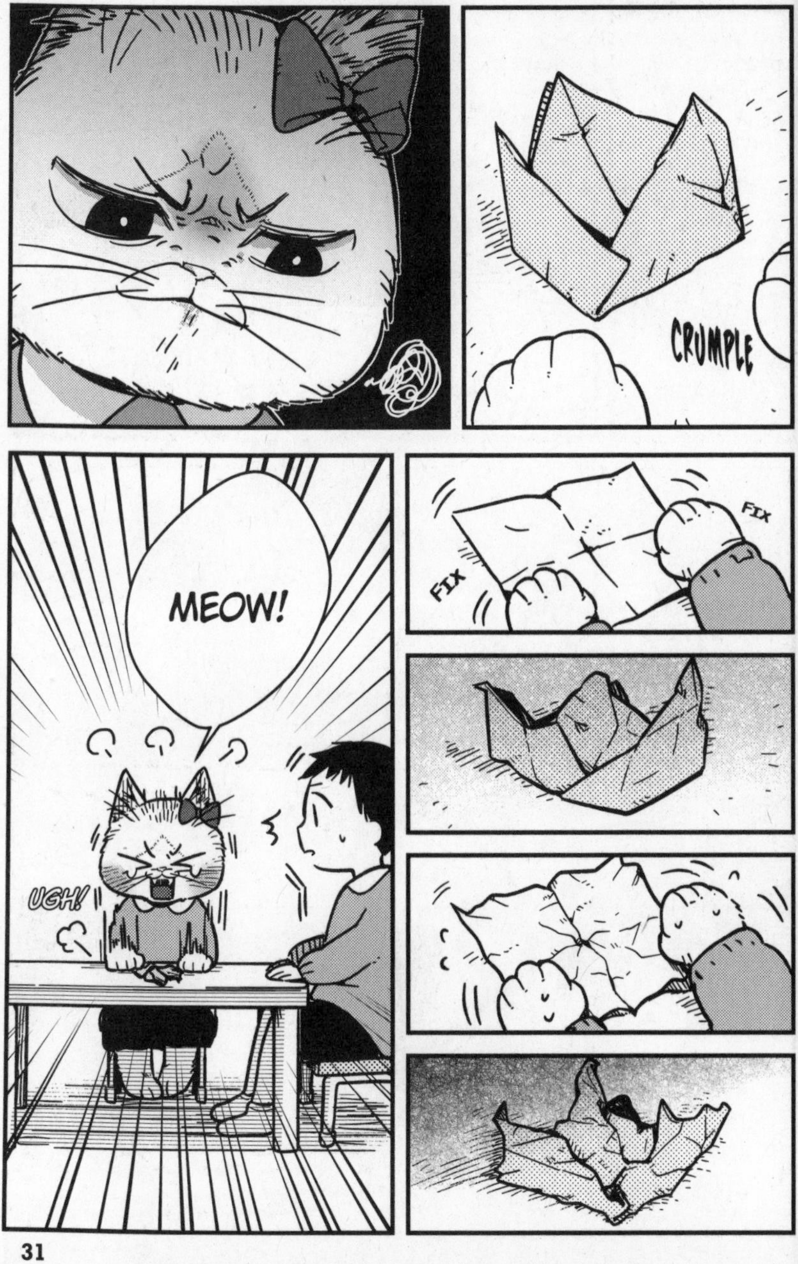
CRUMPLE
FIX
FIX
MEOW!
UGH!

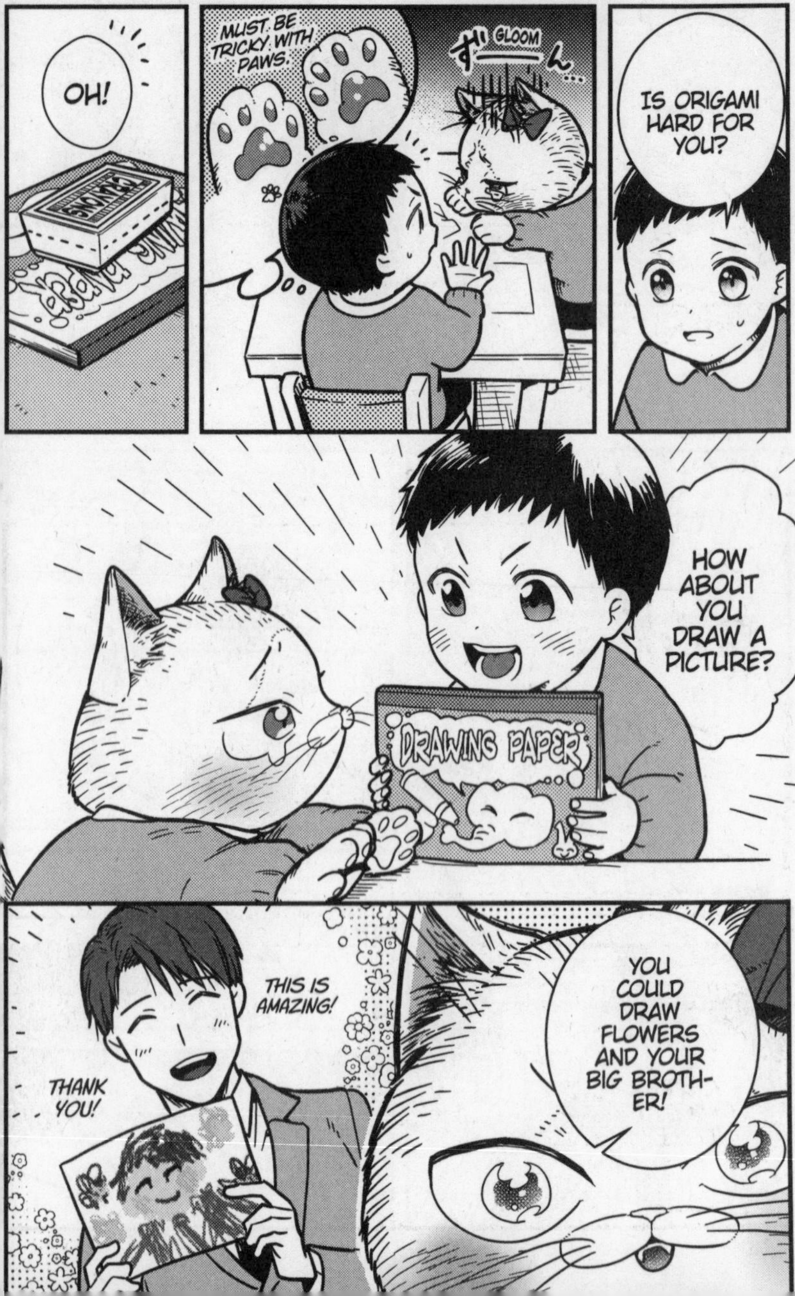
IS ORIGAMI HARD FOR YOU?
GLOOM
MUST BE TRICKY WITH PAWS.
OH!
HOW ABOUT YOU DRAW A PICTURE?
DRAWING PAPER
YOU COULD DRAW FLOWERS AND YOUR BIG BROTH-ER!
THIS IS AMAZING!
THANK YOU!

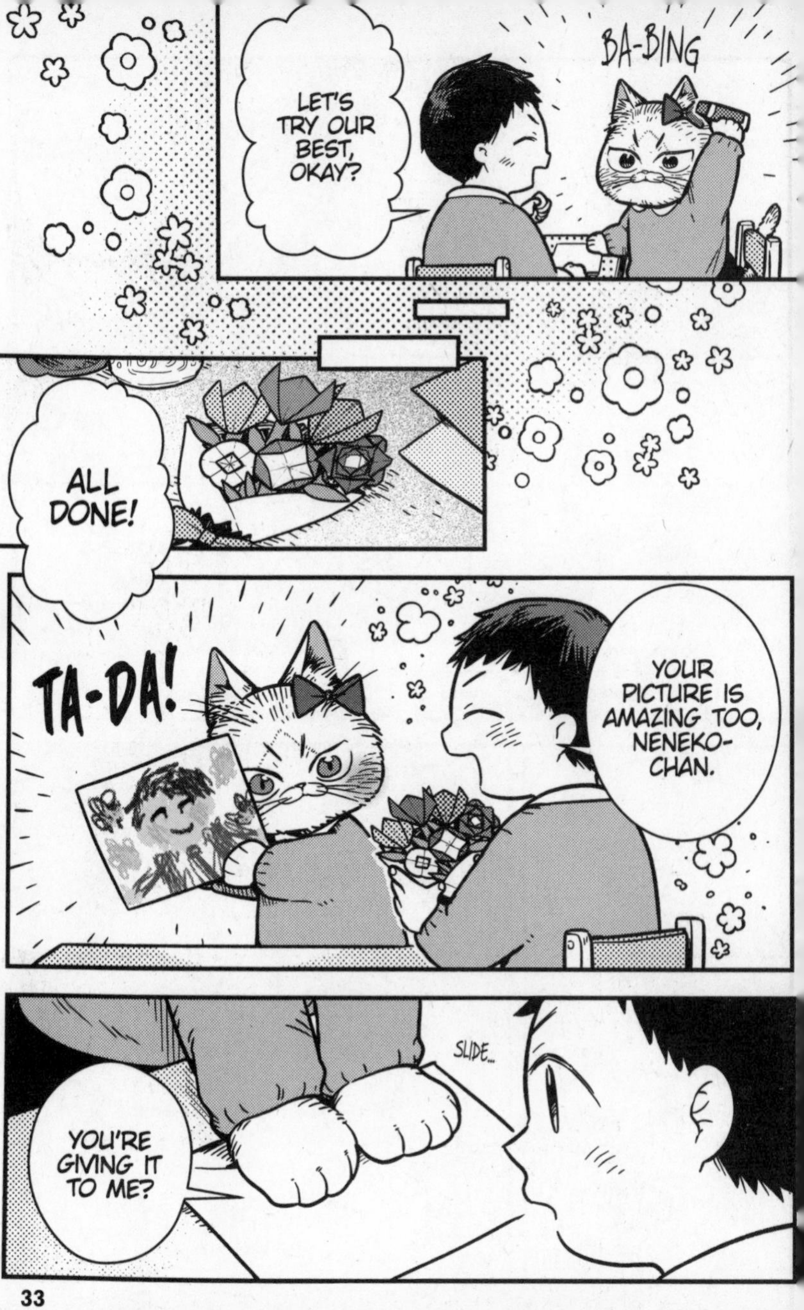
BA-BING
LET'S TRY OUR BEST, OKAY?
ALL DONE!
YOUR PICTURE IS AMAZING TOO, NENEKO-CHAN.
TA-DA!
SLIDE...
YOU'RE GIVING IT TO ME?

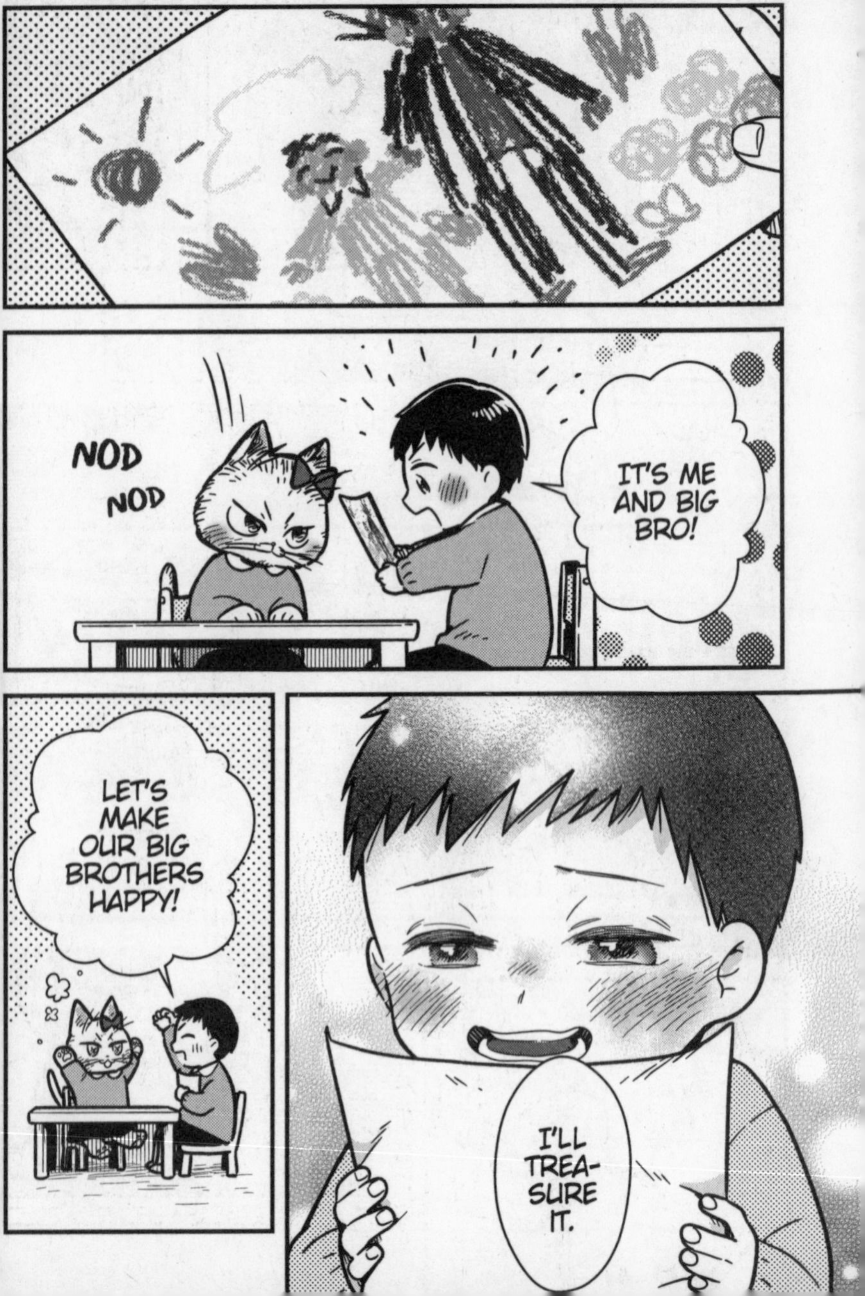
IT'S ME AND BIG BRO!
NOD NOD
I'LL TREASURE IT.
LET'S MAKE OUR BIG BROTHERS HAPPY!

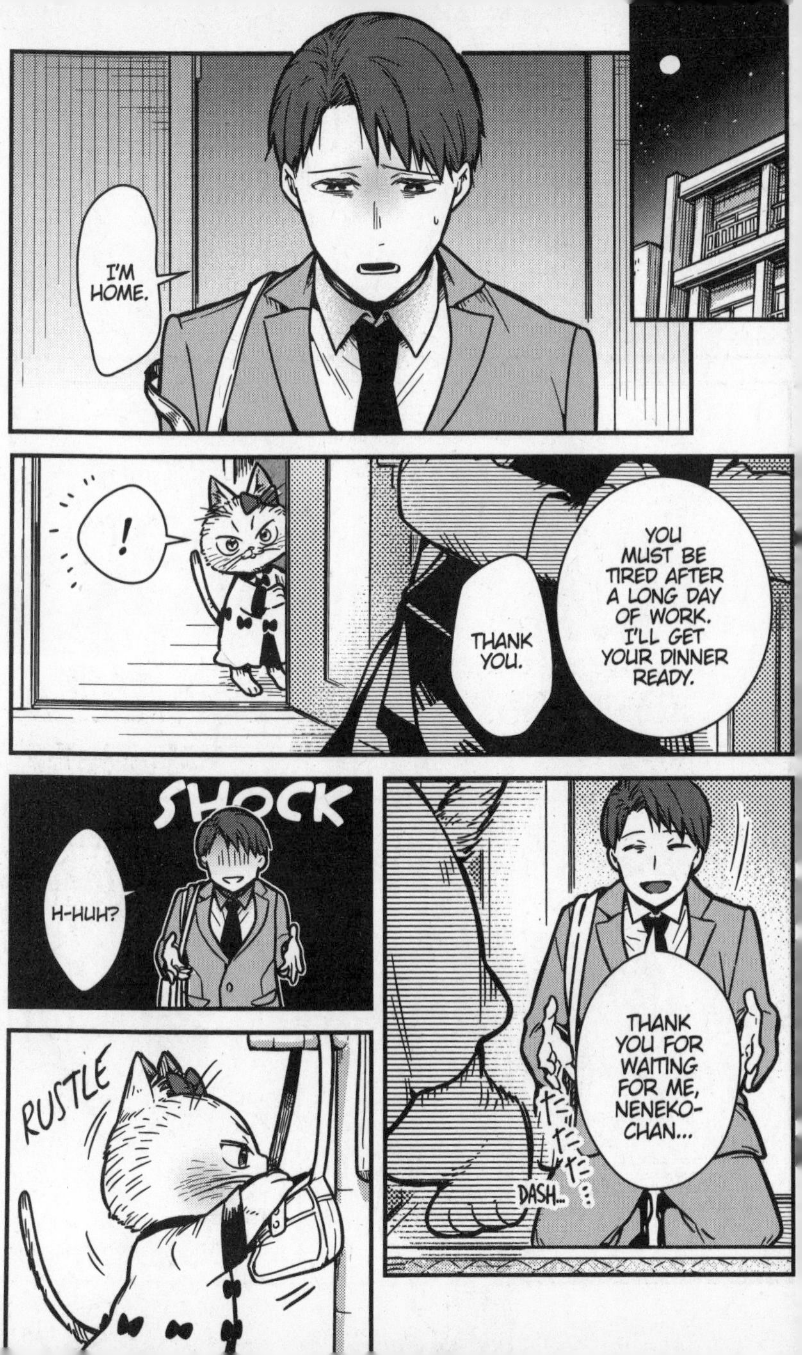
I'M HOME.
YOU MUST BE TIRED AFTER A LONG DAY OF WORK. I'LL GET YOUR DINNER READY.
THANK YOU.
!
THANK YOU FOR WAITING FOR ME, NENEKO-CHAN...
DASH...
SHOCK
H-HUH?
RUSTLE

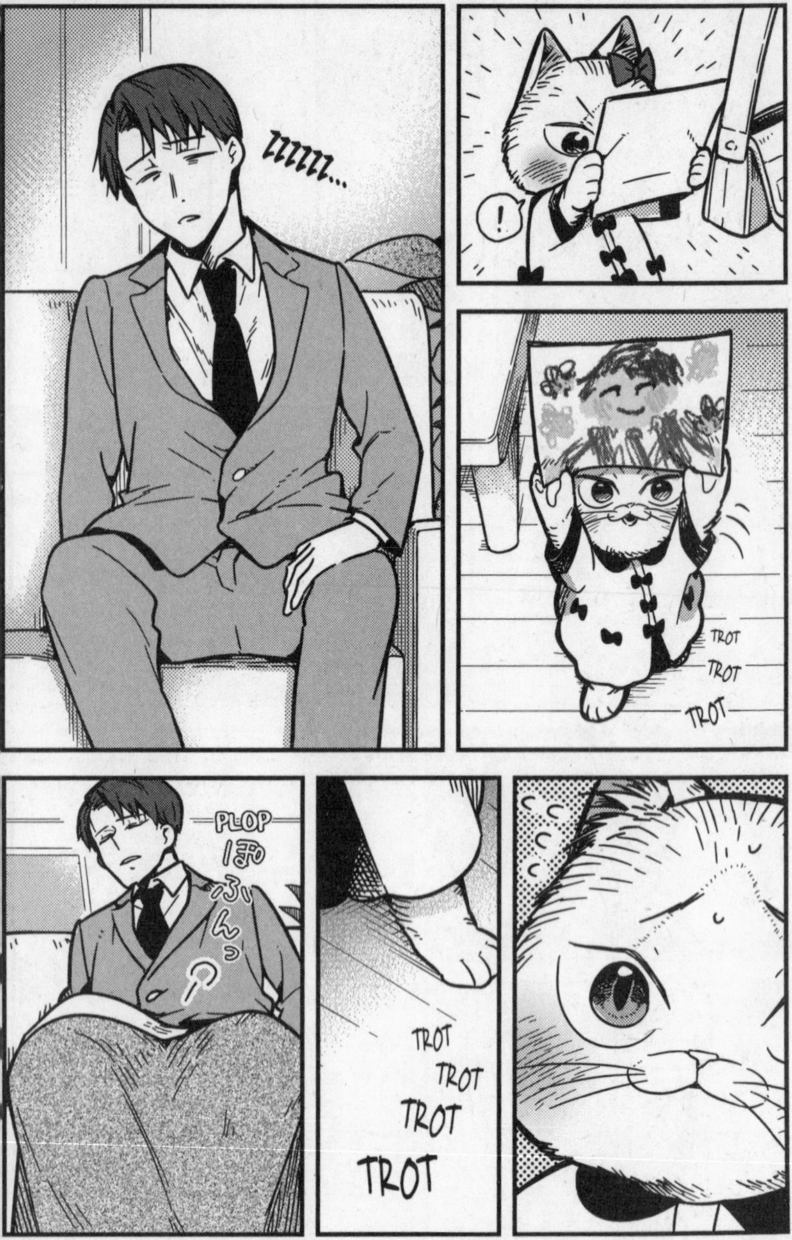
!
TROT
TROT
TROT
ZZZZZZ...
TROT
TROT
TROT
TROT
PLOP
ぽふんっ

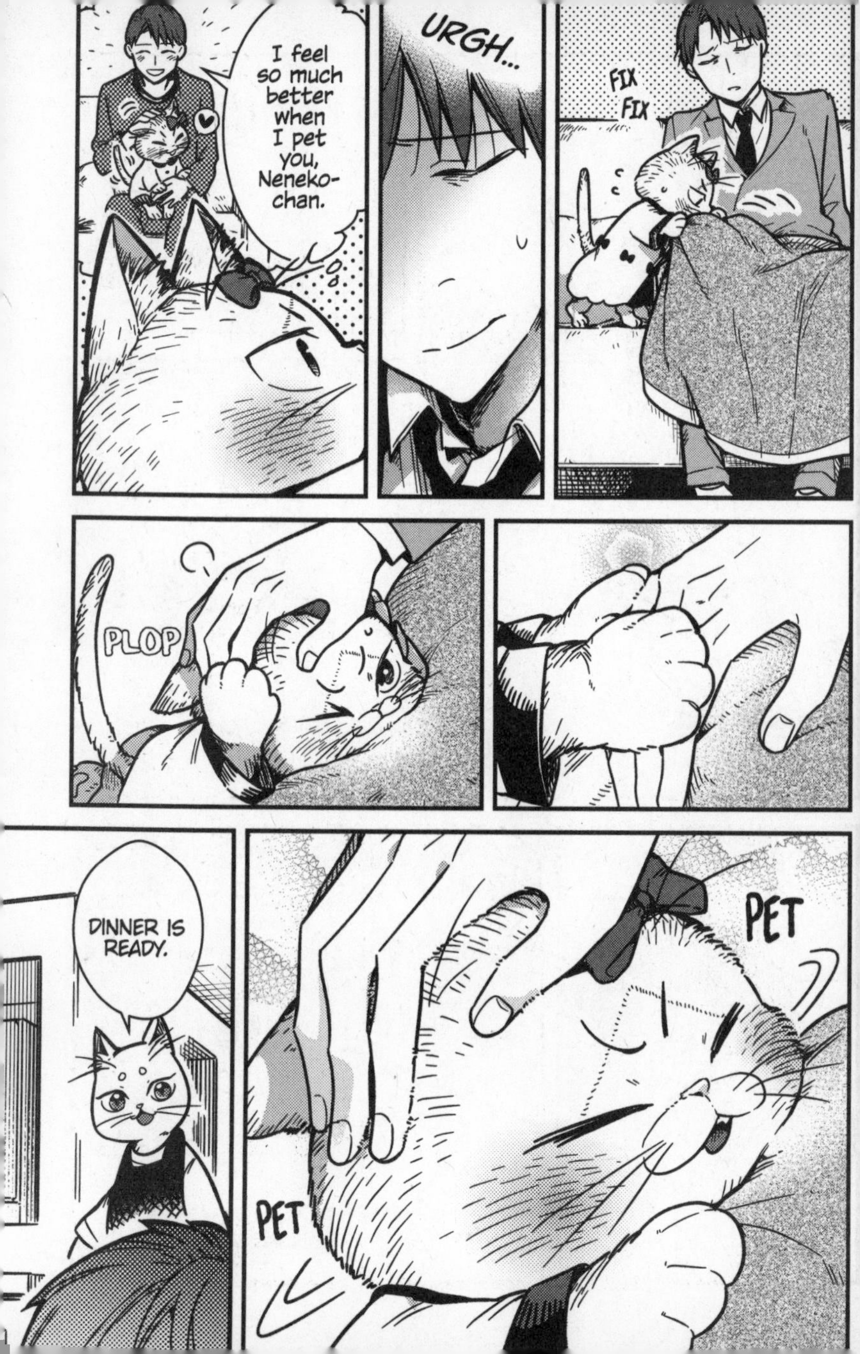
FIX
FIX
URGH...
I feel so much better when I pet you, Neneko-chan.
PLOP
PET
PET
DINNER IS READY.

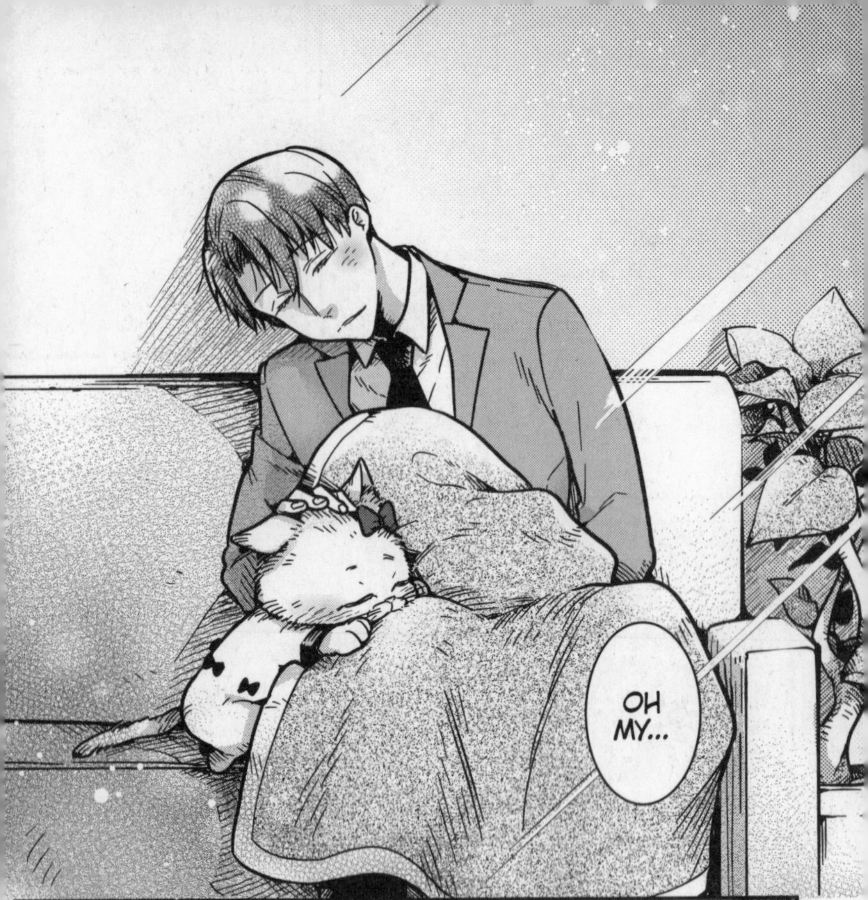
OH MY...

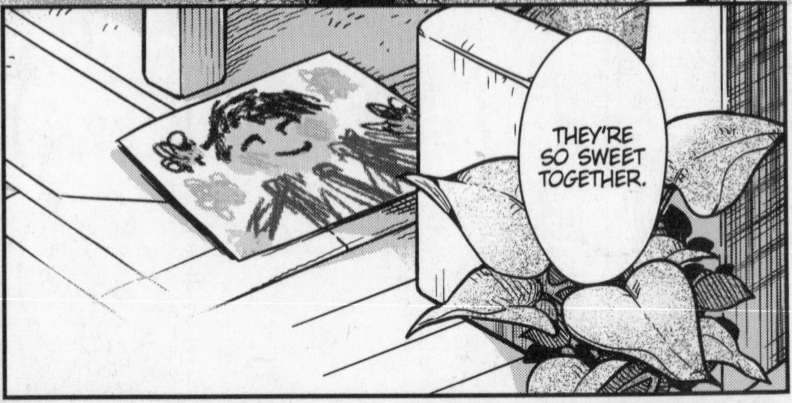
THEY'RE SO SWEET TOGETHER.

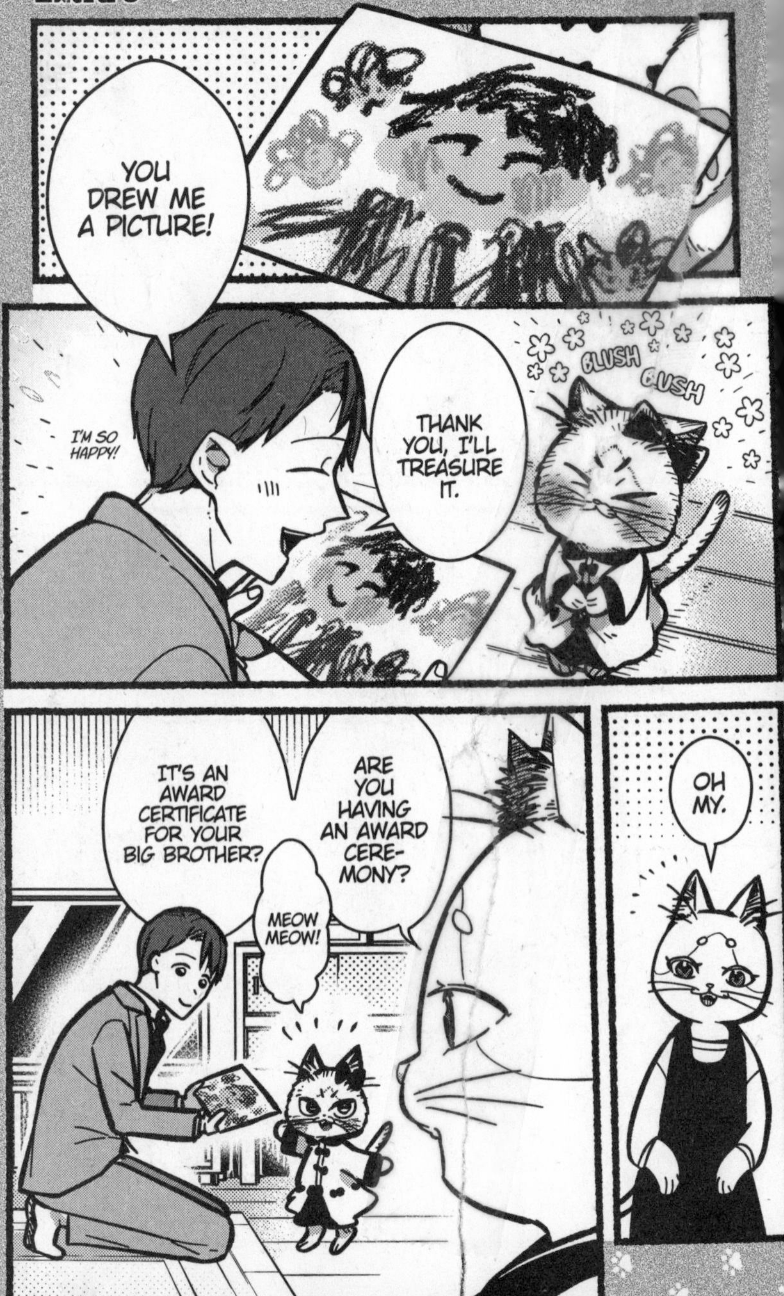
YOU DREW ME A PICTURE!
BLUSH BLUSH
THANK YOU, I'LL TREASURE IT.
I'M SO HAPPY!
OH MY.
ARE YOU HAVING AN AWARD CERE-MONY?
IT'S AN AWARD CERTIFICATE FOR YOUR BIG BROTHER?
MEOW MEOW!

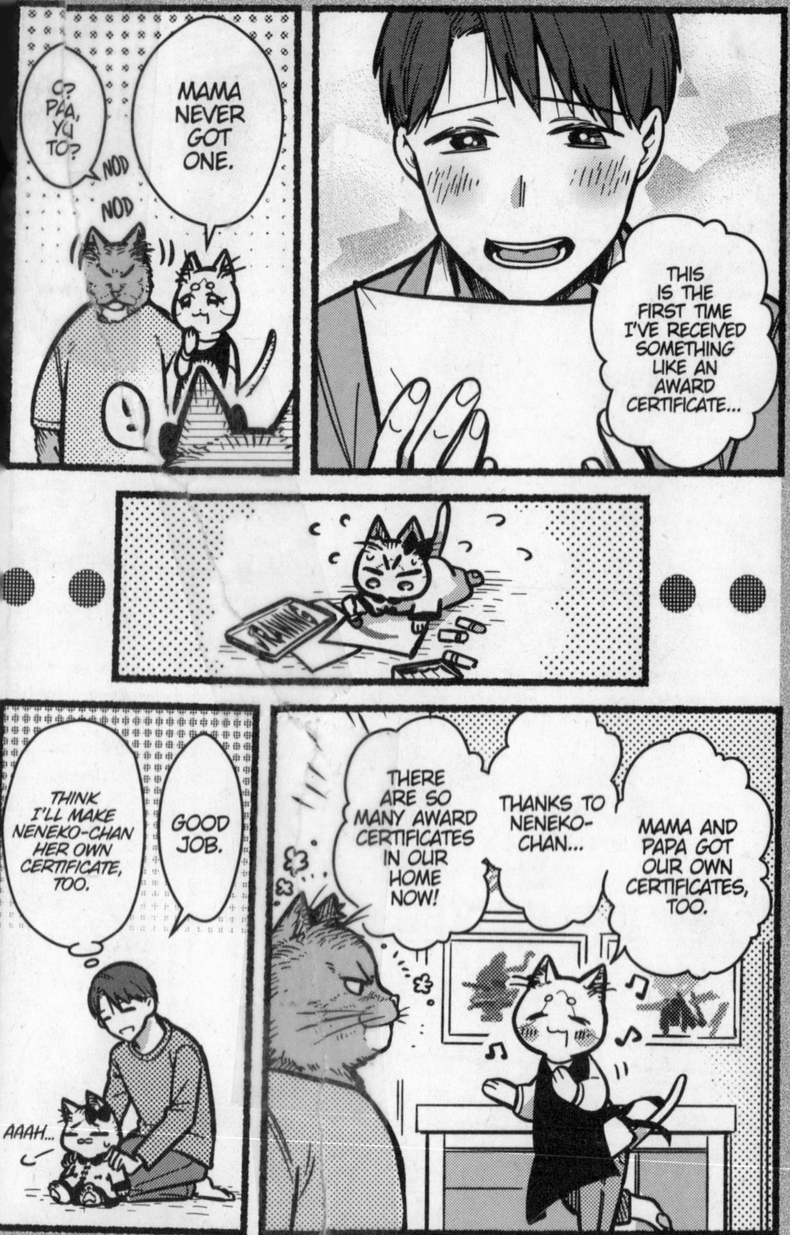
THIS IS THE FIRST TIME I'VE RECEIVED SOMETHING LIKE AN AWARD CERTIFICATE...
MAMA NEVER GOT ONE.
O? PAA, YU TO?
NOD
NOD
!
MAMA AND PAPA GOT OUR OWN CERTIFICATES, TOO.
THANKS TO NENEKO-CHAN...
THERE ARE SO MANY AWARD CERTIFICATES IN OUR HOME NOW!
GOOD JOB.
THINK I'LL MAKE NENEKO-CHAN HER OWN CERTIFICATE, TOO.
AAAH...

Chapter 4: Neneko and the Marathon

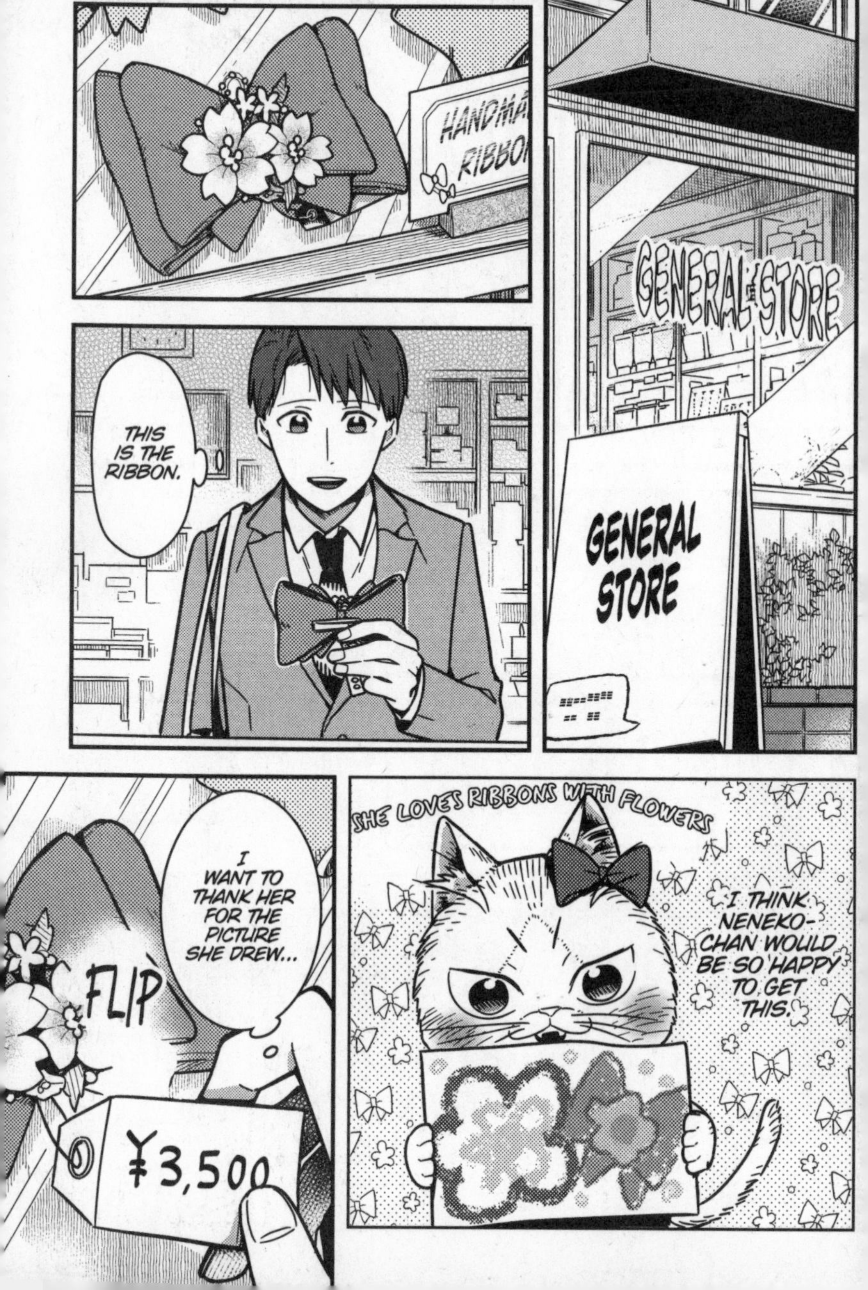
GENERAL STORE
GENERAL STORE
THIS IS THE RIBBON.
SHE LOVES RIBBONS WITH FLOWERS
I THINK NENEKO-CHAN WOULD BE SO HAPPY TO GET THIS.
I WANT TO THANK HER FOR THE PICTURE SHE DREW...
FLIP
¥3,500

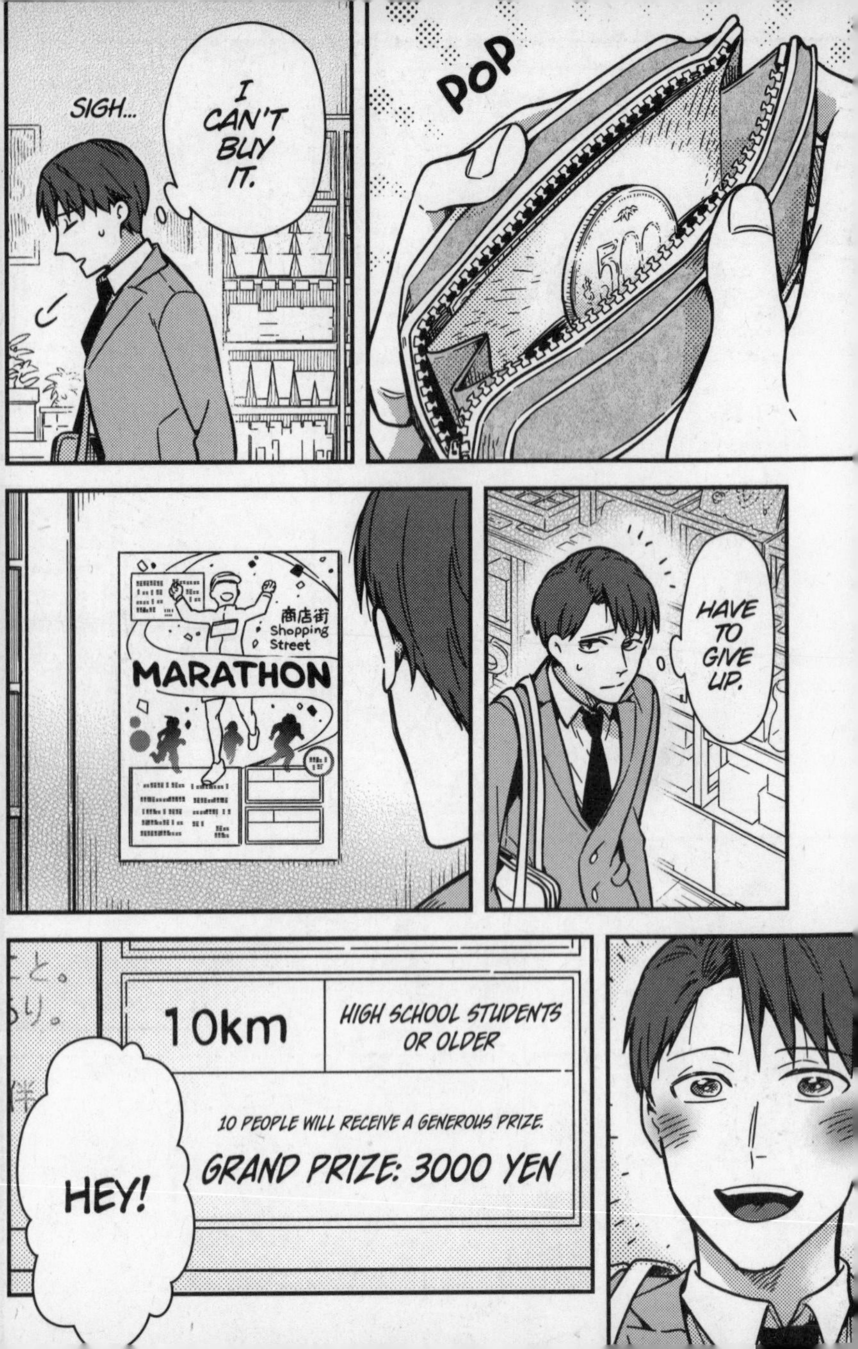
POP
SIGH...
I CAN'T BUY IT.
HAVE TO GIVE UP.
商店街
Shopping Street
MARATHON
10km
HIGH SCHOOL STUDENTS OR OLDER
10 PEOPLE WILL RECEIVE A GENEROUS PRIZE.
GRAND PRIZE: 3000 YEN
HEY!

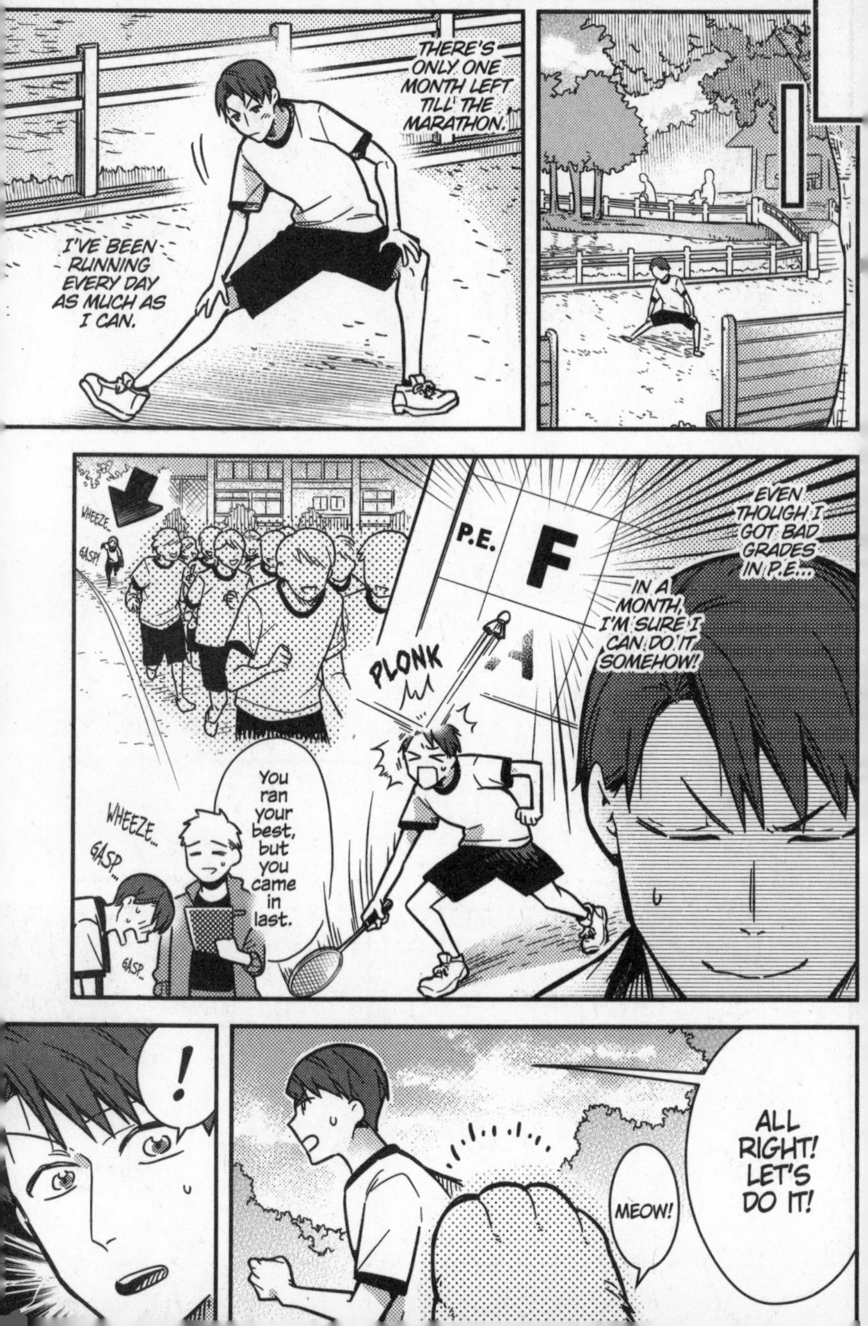
THERE'S ONLY ONE MONTH LEFT TILL THE MARATHON.
I'VE BEEN RUNNING EVERY DAY AS MUCH AS I CAN.
EVEN THOUGH I GOT BAD GRADES IN P.E...
IN A MONTH, I'M SURE I CAN DO IT SOMEHOW!
P.E.
F
PLONK
WHEEZE...
GASP!
You ran your best, but you came in last.
WHEEZE...
GASP...
GASP...
ALL RIGHT! LET'S DO IT!
MEOW!
!

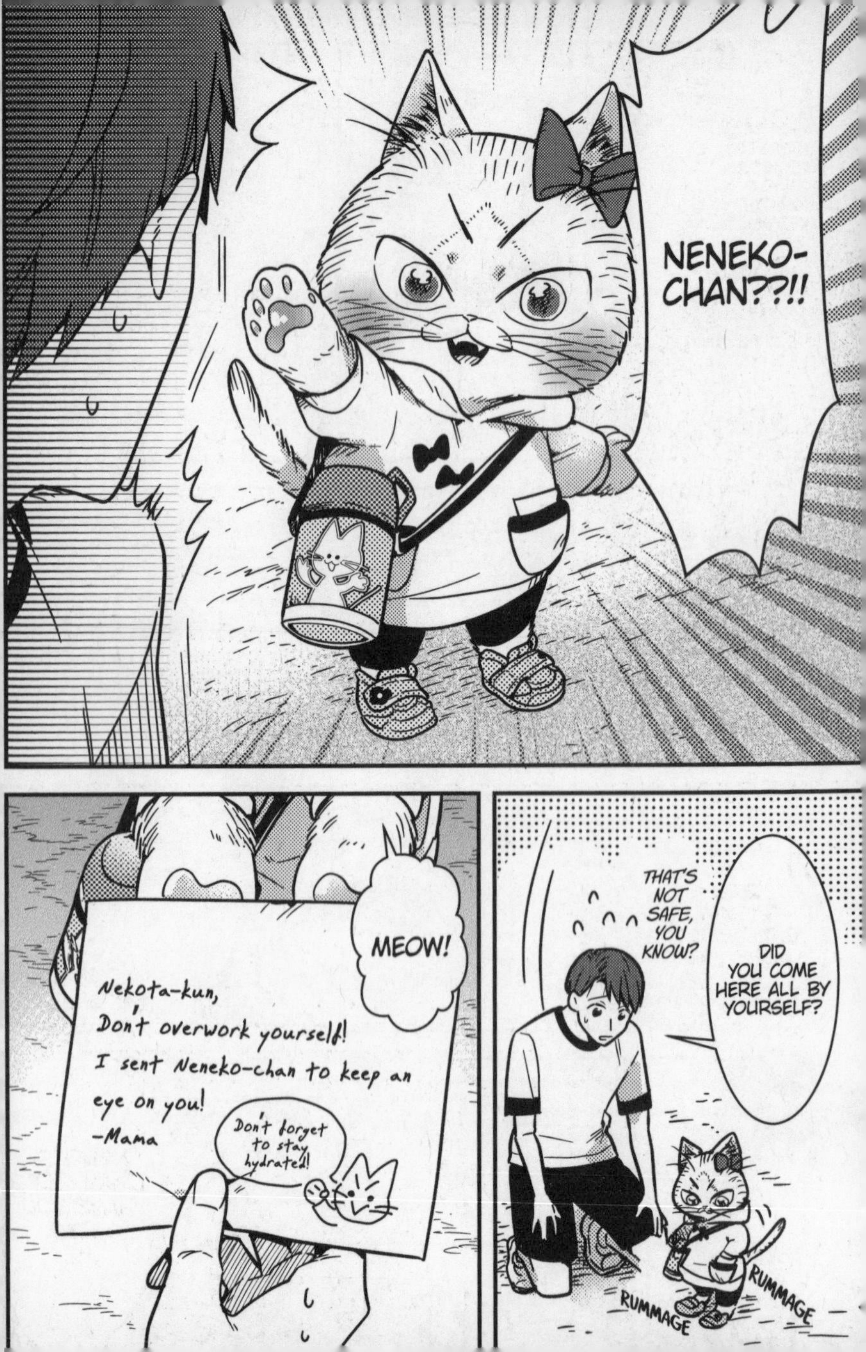
NENEKO-CHAN??!!
MEOW!
Nekota-kun,
Don't overwork yourself!
I sent Neneko-chan to keep an eye on you!
-Mama
Don't forget to stay hydrated!
DID YOU COME HERE ALL BY YOURSELF?
THAT'S NOT SAFE, YOU KNOW?
RUMMAGE
RUMMAGE

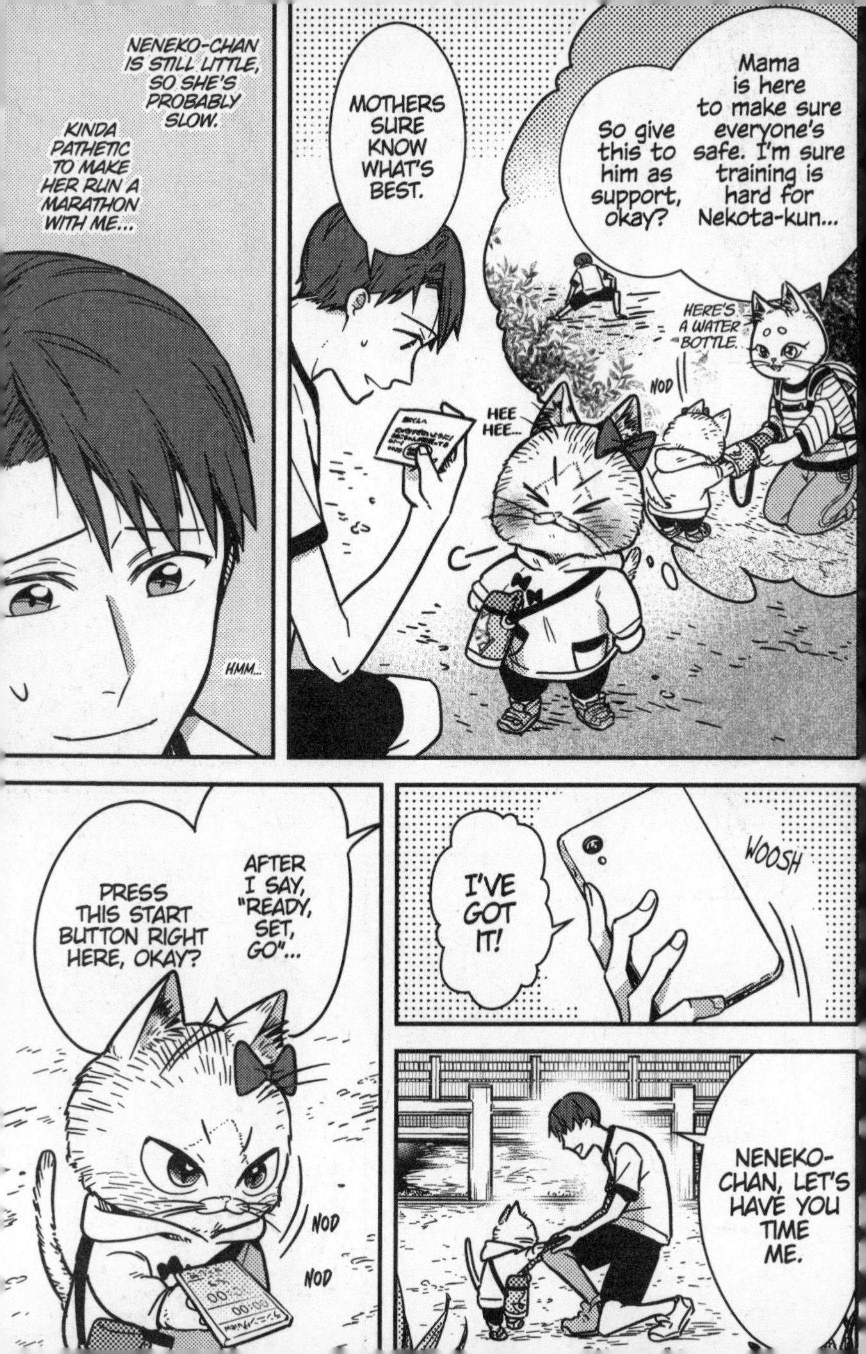

Mama is here to make sure everyone's safe. I'm sure training is hard for Nekota-kun...
So give this to him as support, okay?
HERE'S A WATER BOTTLE.
NOD
HEE HEE...
MOTHERS SURE KNOW WHAT'S BEST.
NENEKO-CHAN IS STILL LITTLE, SO SHE'S PROBABLY SLOW.
KINDA PATHETIC TO MAKE HER RUN A MARATHON WITH ME...
HMM...
NENEKO-CHAN, LET'S HAVE YOU TIME ME.
WOOSH
I'VE GOT IT!
AFTER I SAY, "READY, SET, GO"...
PRESS THIS START BUTTON RIGHT HERE, OKAY?
NOD
NOD

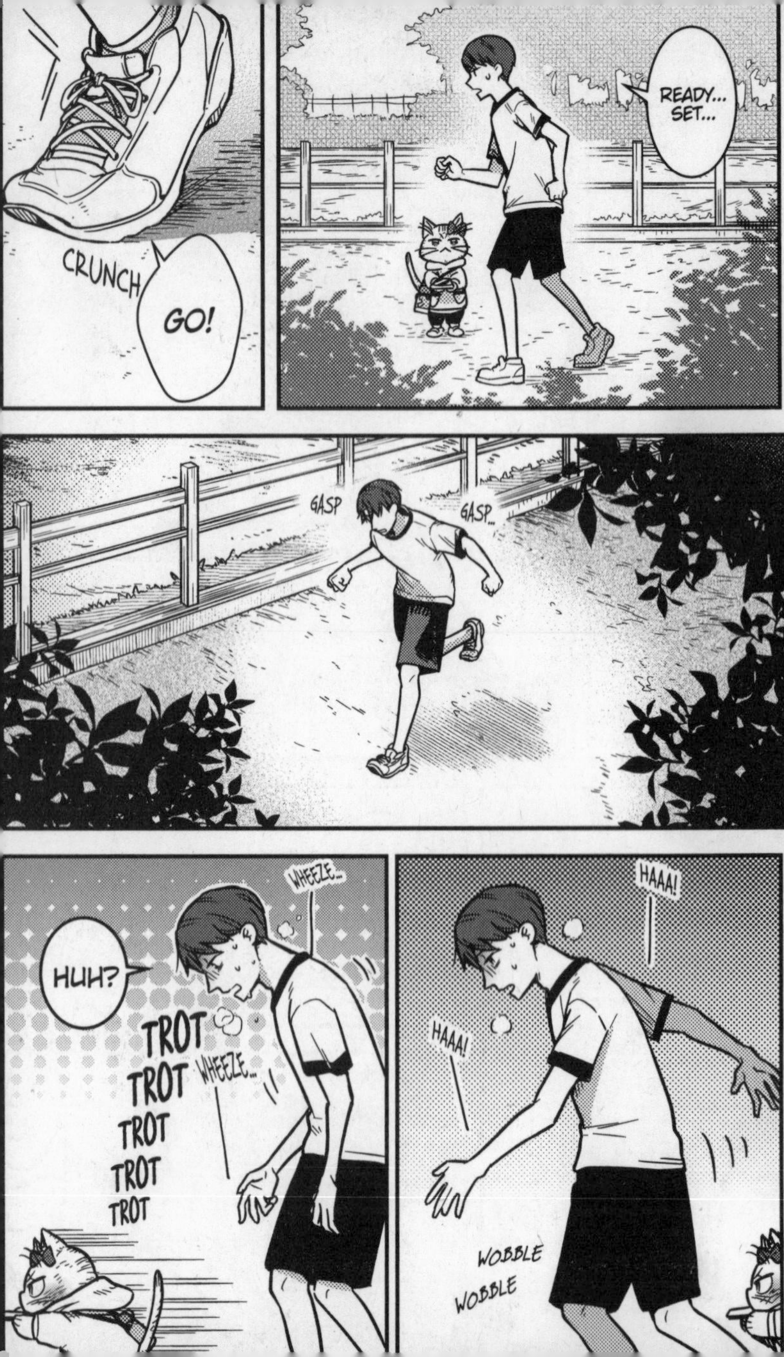
READY... SET...
GO!
CRUNCH
GASP...
GASP
HAAA!
HAAA!
WOBBLE
WOBBLE
WHEEZE...
HUH?
WHEEZE...
TROT
TROT
TROT
TROT
TROT

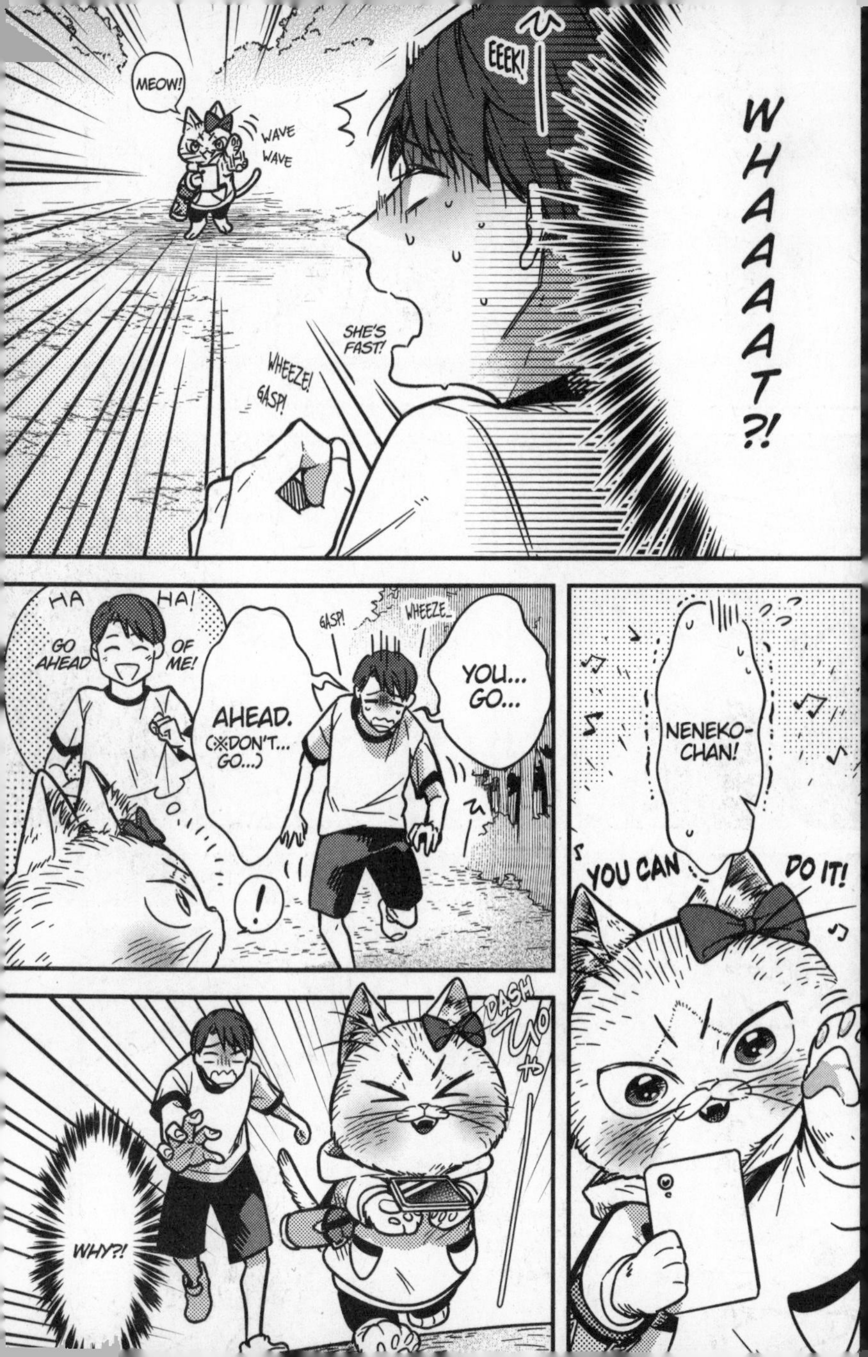
EEEK!
WHAAAAAT?!
MEOW!
WAVE WAVE
SHE'S FAST!
WHEEZE!
GASP!
NENEKO-CHAN!
YOU CAN DO IT!
YOU... GO...
WHEEZE...
GASP!
AHEAD. (※DON'T... GO...)
HA HA!
GO AHEAD OF ME!
!
DASH
WHY?!

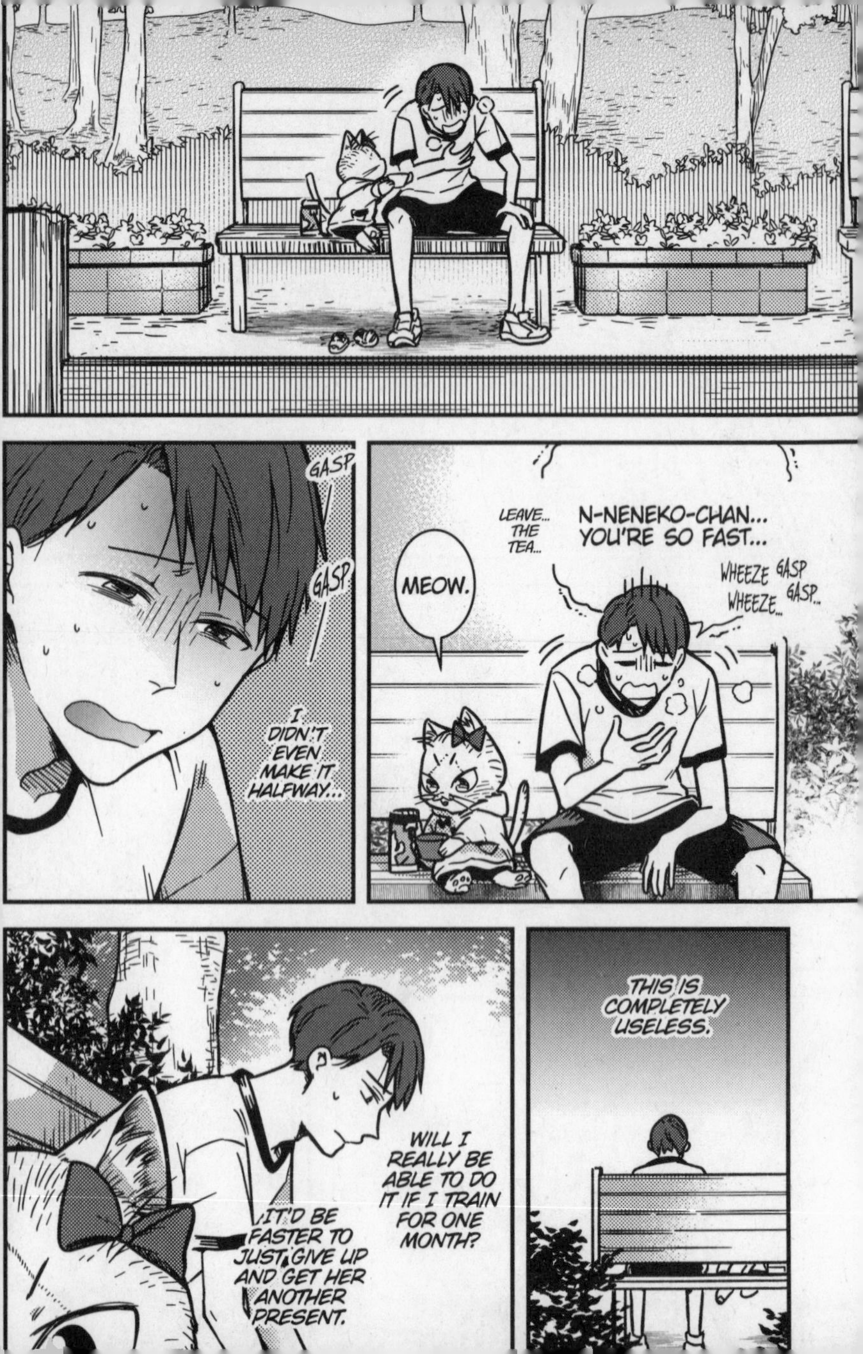
N-NENEKO-CHAN... YOU'RE SO FAST...
WHEEZE WHEEZE...
GASP GASP...
LEAVE... THE TEA...
MEOW.
GASP
GASP
I DIDN'T EVEN MAKE IT HALFWAY...
THIS IS COMPLETELY USELESS.
WILL I REALLY BE ABLE TO DO IT IF I TRAIN FOR ONE MONTH?
IT'D BE FASTER TO JUST GIVE UP AND GET HER ANOTHER PRESENT.

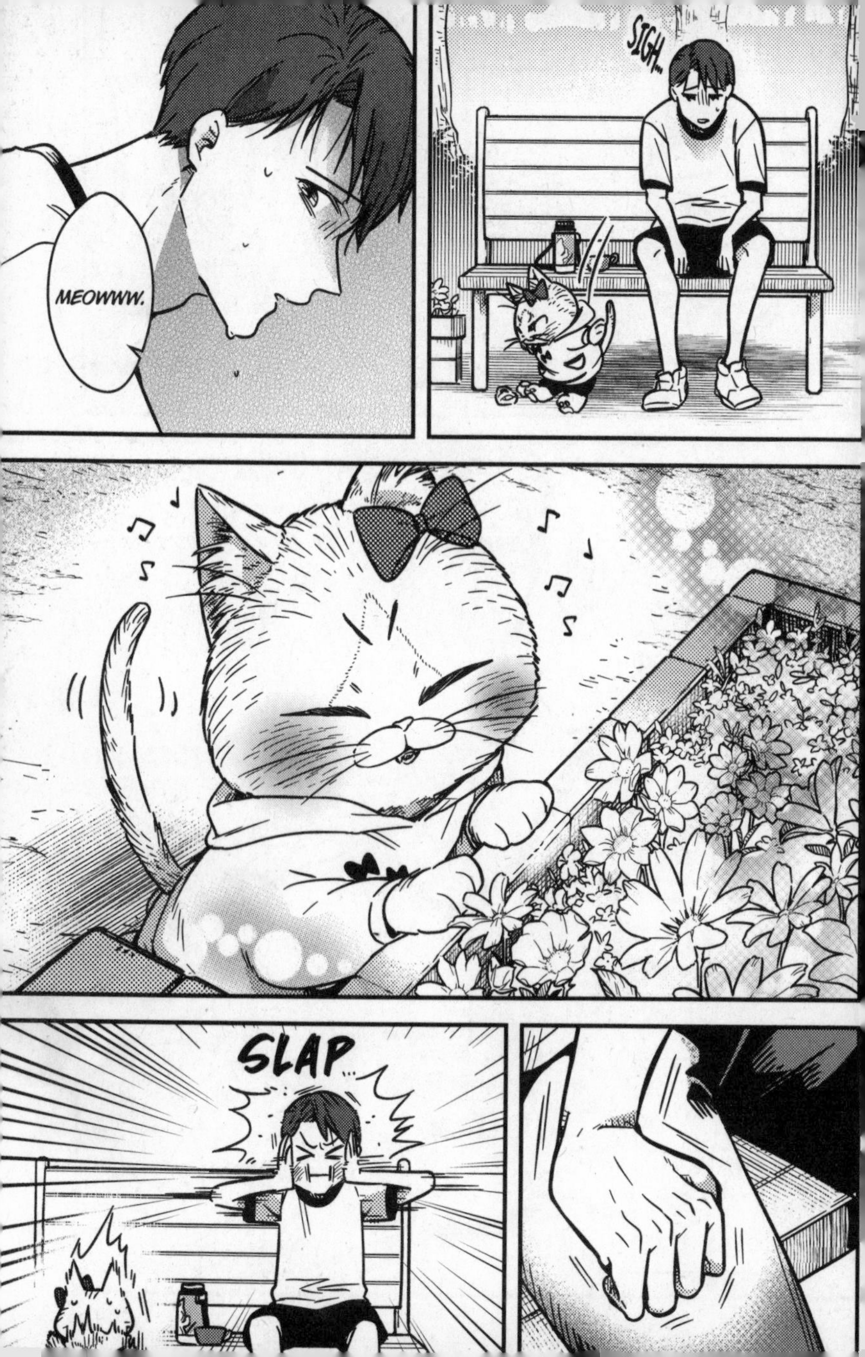
SIGH...
MEOWWW.
SLAP...

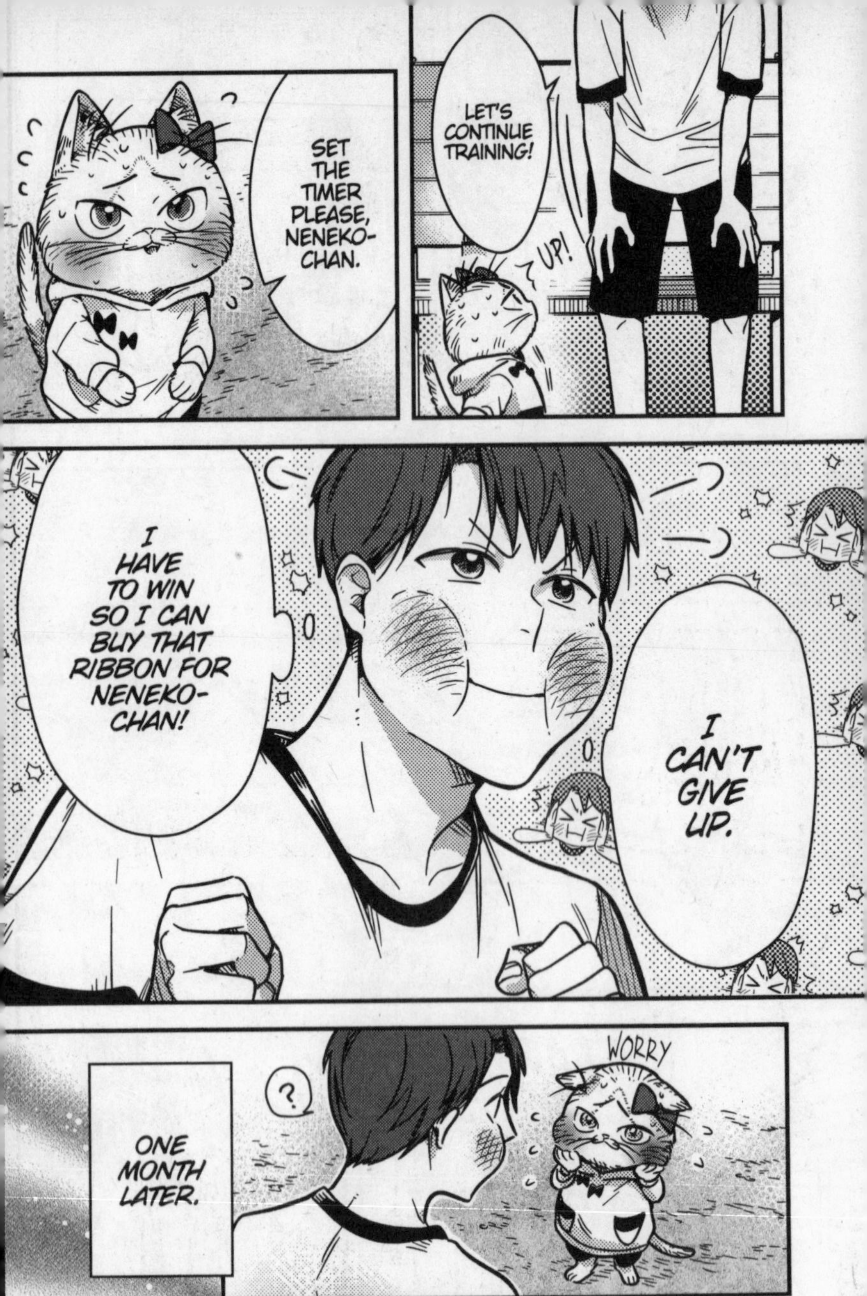
LET'S CONTINUE TRAINING!
UP!
SET THE TIMER PLEASE, NENEKO-CHAN.
I CAN'T GIVE UP.
I HAVE TO WIN SO I CAN BUY THAT RIBBON FOR NENEKO-CHAN!
WORRY
?
ONE MONTH LATER.

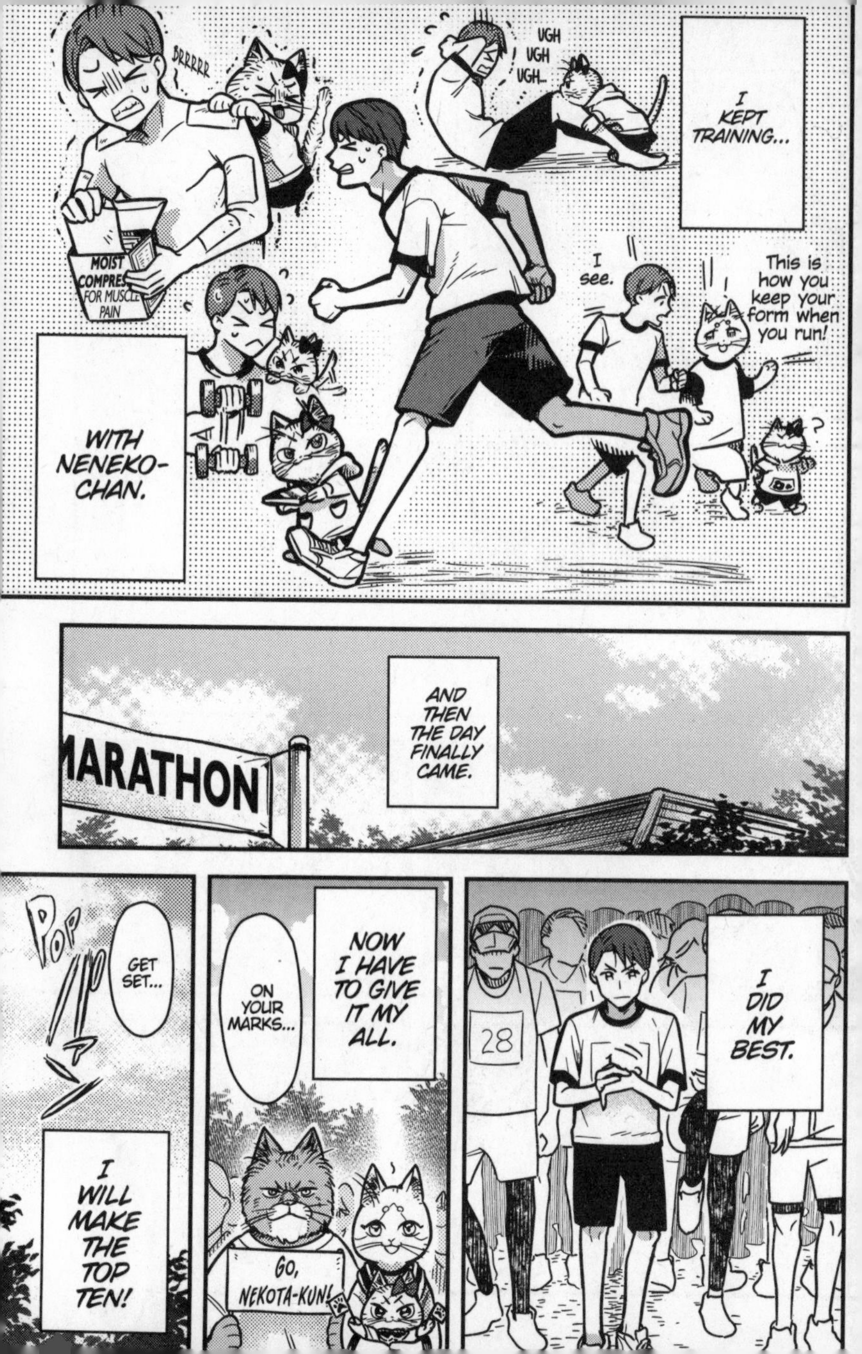
I KEPT TRAINING...
UGH UGH UGH...
This is how you keep your form when you run!
I see.
BRRRRR
MOIST COMPRES FOR MUSCLE PAIN
WITH NENEKO-CHAN.
AND THEN THE DAY FINALLY CAME.
MARATHON
I DID MY BEST.
28
NOW I HAVE TO GIVE IT MY ALL.
ON YOUR MARKS...
GO, NEKOTA-KUN!
GET SET...
POP
I WILL MAKE THE TOP TEN!

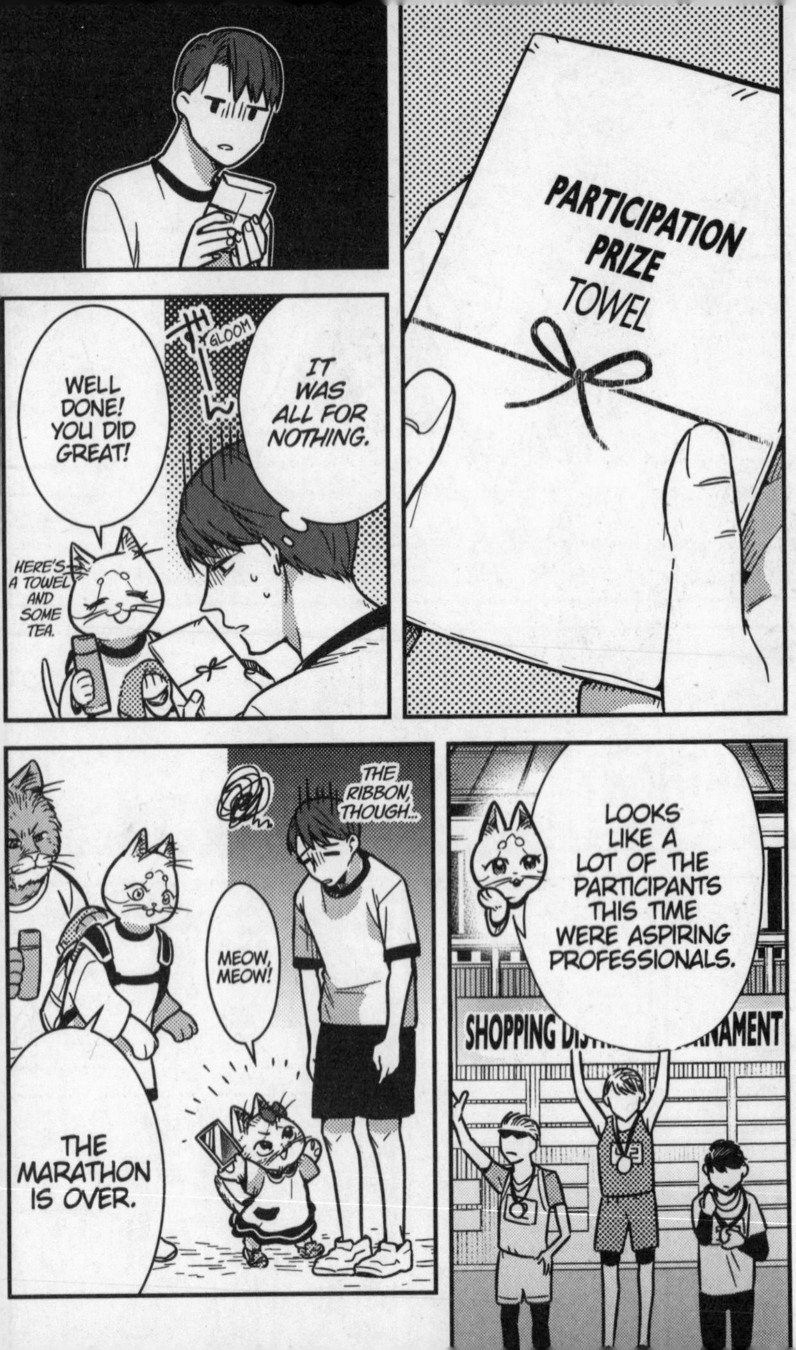
PARTICIPATION PRIZE
TOWEL
IT WAS ALL FOR NOTHING.
GLOOM
WELL DONE! YOU DID GREAT!
HERE'S A TOWEL AND SOME TEA.
LOOKS LIKE A LOT OF THE PARTICIPANTS THIS TIME WERE ASPIRING PROFESSIONALS.
SHOPPING DIS
NAMENT
THE RIBBON, THOUGH...
MEOW, MEOW!
THE MARATHON IS OVER.

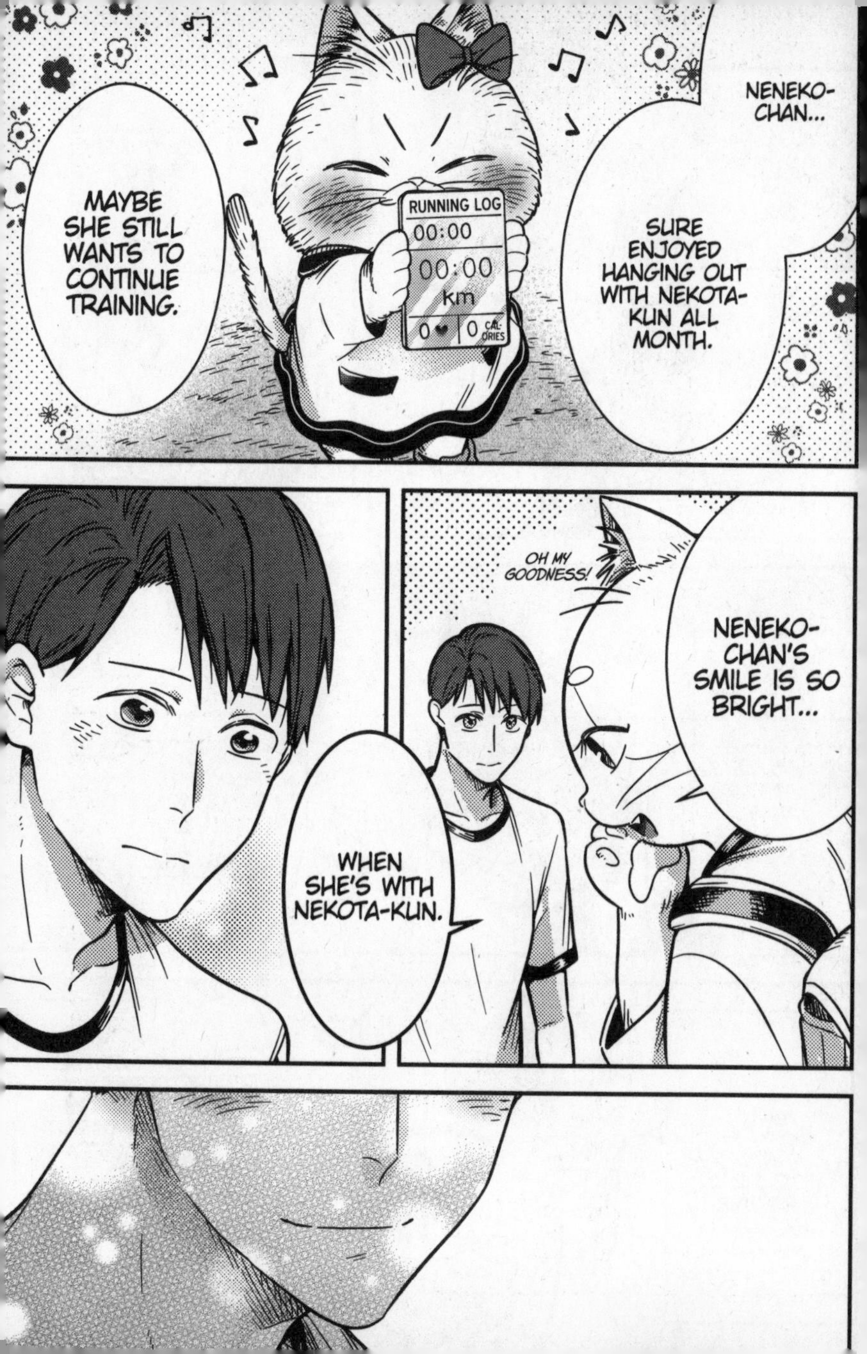
NENEKO-CHAN... SURE ENJOYED HANGING OUT WITH NEKOTA-KUN ALL MONTH.
RUNNING LOG
00:00
00:00 km
0 0 CAL-ORIES
MAYBE SHE STILL WANTS TO CONTINUE TRAINING.
NENEKO-CHAN'S SMILE IS SO BRIGHT...
OH MY GOODNESS!
WHEN SHE'S WITH NEKOTA-KUN.

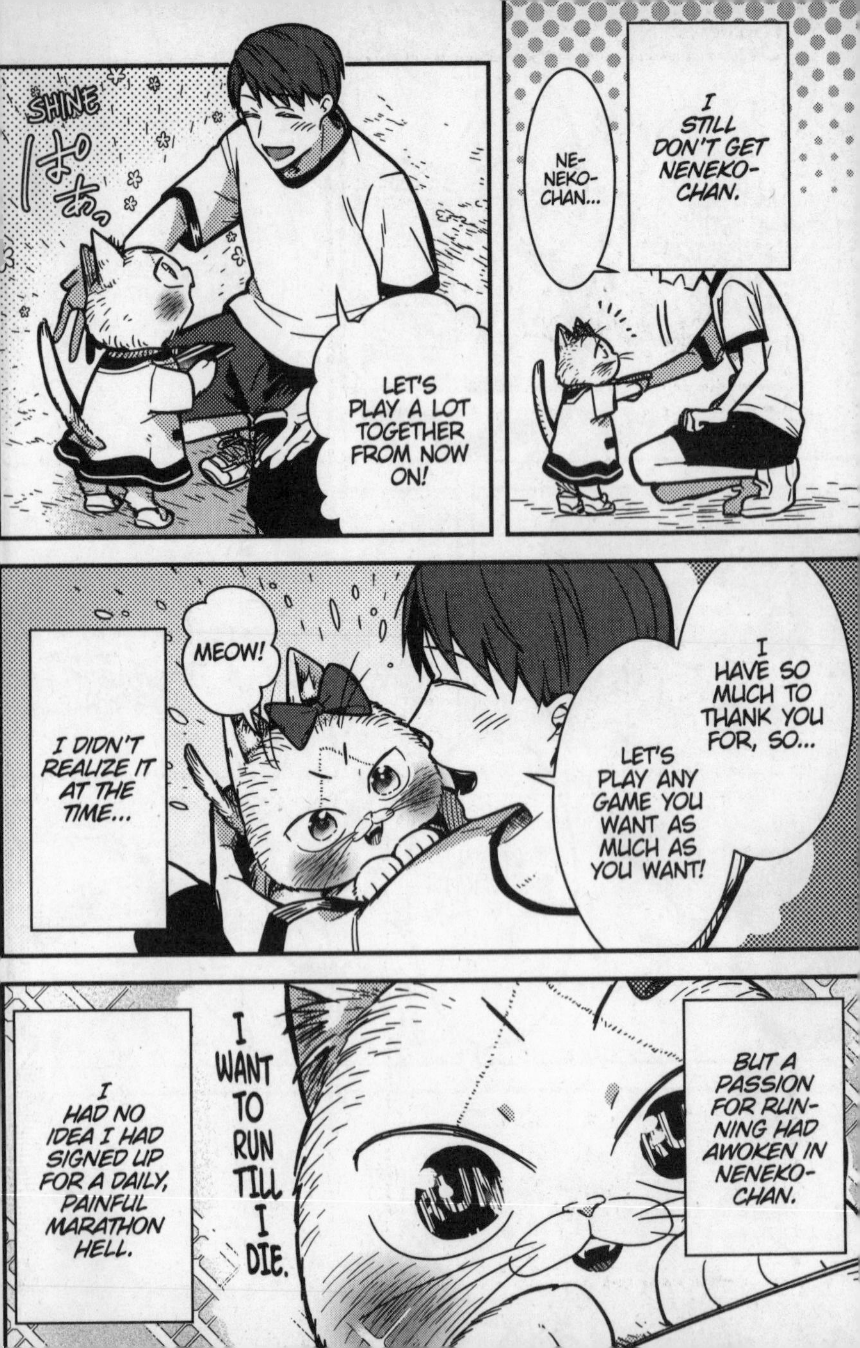
I STILL DON'T GET NENEKO-CHAN.
NE-NEKO-CHAN...
SHINE
LET'S PLAY A LOT TOGETHER FROM NOW ON!
I HAVE SO MUCH TO THANK YOU FOR, SO...
LET'S PLAY ANY GAME YOU WANT AS MUCH AS YOU WANT!
MEOW!
I DIDN'T REALIZE IT AT THE TIME...
BUT A PASSION FOR RUN-NING HAD AWOKEN IN NENEKO-CHAN.
I WANT TO RUN TILL I DIE.
I HAD NO IDEA I HAD SIGNED UP FOR A DAILY, PAINFUL MARATHON HELL.

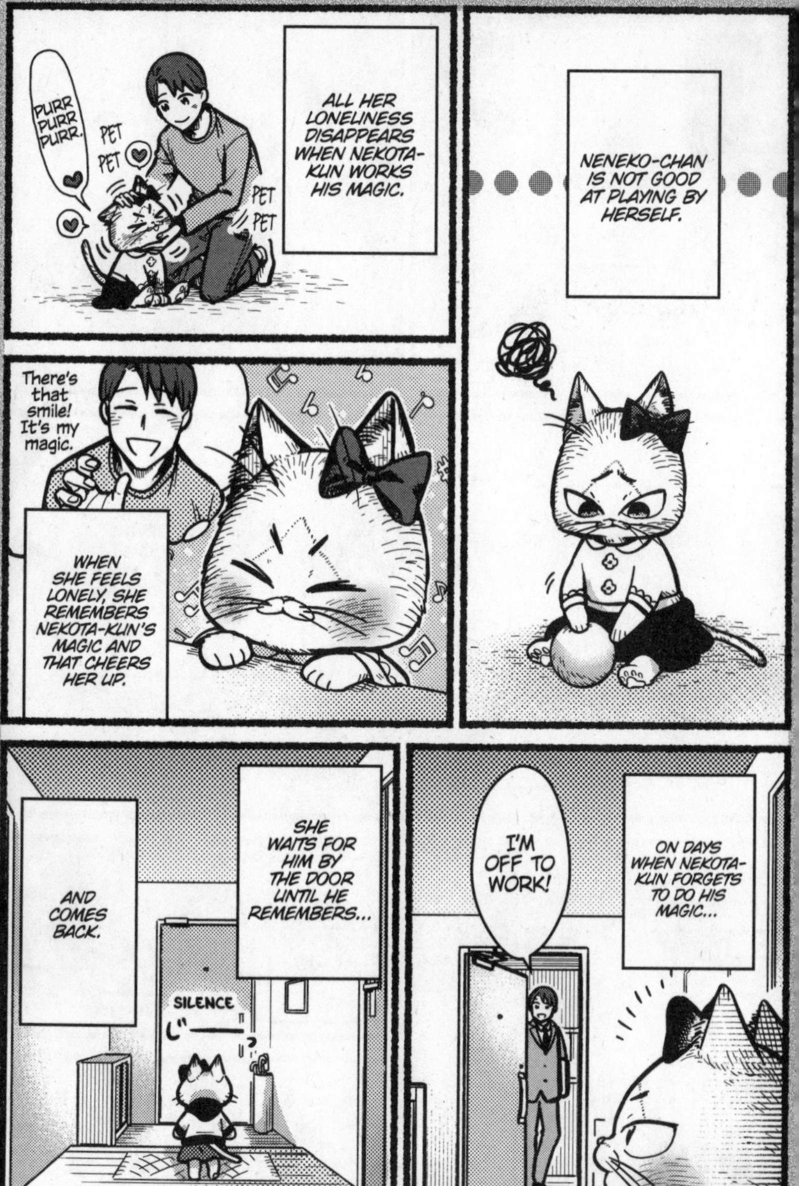
NENEKO-CHAN IS NOT GOOD AT PLAYING BY HERSELF.
ALL HER LONELINESS DISAPPEARS WHEN NEKOTA-KUN WORKS HIS MAGIC.
PURR PURR PURR.
PET PET
PET PET
There's that smile! It's my magic.
WHEN SHE FEELS LONELY, SHE REMEMBERS NEKOTA-KUN'S MAGIC AND THAT CHEERS HER UP.
ON DAYS WHEN NEKOTA-KUN FORGETS TO DO HIS MAGIC...
I'M OFF TO WORK!
SHE WAITS FOR HIM BY THE DOOR UNTIL HE REMEMBERS...
AND COMES BACK.
SILENCE
じー

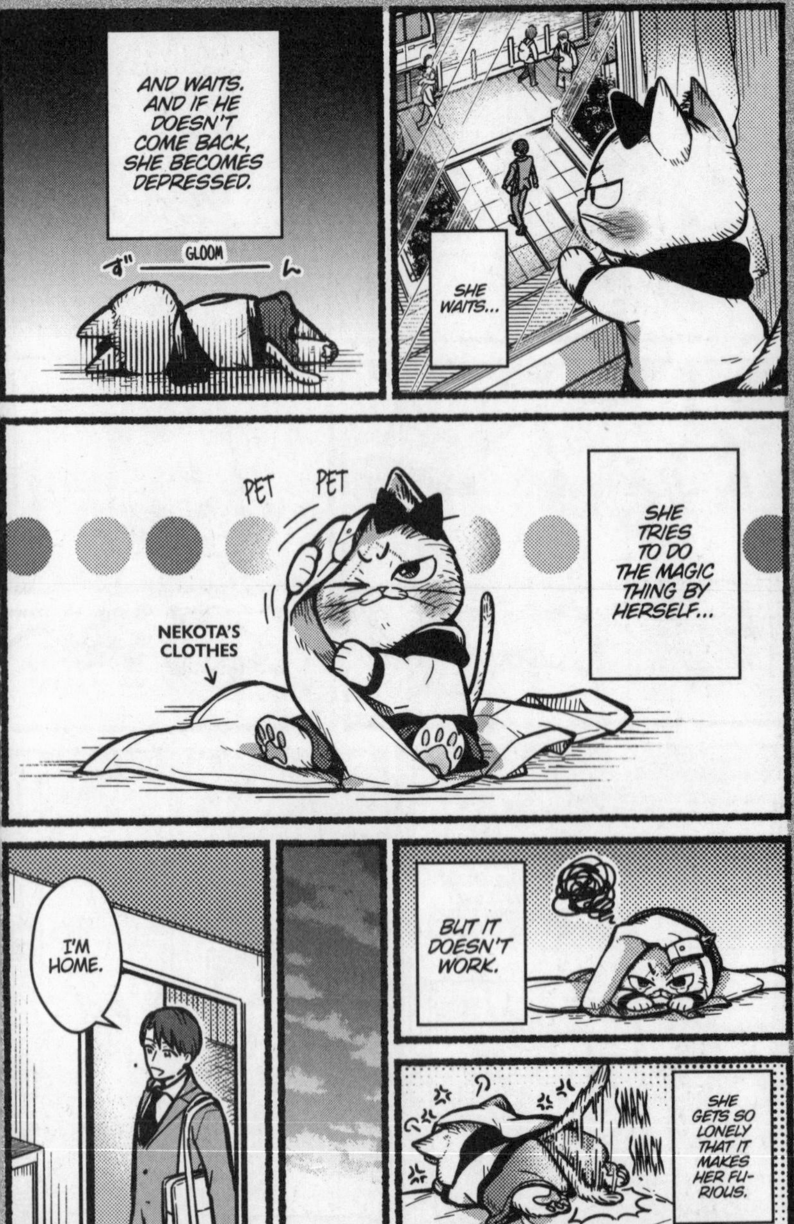
SHE WAITS...
AND WAITS. AND IF HE DOESN'T COME BACK, SHE BECOMES DEPRESSED.
GLOOM
ずーん
SHE TRIES TO DO THE MAGIC THING BY HERSELF...
PET PET
NEKOTA'S CLOTHES
BUT IT DOESN'T WORK.
SHE GETS SO LONELY THAT IT MAKES HER FURIOUS.
SMACK
SMACK
I'M HOME.

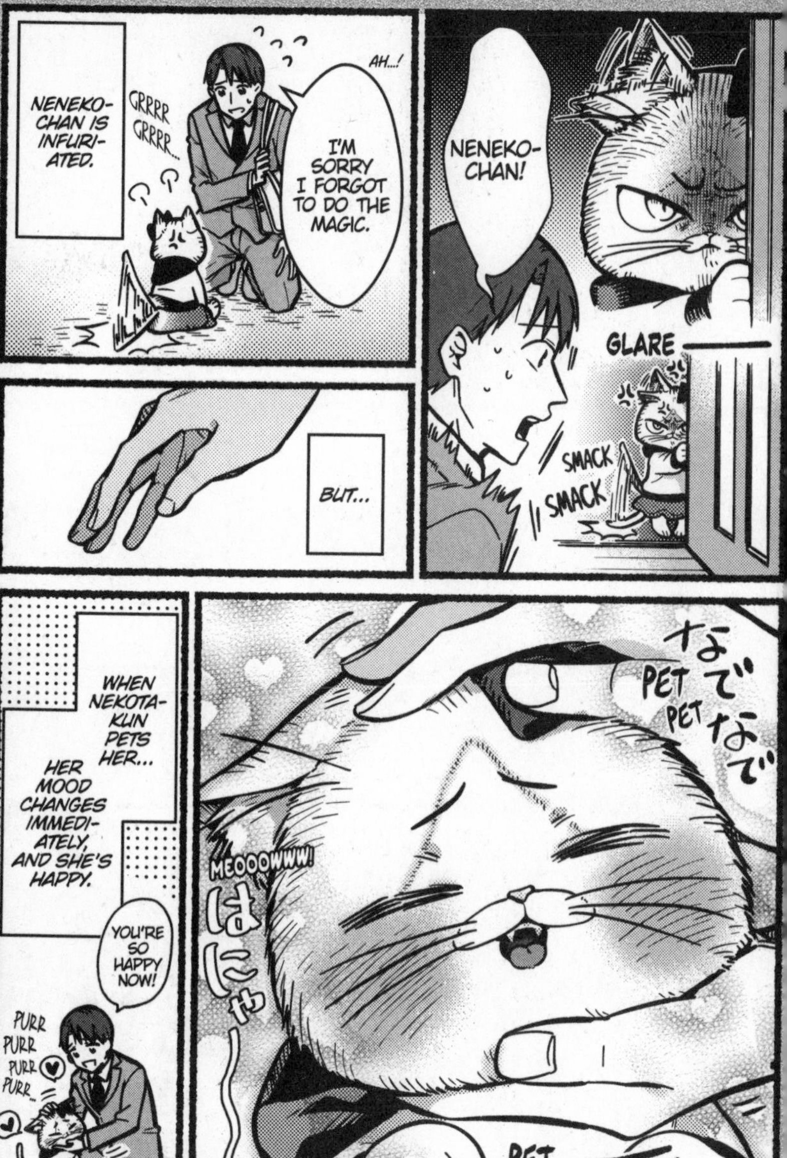
NENEKO-CHAN!
GLARE
SMACK SMACK
AH...!
I'M SORRY I FORGOT TO DO THE MAGIC.
GRRRR GRRRR...
NENEKO-CHAN IS INFURIATED.
BUT...
なでなで
PET PET
MEOOOWWW!
はにゃ〜
PET PET
WHEN NEKOTA-KUN PETS HER...
HER MOOD CHANGES IMMEDIATELY, AND SHE'S HAPPY.
YOU'RE SO HAPPY NOW!
PURR PURR PURR PURR...

My
Sister,
the
Cat

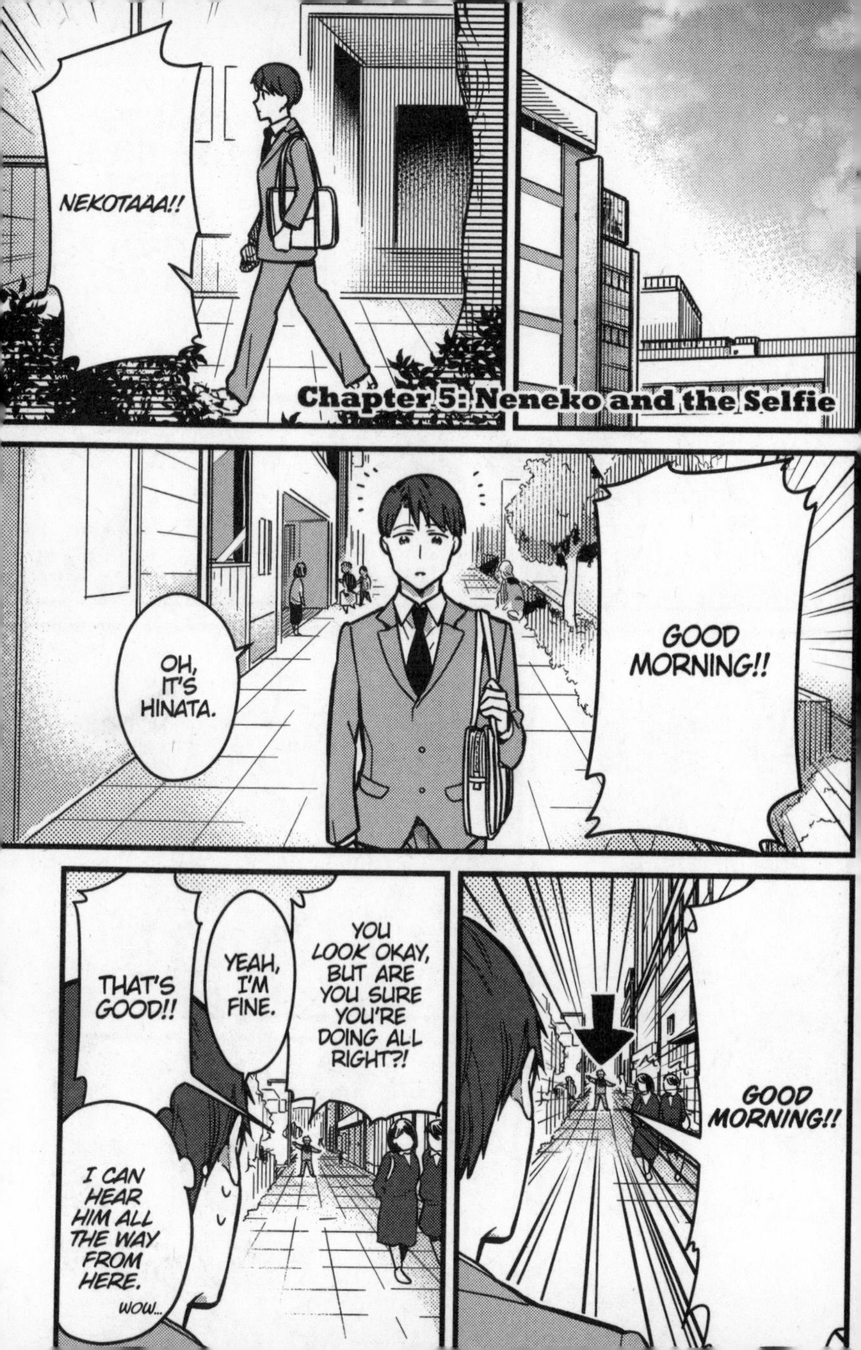
NEKOTAAA!!
Chapter 5: Neneko and the Selfie
GOOD MORNING!!
OH, IT'S HINATA.
GOOD MORNING!!
YOU LOOK OKAY, BUT ARE YOU SURE YOU'RE DOING ALL RIGHT?!
YEAH, I'M FINE.
THAT'S GOOD!!
I CAN HEAR HIM ALL THE WAY FROM HERE.
WOW...

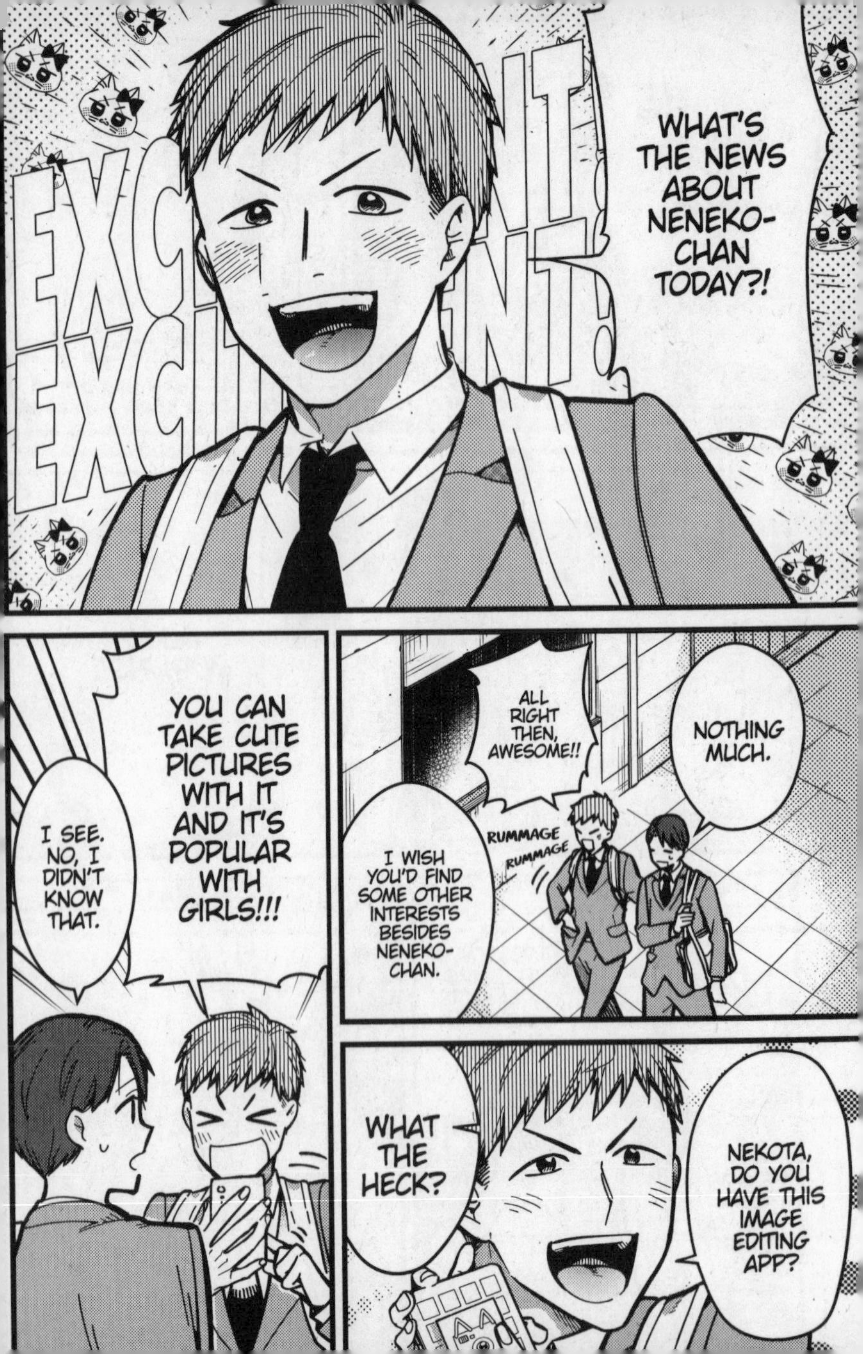
WHAT'S THE NEWS ABOUT NENEKO-CHAN TODAY?!
NOTHING MUCH.
ALL RIGHT THEN, AWESOME!!
RUMMAGE RUMMAGE
I WISH YOU'D FIND SOME OTHER INTERESTS BESIDES NENEKO-CHAN.
NEKOTA, DO YOU HAVE THIS IMAGE EDITING APP?
WHAT THE HECK?
YOU CAN TAKE CUTE PICTURES WITH IT AND IT'S POPULAR WITH GIRLS!!!
I SEE. NO, I DIDN'T KNOW THAT.

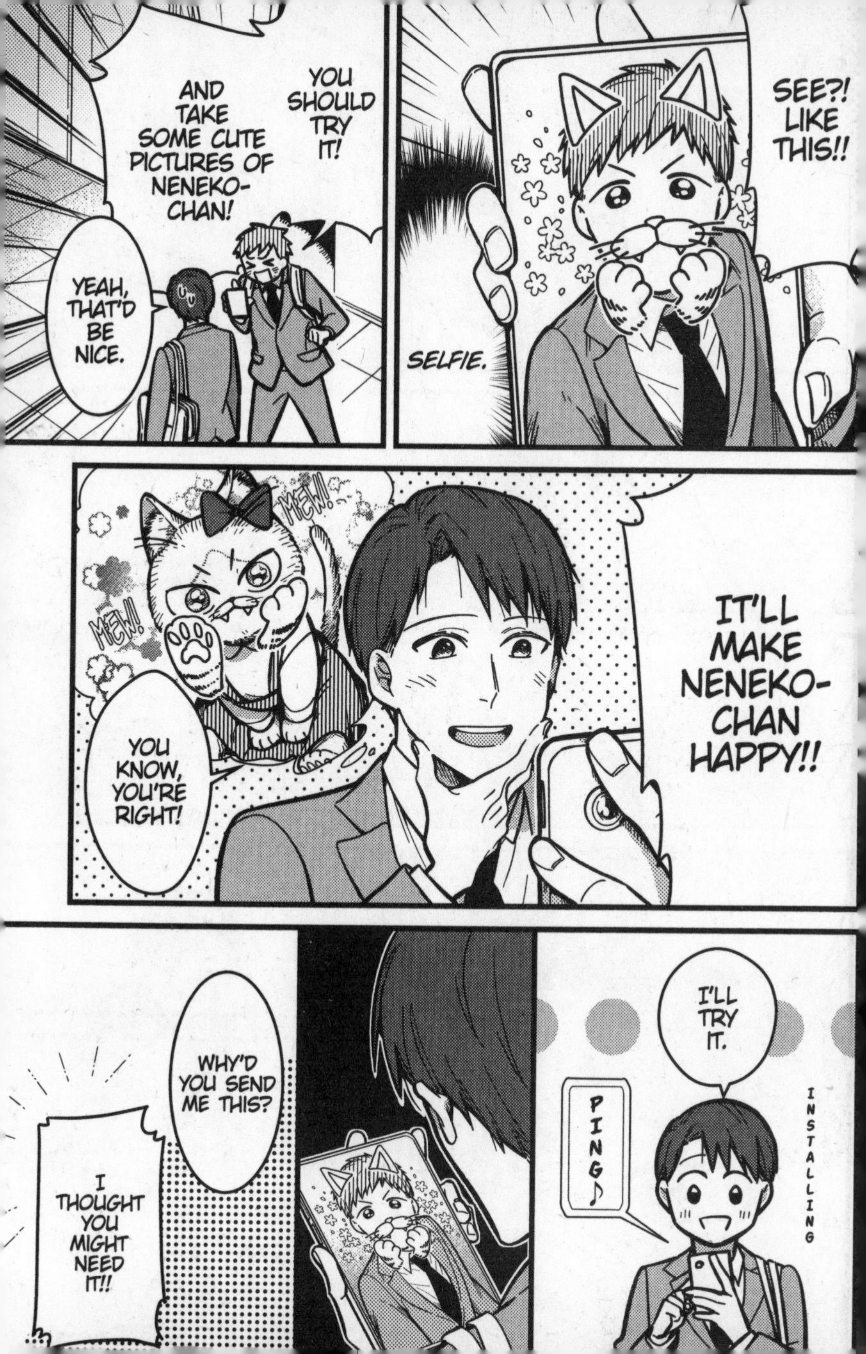
SEE?! LIKE THIS!!
SELFIE.
YOU SHOULD TRY IT!
AND TAKE SOME CUTE PICTURES OF NENEKO-CHAN!
YEAH, THAT'D BE NICE.
IT'LL MAKE NENEKO-CHAN HAPPY!!
MEW!
MEW!
YOU KNOW, YOU'RE RIGHT!
I'LL TRY IT.
INSTALLING
PING♪
WHY'D YOU SEND ME THIS?
I THOUGHT YOU MIGHT NEED IT!!

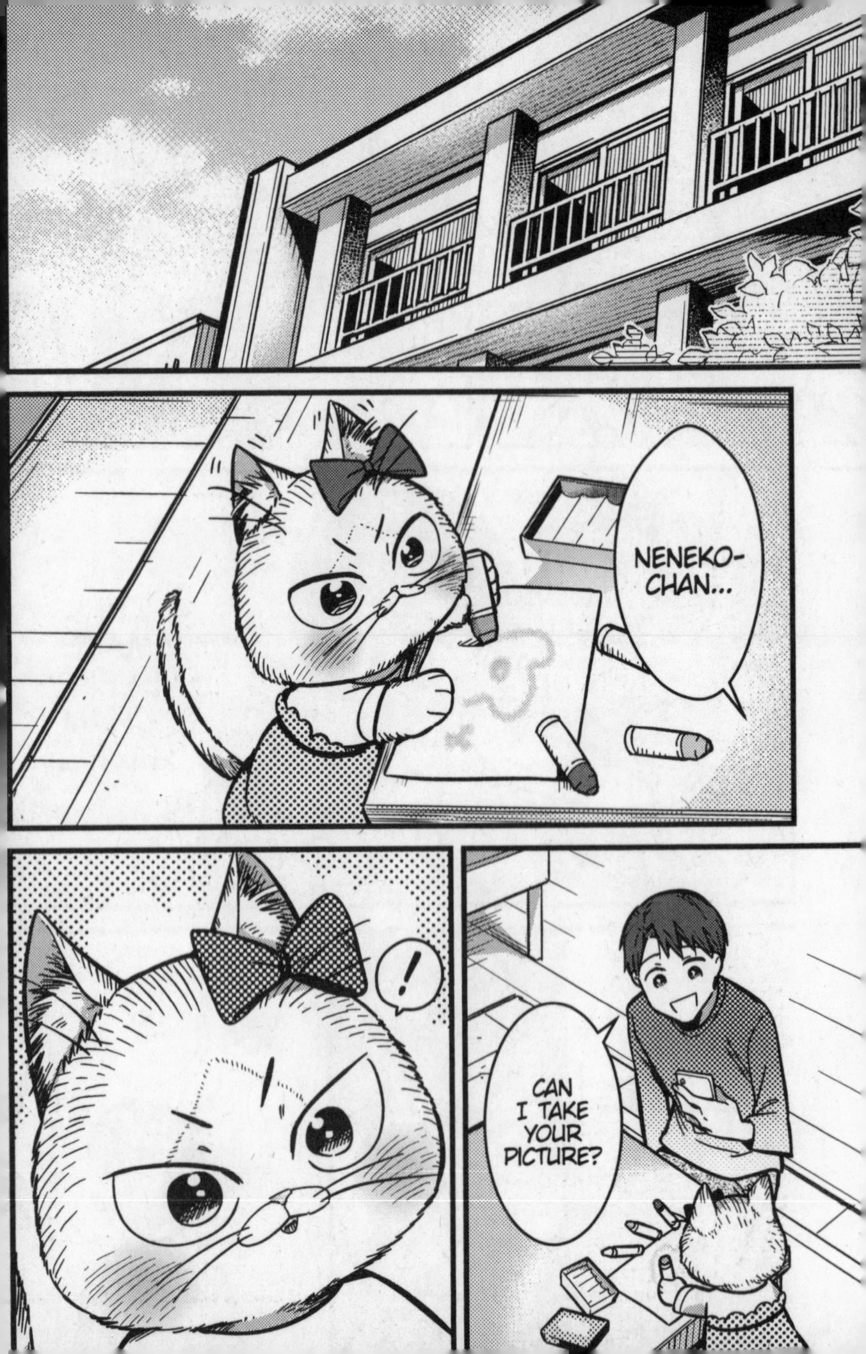
NENEKO-CHAN...
CAN I TAKE YOUR PICTURE?
!

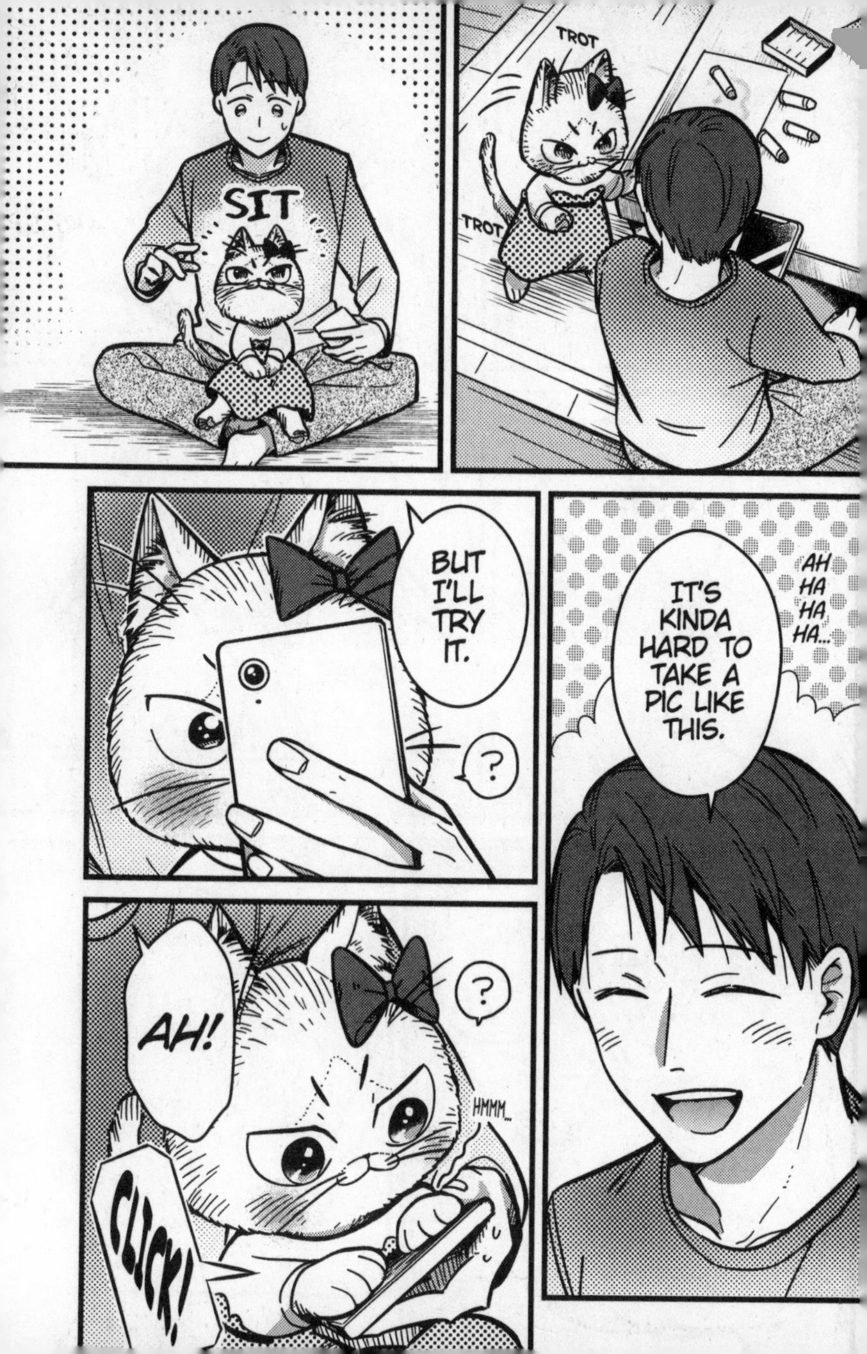
TROT
TROT
SIT
AH HA HA HA...
IT'S KINDA HARD TO TAKE A PIC LIKE THIS.
BUT I'LL TRY IT.
?
?
AH!
HMMM...
CLICK!

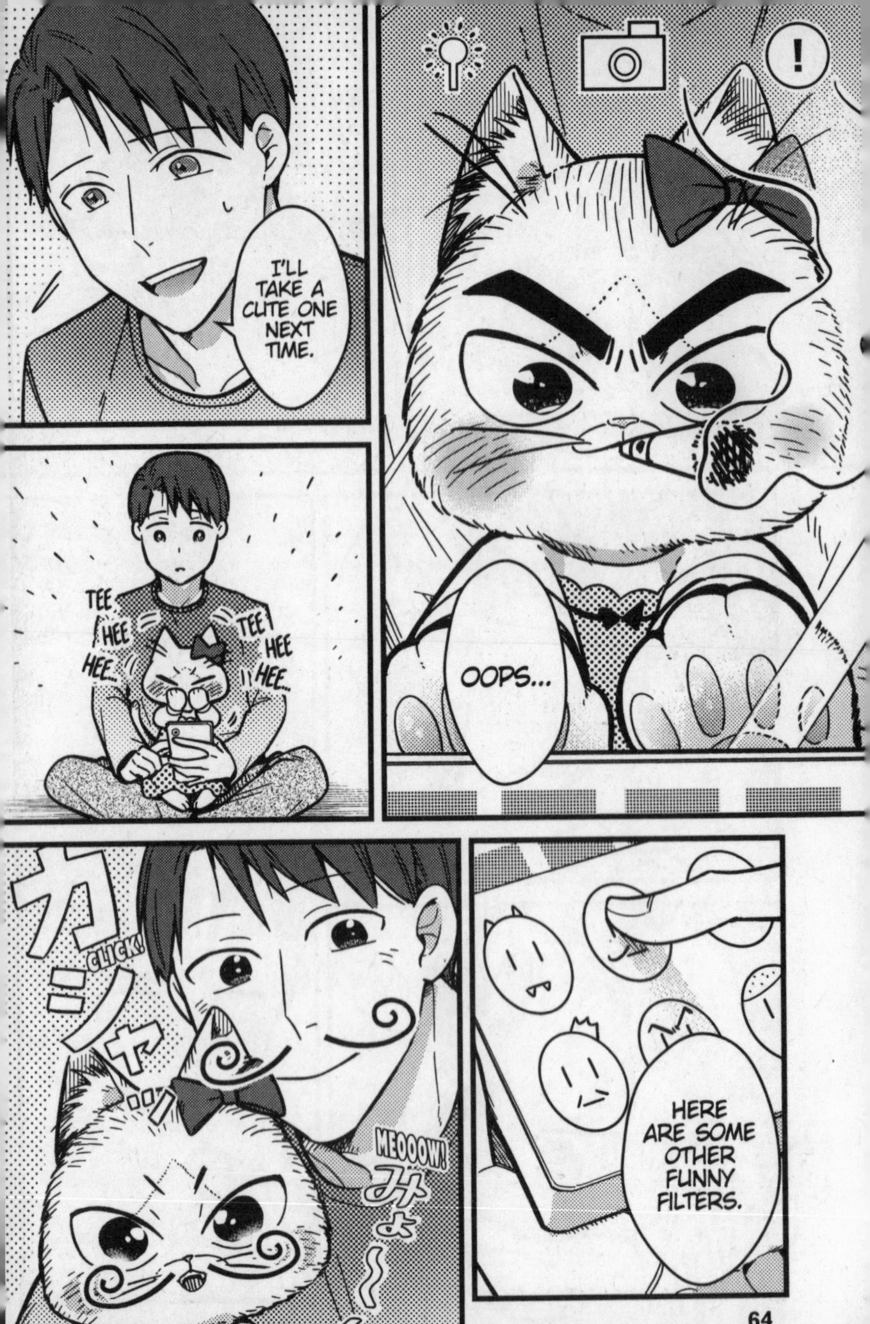
OOPS...
I'LL TAKE A CUTE ONE NEXT TIME.
TEE HEE HEE...
TEE HEE HEE...
HERE ARE SOME OTHER FUNNY FILTERS.
CLICK!
MEOOOW!

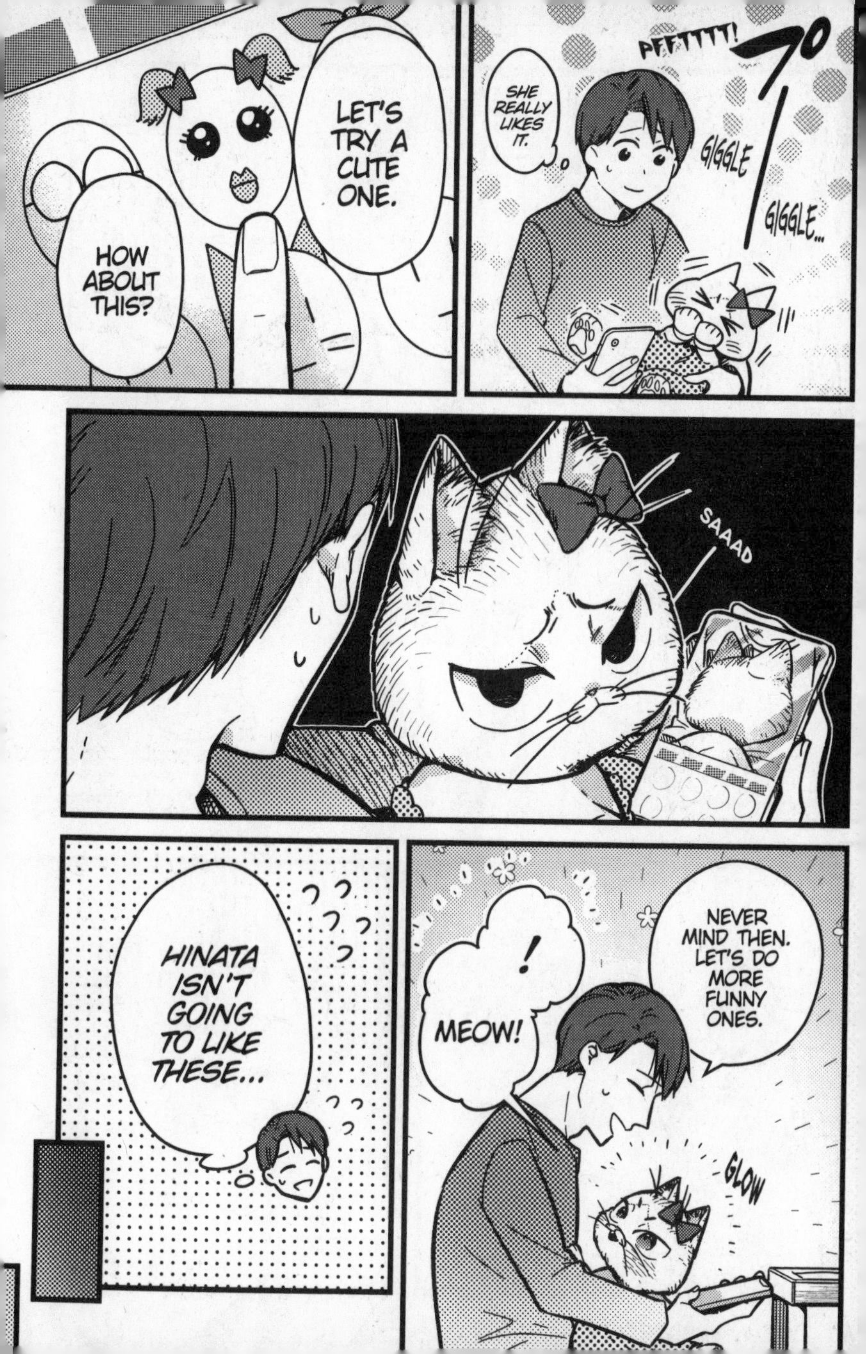
PFFTTTT!
SHE REALLY LIKES IT.
GIGGLE
GIGGLE...
LET'S TRY A CUTE ONE.
HOW ABOUT THIS?
SAAAD
NEVER MIND THEN. LET'S DO MORE FUNNY ONES.
!
MEOW!
GLOW
HINATA ISN'T GOING TO LIKE THESE...

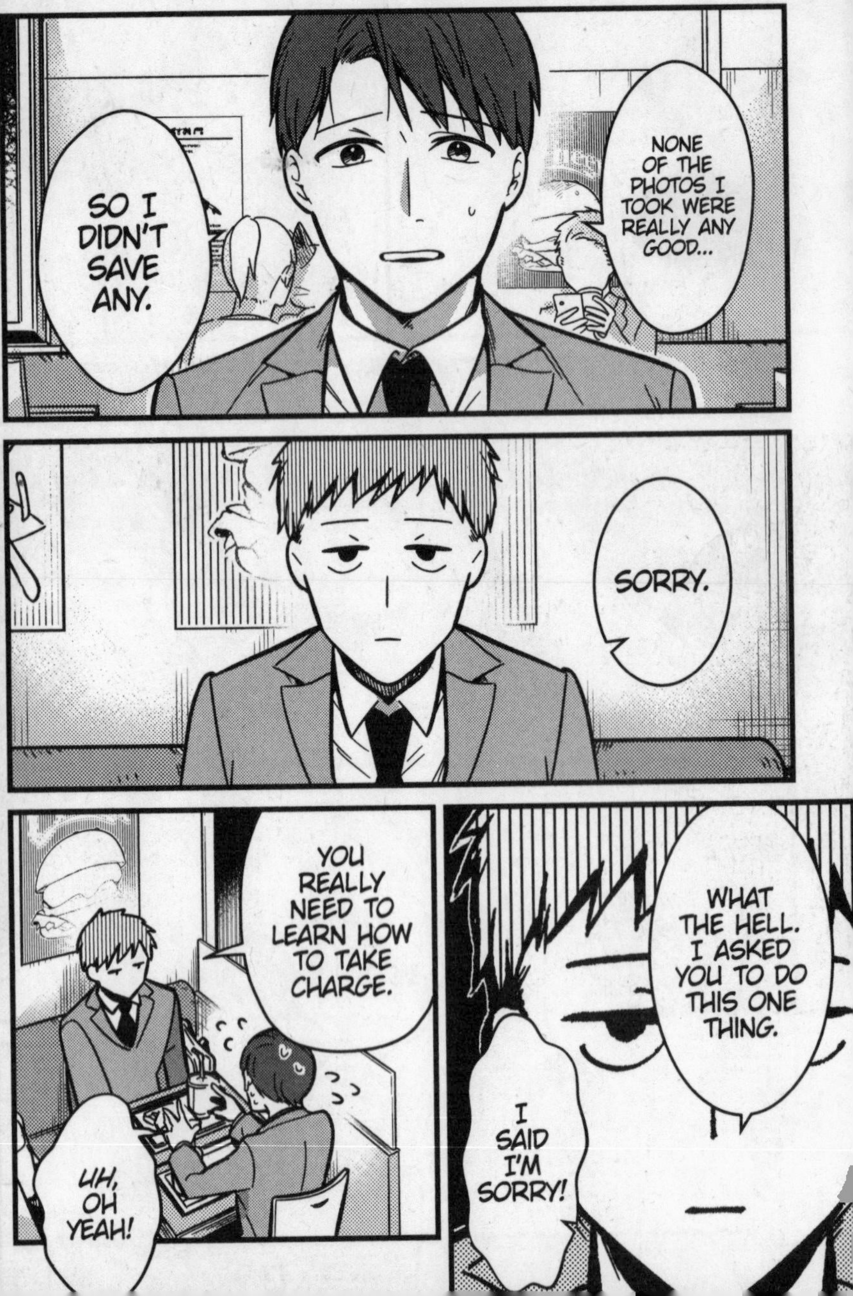
NONE OF THE PHOTOS I TOOK WERE REALLY ANY GOOD...
SO I DIDN'T SAVE ANY.
SORRY.
WHAT THE HELL. I ASKED YOU TO DO THIS ONE THING.
I SAID I'M SORRY!
YOU REALLY NEED TO LEARN HOW TO TAKE CHARGE.
UH, OH YEAH!

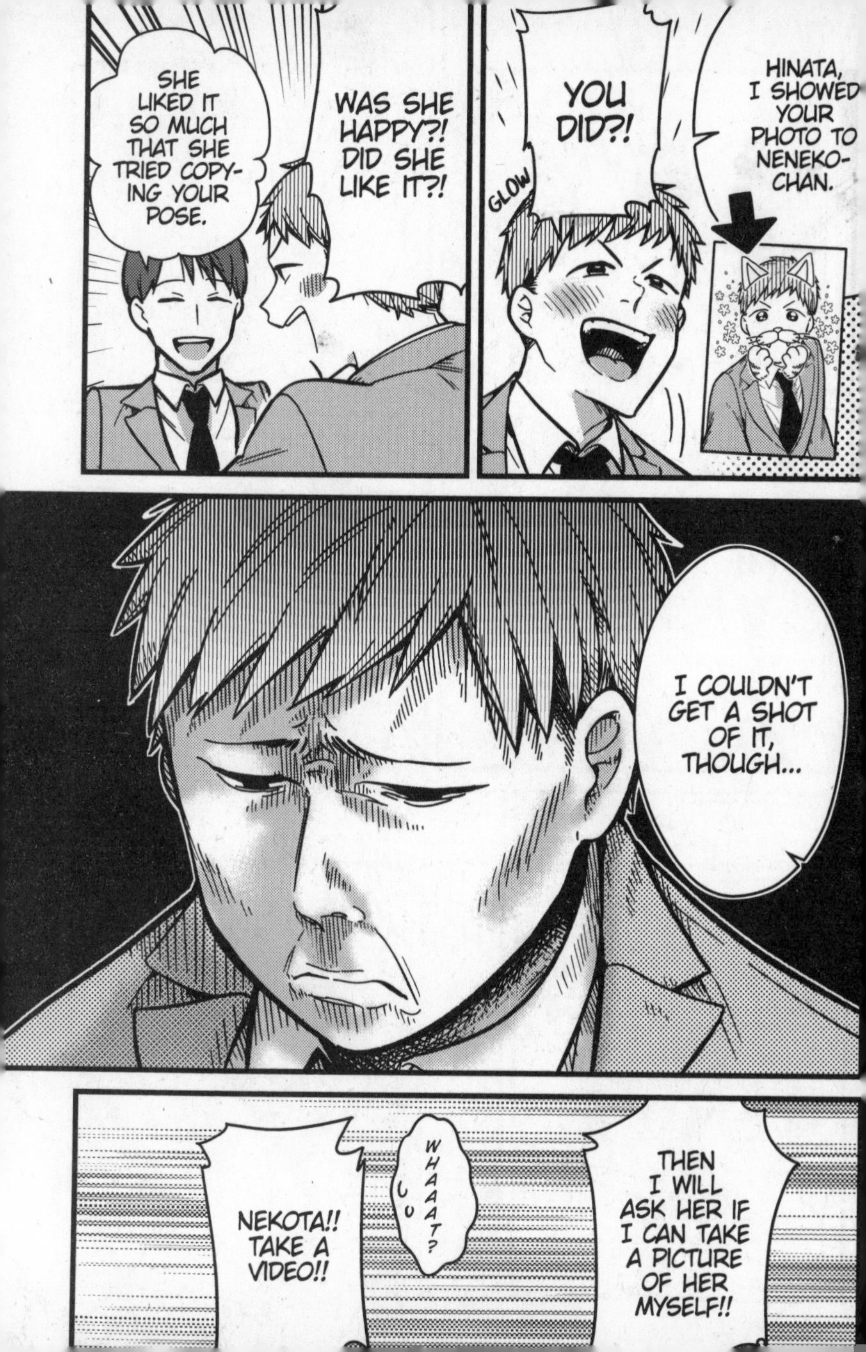
HINATA, I SHOWED YOUR PHOTO TO NENEKO-CHAN.
YOU DID?!
GLOW
WAS SHE HAPPY?! DID SHE LIKE IT?!
SHE LIKED IT SO MUCH THAT SHE TRIED COPY-ING YOUR POSE.
I COULDN'T GET A SHOT OF IT, THOUGH...
THEN I WILL ASK HER IF I CAN TAKE A PICTURE OF HER MYSELF!!
WHAAAT?
NEKOTA!! TAKE A VIDEO!!

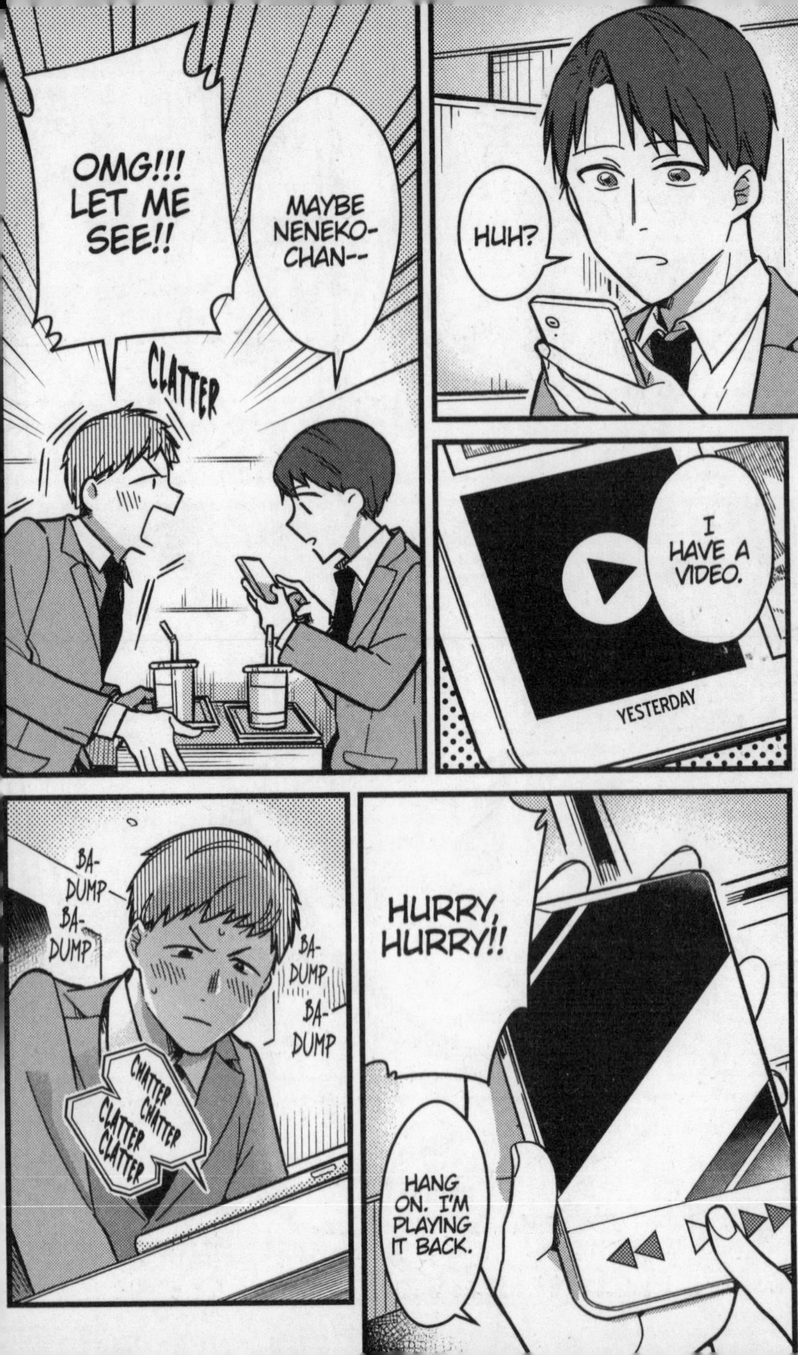
HUH?
I HAVE A VIDEO.
YESTERDAY
MAYBE NENEKO-CHAN--
OMG!!! LET ME SEE!!
CLATTER
HURRY, HURRY!!
HANG ON. I'M PLAYING IT BACK.
BA-DUMP BA-DUMP
BA-DUMP BA-DUMP
CHATTER CHATTER CLATTER CLATTER

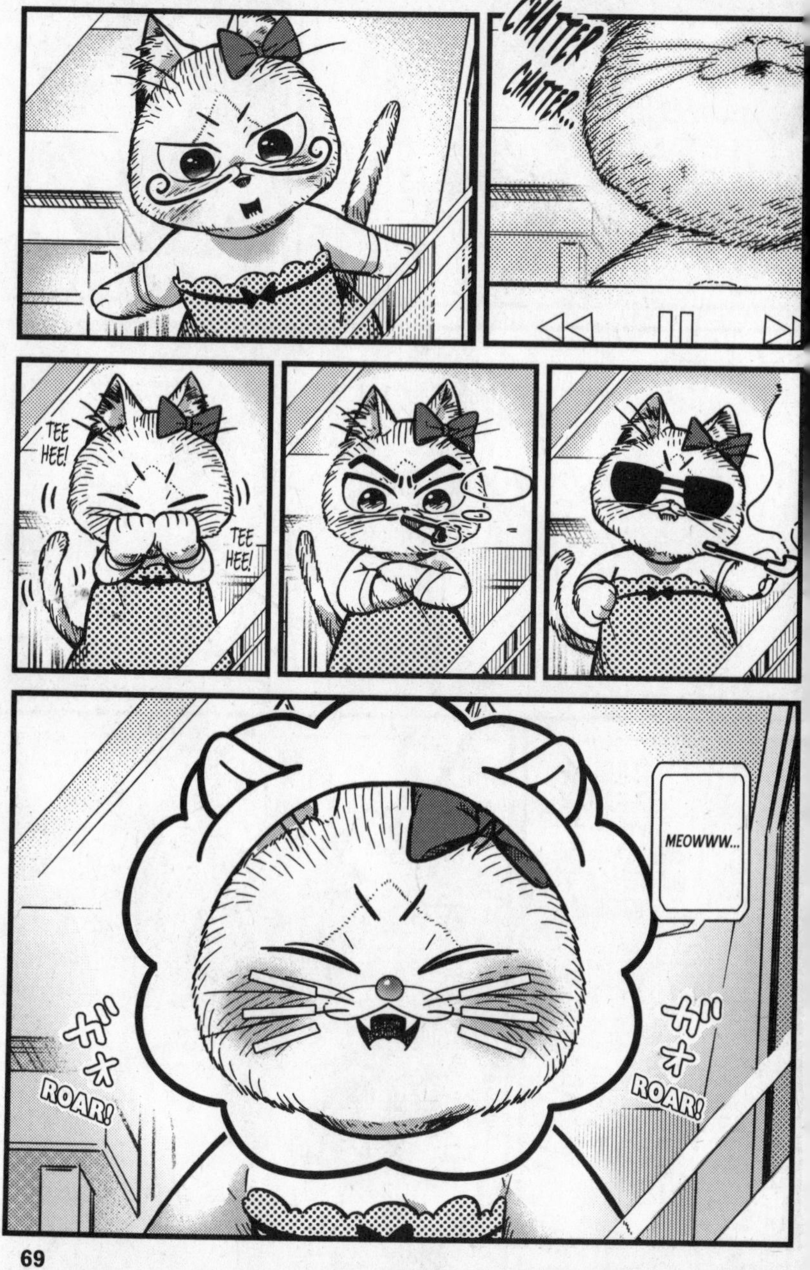
CHATTER CHATTER...
TEE HEE!
TEE HEE!
MEOWWW...
ガオ
ROAR!
ガオ
ROAR!

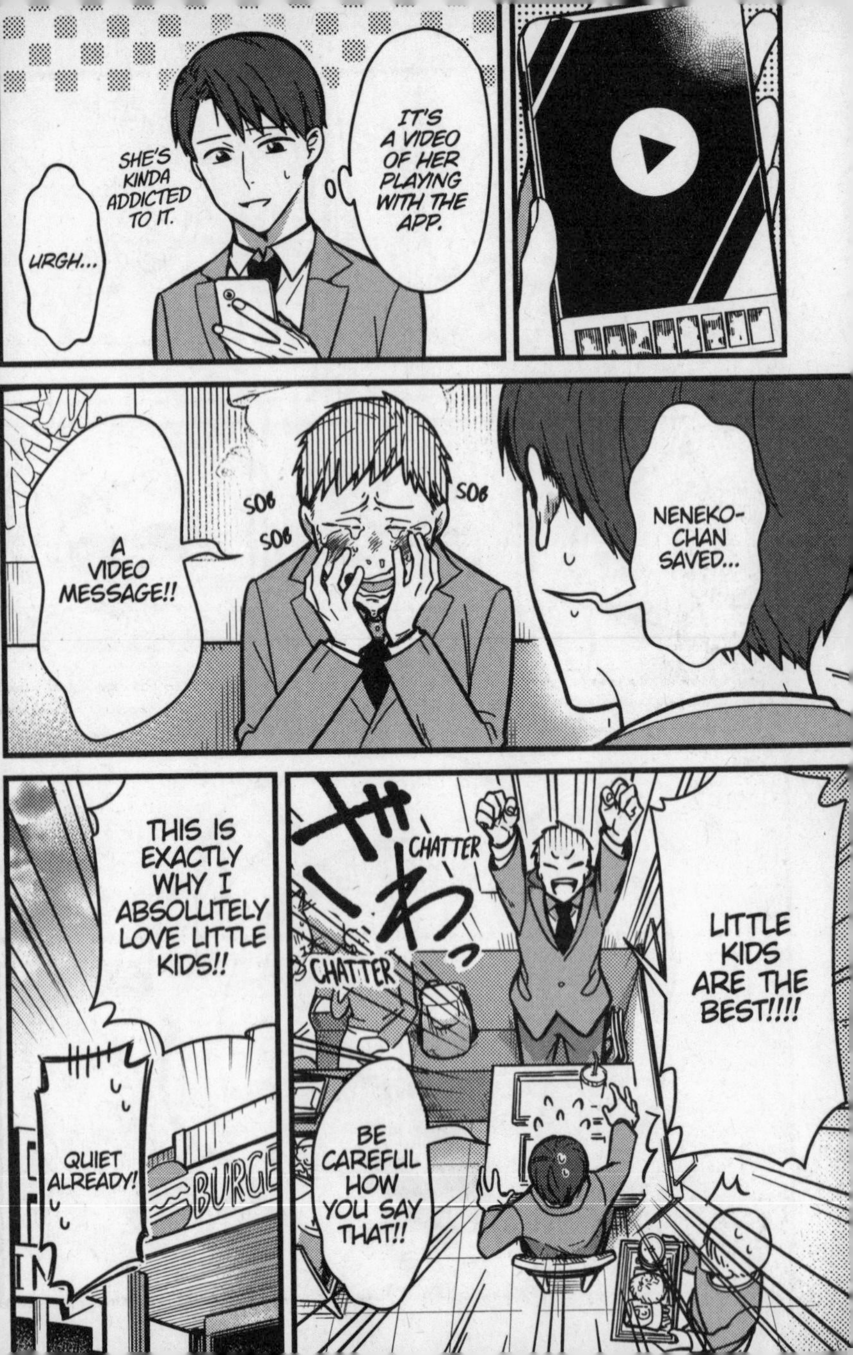
IT'S A VIDEO OF HER PLAYING WITH THE APP.
SHE'S KINDA ADDICTED TO IT.
URGH...
NENEKO-CHAN SAVED...
SOB
SOB
SOB
A VIDEO MESSAGE!!
LITTLE KIDS ARE THE BEST!!!!
ざわっ
CHATTER
CHATTER
BE CAREFUL HOW YOU SAY THAT!!
THIS IS EXACTLY WHY I ABSOLUTELY LOVE LITTLE KIDS!!
QUIET ALREADY!
BURGE

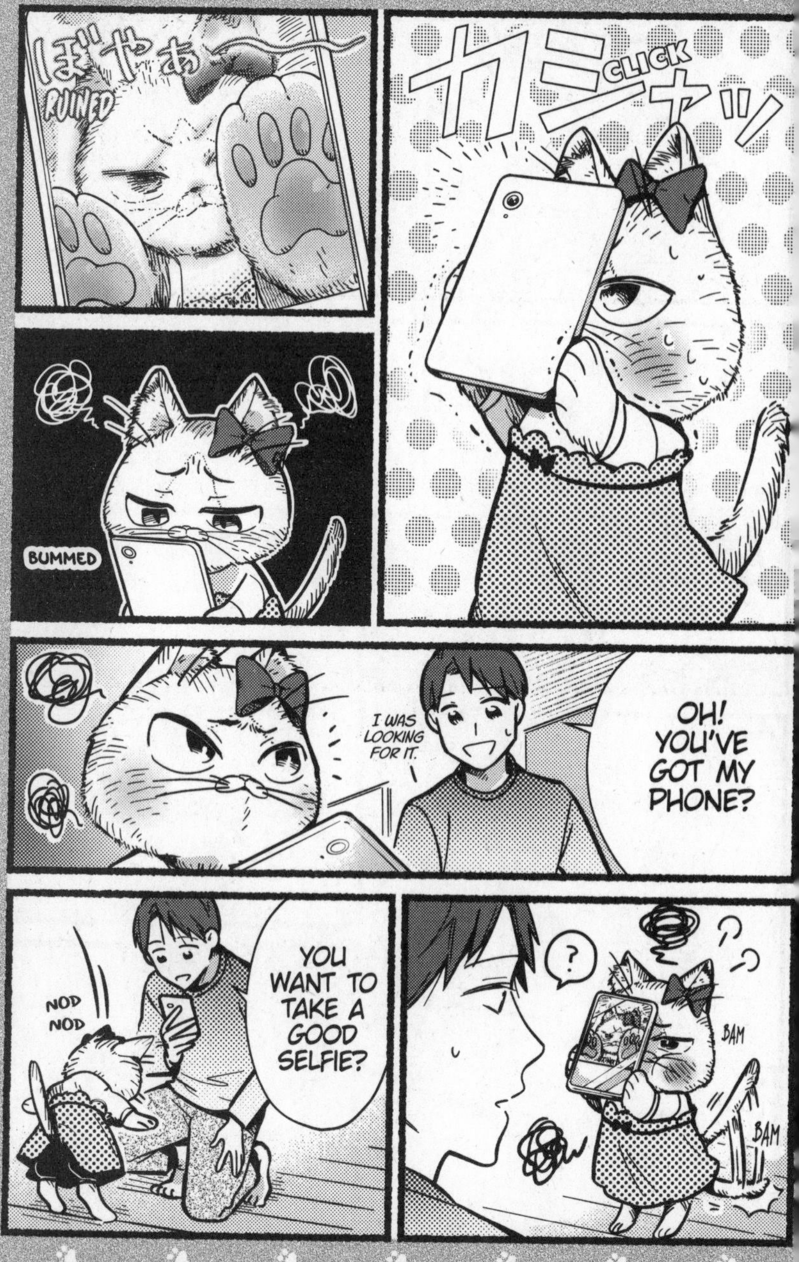
カシャッ
CLICK
ぼやあ
RUINED
BUMMED
OH! YOU'VE GOT MY PHONE?
I WAS LOOKING FOR IT.
?
BAM
BAM
YOU WANT TO TAKE A GOOD SELFIE?
NOD NOD

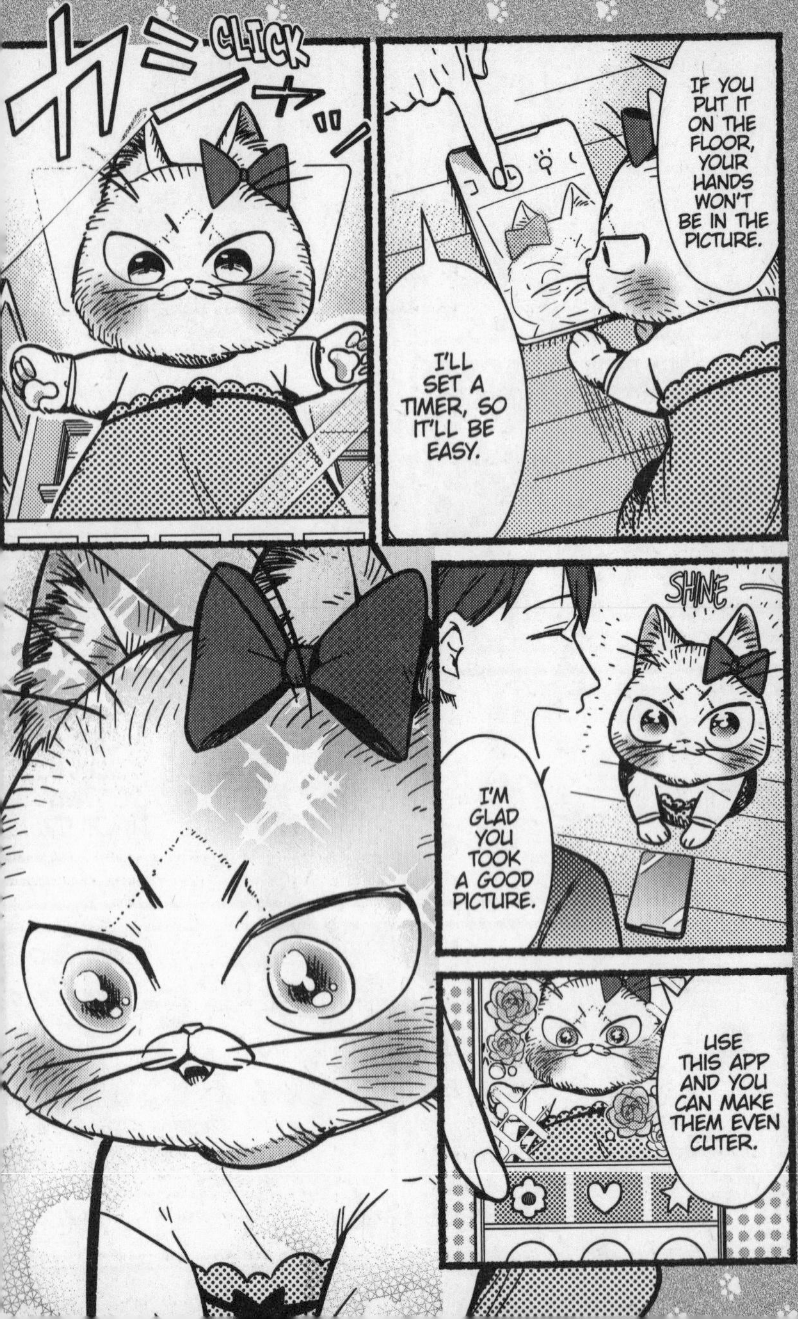
IF YOU PUT IT ON THE FLOOR, YOUR HANDS WON'T BE IN THE PICTURE.
I'LL SET A TIMER, SO IT'LL BE EASY.
CLICK
SHINE
I'M GLAD YOU TOOK A GOOD PICTURE.
USE THIS APP AND YOU CAN MAKE THEM EVEN CUTER.

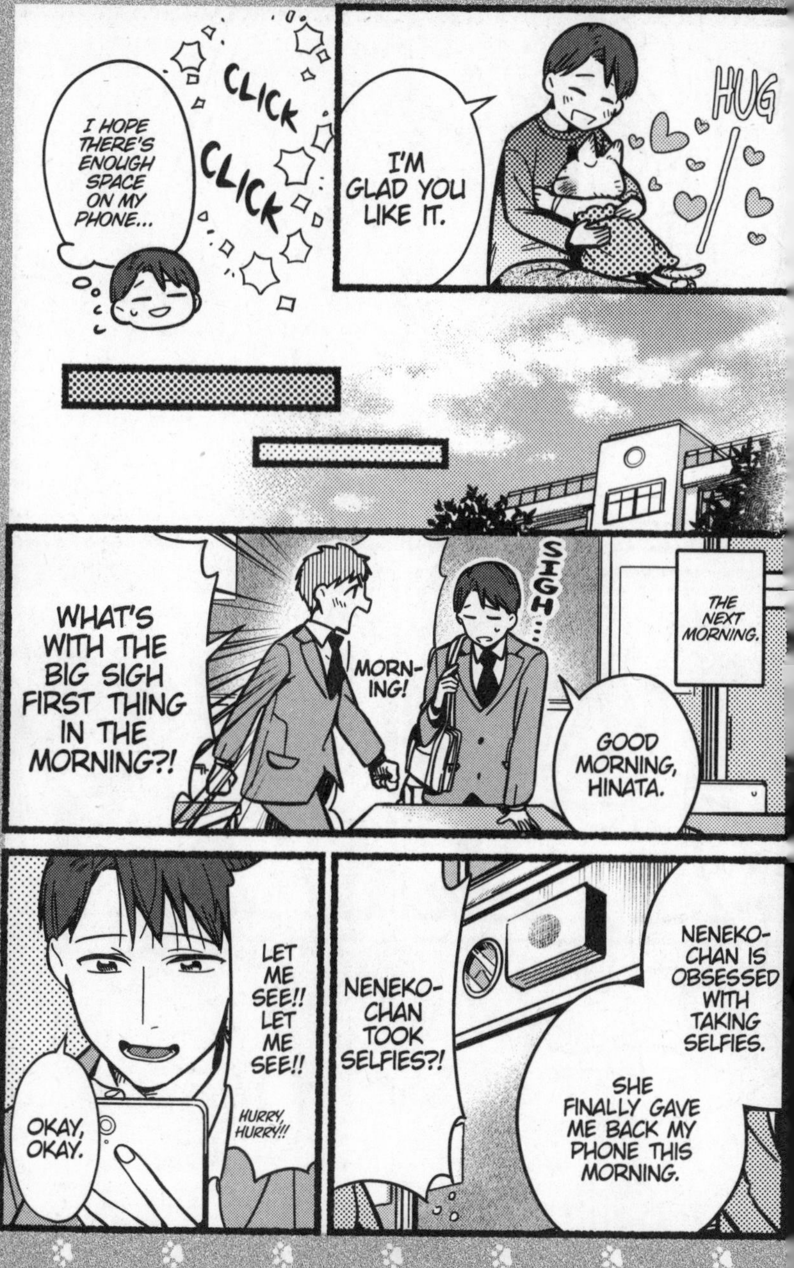
HUG
I'M GLAD YOU LIKE IT.
CLICK
CLICK
I HOPE THERE'S ENOUGH SPACE ON MY PHONE...
THE NEXT MORNING.
SIGH...
GOOD MORNING, HINATA.
MORNING!
WHAT'S WITH THE BIG SIGH FIRST THING IN THE MORNING?!
NENEKO-CHAN IS OBSESSED WITH TAKING SELFIES.
SHE FINALLY GAVE ME BACK MY PHONE THIS MORNING.
NENEKO-CHAN TOOK SELFIES?!
LET ME SEE!! LET ME SEE!!
HURRY, HURRY!!
OKAY, OKAY.

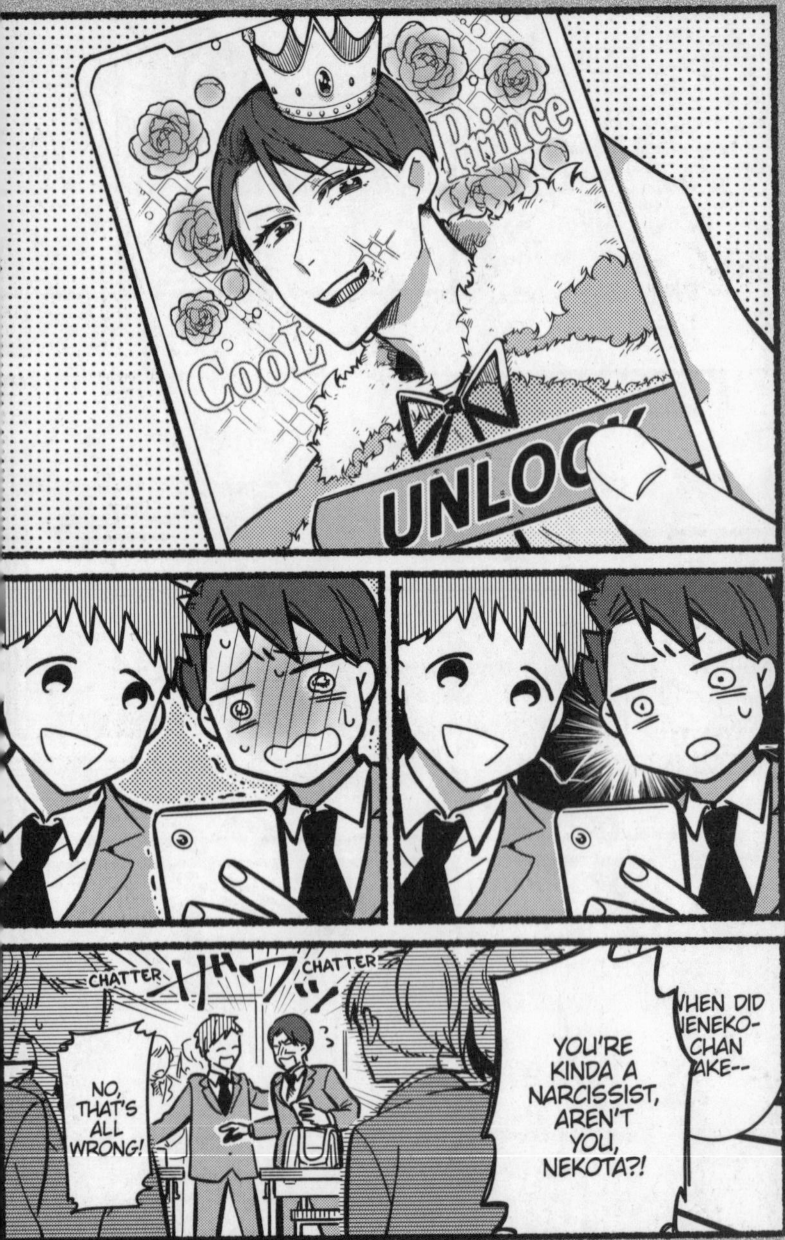
Prince
CooL
UNLOCK
WHEN DID
ENEKO-
CHAN
AKE--
YOU'RE KINDA A NARCISSIST, AREN'T YOU, NEKOTA?!
CHATTER
CHATTER
NO, THAT'S ALL WRONG!

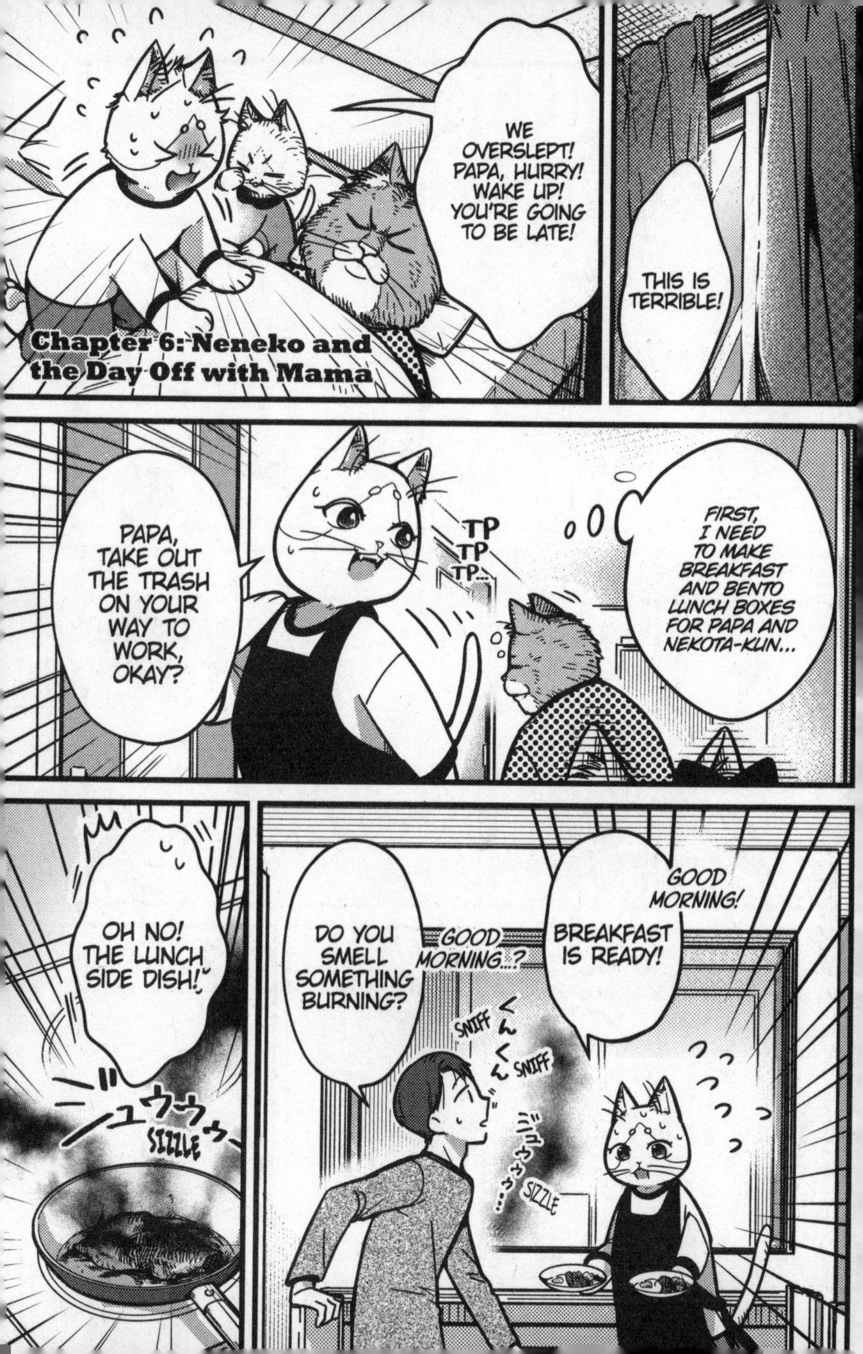
THIS IS TERRIBLE!
WE OVERSLEPT! PAPA, HURRY! WAKE UP! YOU'RE GOING TO BE LATE!
Chapter 6: Neneko and the Day Off with Mama
FIRST, I NEED TO MAKE BREAKFAST AND BENTO LUNCH BOXES FOR PAPA AND NEKOTA-KUN...
TP TP TP...
PAPA, TAKE OUT THE TRASH ON YOUR WAY TO WORK, OKAY?
GOOD MORNING!
BREAKFAST IS READY!
SNIFF
SNIFF
GOOD MORNING...?
DO YOU SMELL SOMETHING BURNING?
SIZZLE
OH NO! THE LUNCH SIDE DISH!
SIZZLE

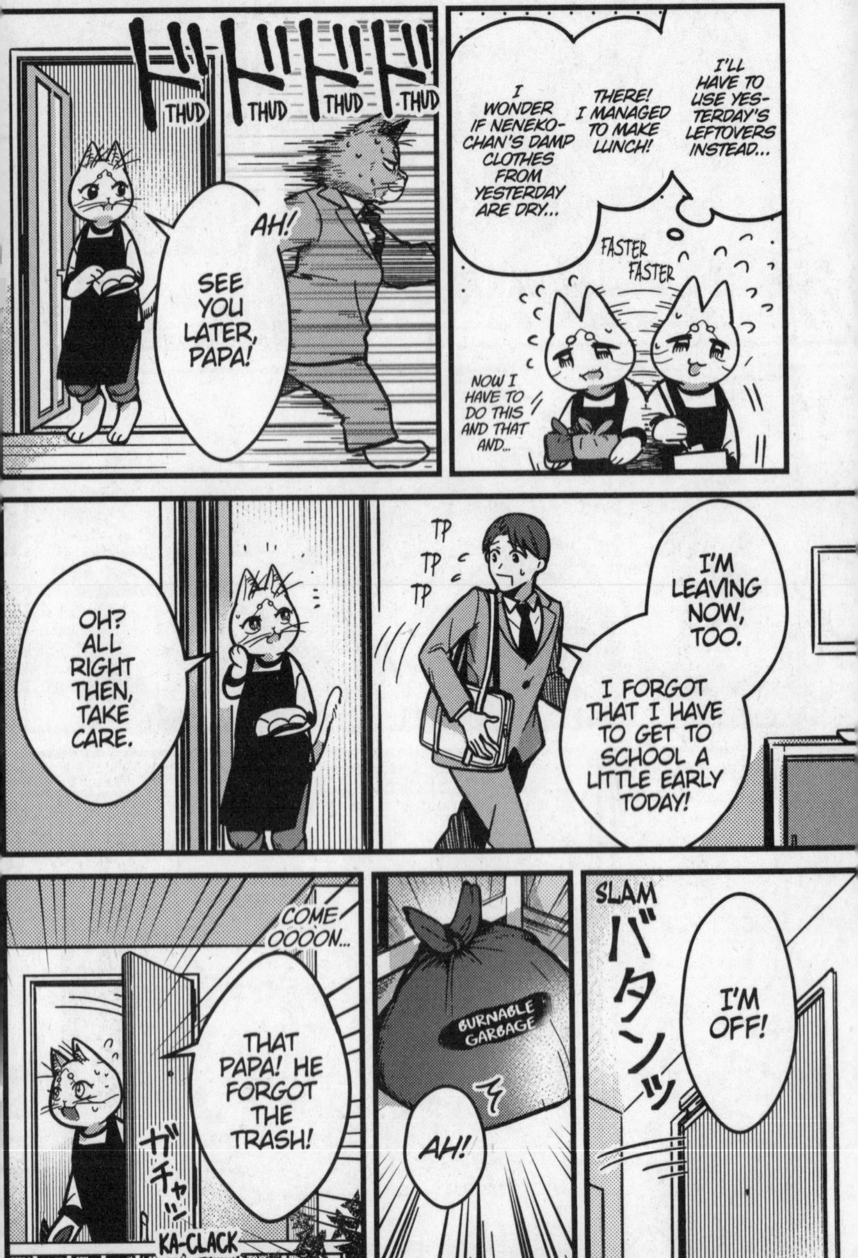
I'LL HAVE TO USE YESTERDAY'S LEFTOVERS INSTEAD...
THERE! I MANAGED TO MAKE LUNCH!
I WONDER IF NENEKO-CHAN'S DAMP CLOTHES FROM YESTERDAY ARE DRY...
FASTER FASTER
NOW I HAVE TO DO THIS AND THAT AND...
ドッドッドッドッ
THUD THUD THUD THUD
AH!
SEE YOU LATER, PAPA!
I'M LEAVING NOW, TOO.
I FORGOT THAT I HAVE TO GET TO SCHOOL A LITTLE EARLY TODAY!
TP TP TP
OH? ALL RIGHT THEN, TAKE CARE.
SLAM
バターンッ
I'M OFF!
BURNABLE GARBAGE
AH!
COME OOOON...
THAT PAPA! HE FORGOT THE TRASH!
ガチャッ
KA-CLACK

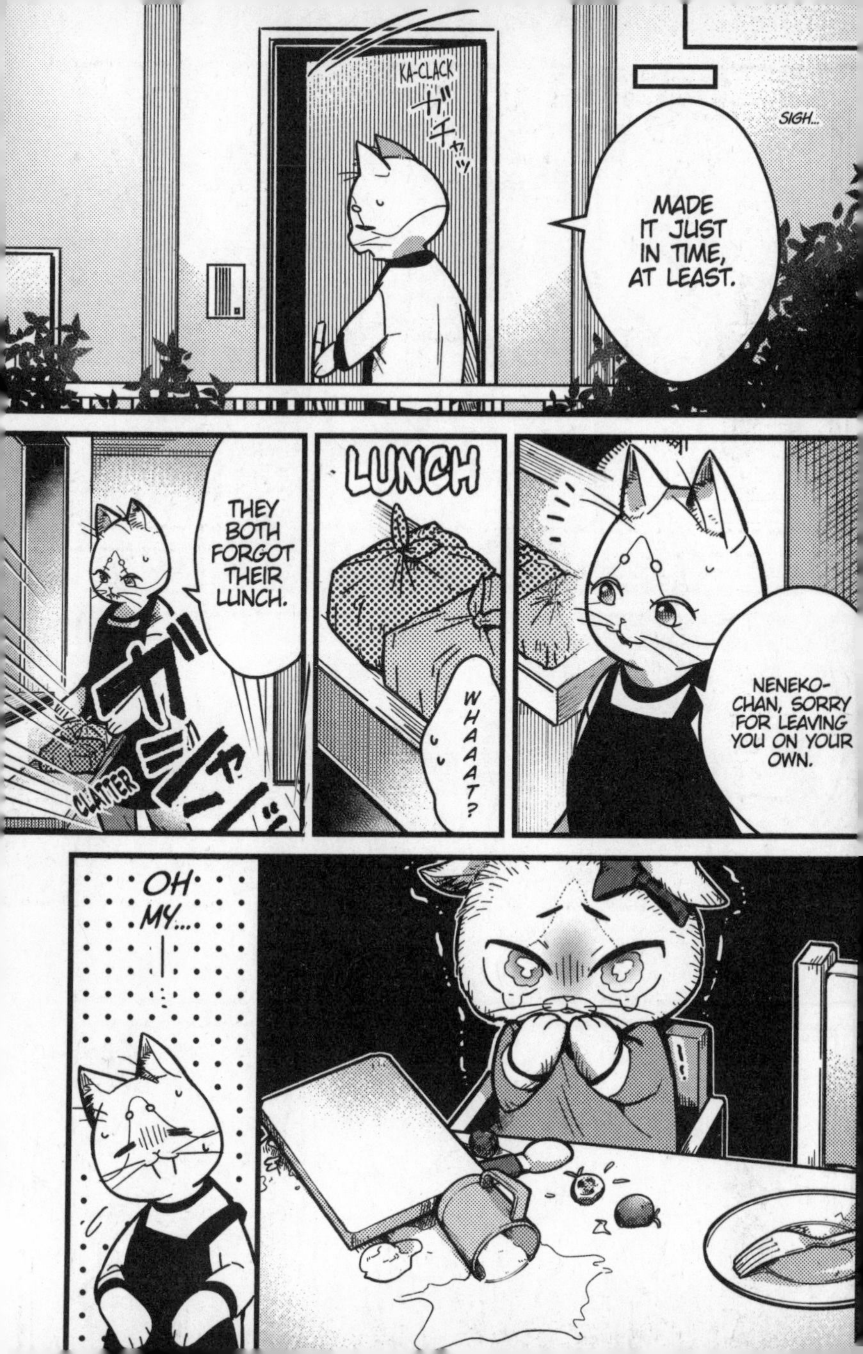
SIGH...
MADE IT JUST IN TIME, AT LEAST.
KA-CLACK
ガチャッ
NENEKO-CHAN, SORRY FOR LEAVING YOU ON YOUR OWN.
LUNCH
WHAAAAT?
THEY BOTH FORGOT THEIR LUNCH.
CLATTER
OH MY...

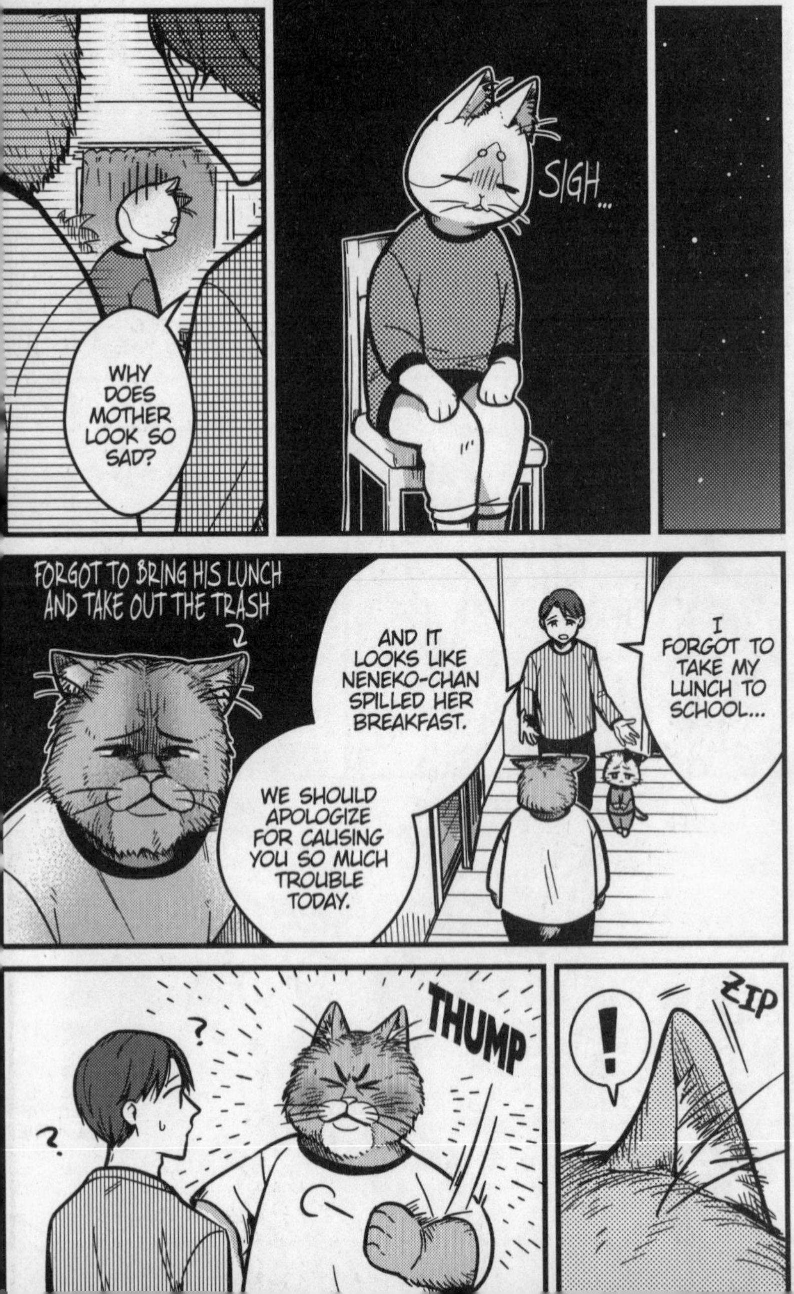
SIGH...
WHY DOES MOTHER LOOK SO SAD?
I FORGOT TO TAKE MY LUNCH TO SCHOOL...
AND IT LOOKS LIKE NENEKO-CHAN SPILLED HER BREAKFAST.
WE SHOULD APOLOGIZE FOR CAUSING YOU SO MUCH TROUBLE TODAY.
FORGOT TO BRING HIS LUNCH AND TAKE OUT THE TRASH
ZIP
!
THUMP
?
?

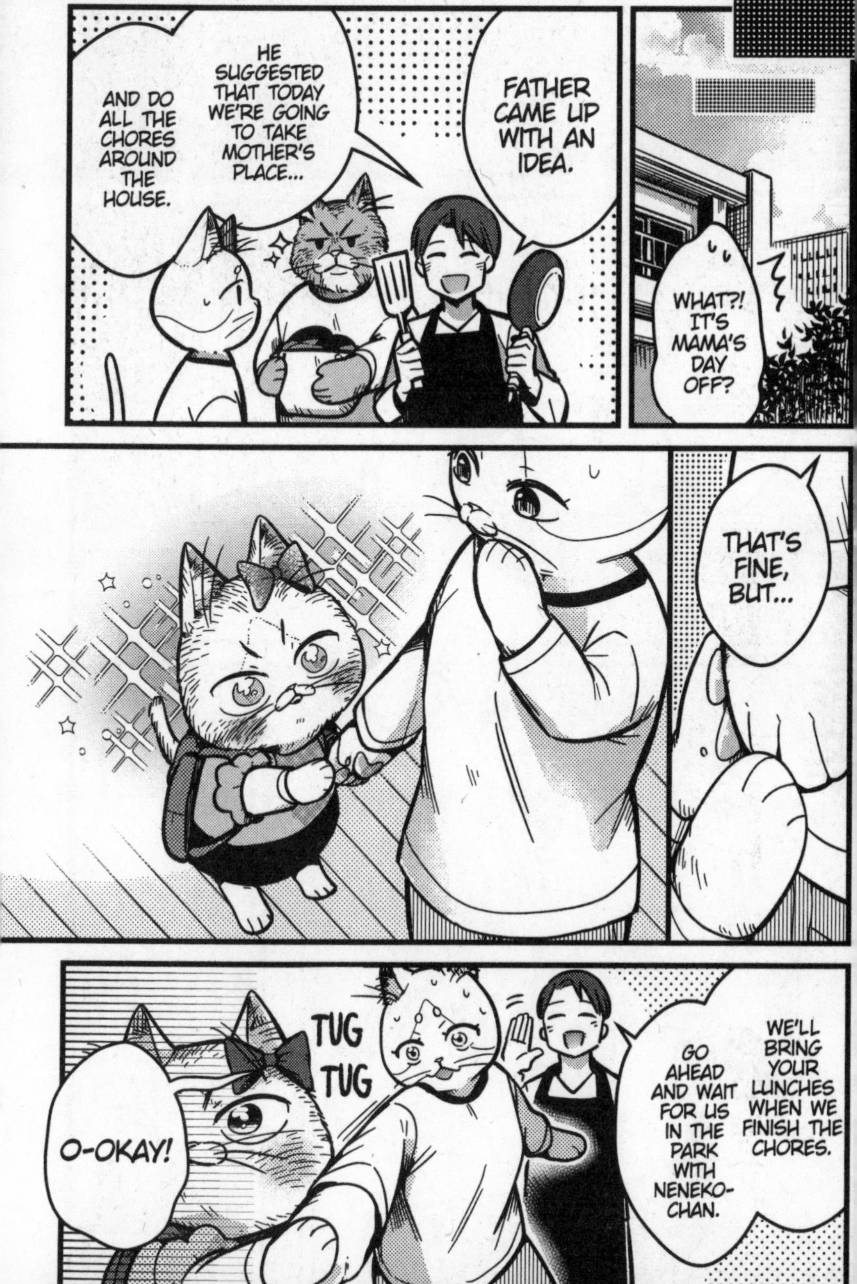
WHAT?! IT'S MAMA'S DAY OFF?
FATHER CAME UP WITH AN IDEA.
HE SUGGESTED THAT TODAY WE'RE GOING TO TAKE MOTHER'S PLACE...
AND DO ALL THE CHORES AROUND THE HOUSE.
THAT'S FINE, BUT...
WE'LL BRING YOUR LUNCHES WHEN WE FINISH THE CHORES.
GO AHEAD AND WAIT FOR US IN THE PARK WITH NENEKO-CHAN.
TUG TUG
O-OKAY!

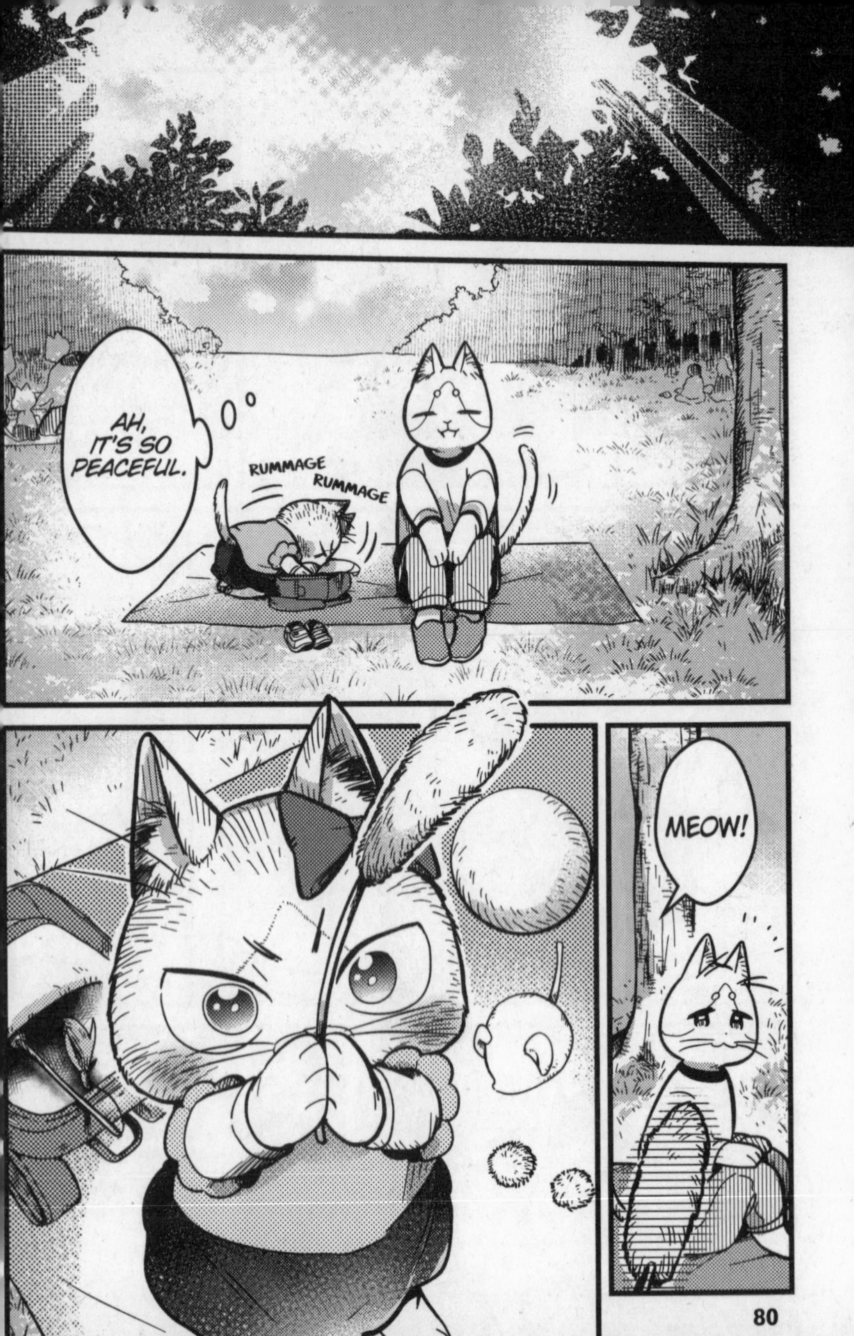
RUMMAGE RUMMAGE
AH, IT'S SO PEACEFUL.
MEOW!

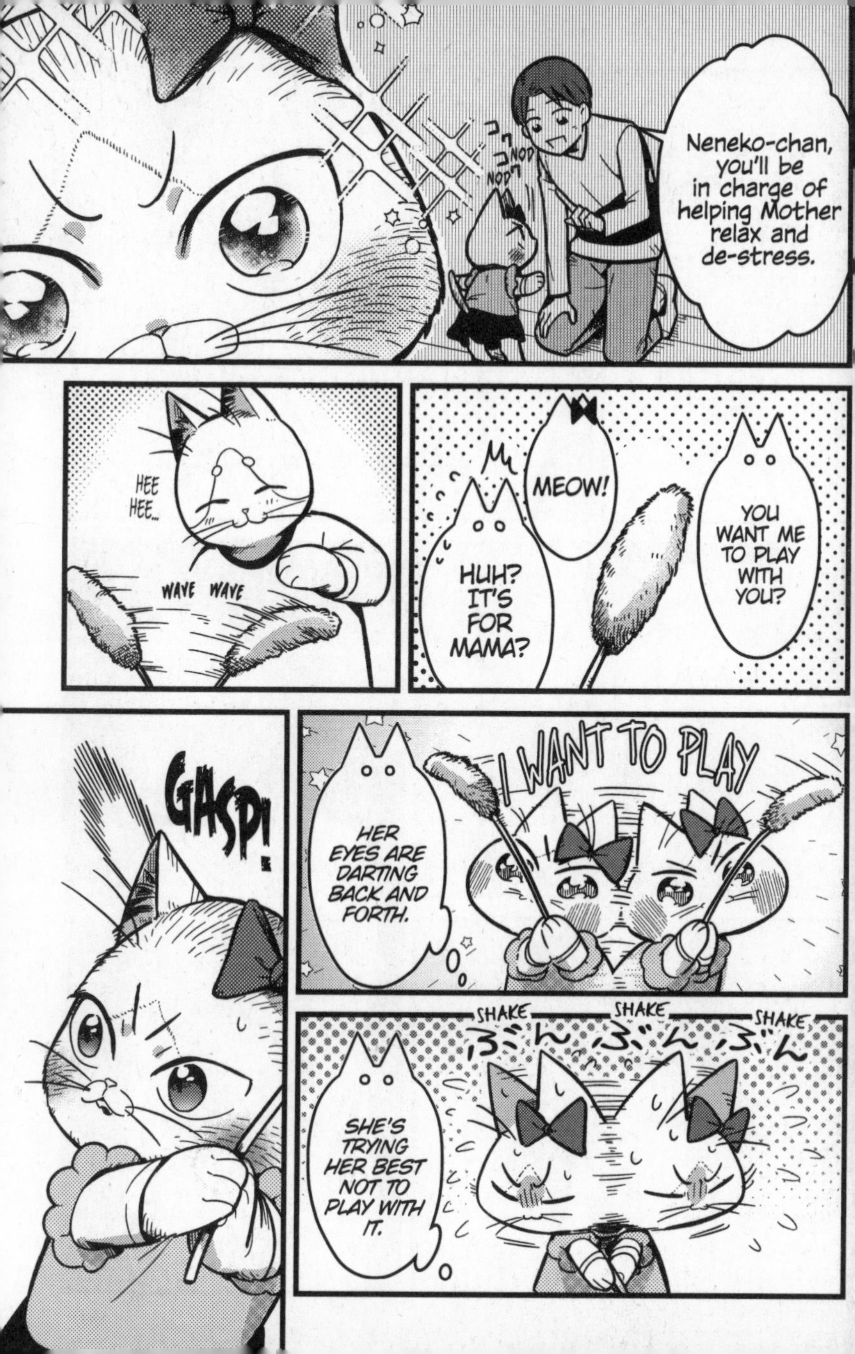
Neneko-chan, you'll be in charge of helping Mother relax and de-stress.
NOD NOD
YOU WANT ME TO PLAY WITH YOU?
MEOW!
HUH? IT'S FOR MAMA?
HEE HEE...
WAVE WAVE
I WANT TO PLAY
HER EYES ARE DARTING BACK AND FORTH.
SHAKE SHAKE SHAKE
ぶんぶんぶん
SHE'S TRYING HER BEST NOT TO PLAY WITH IT.
GASP!

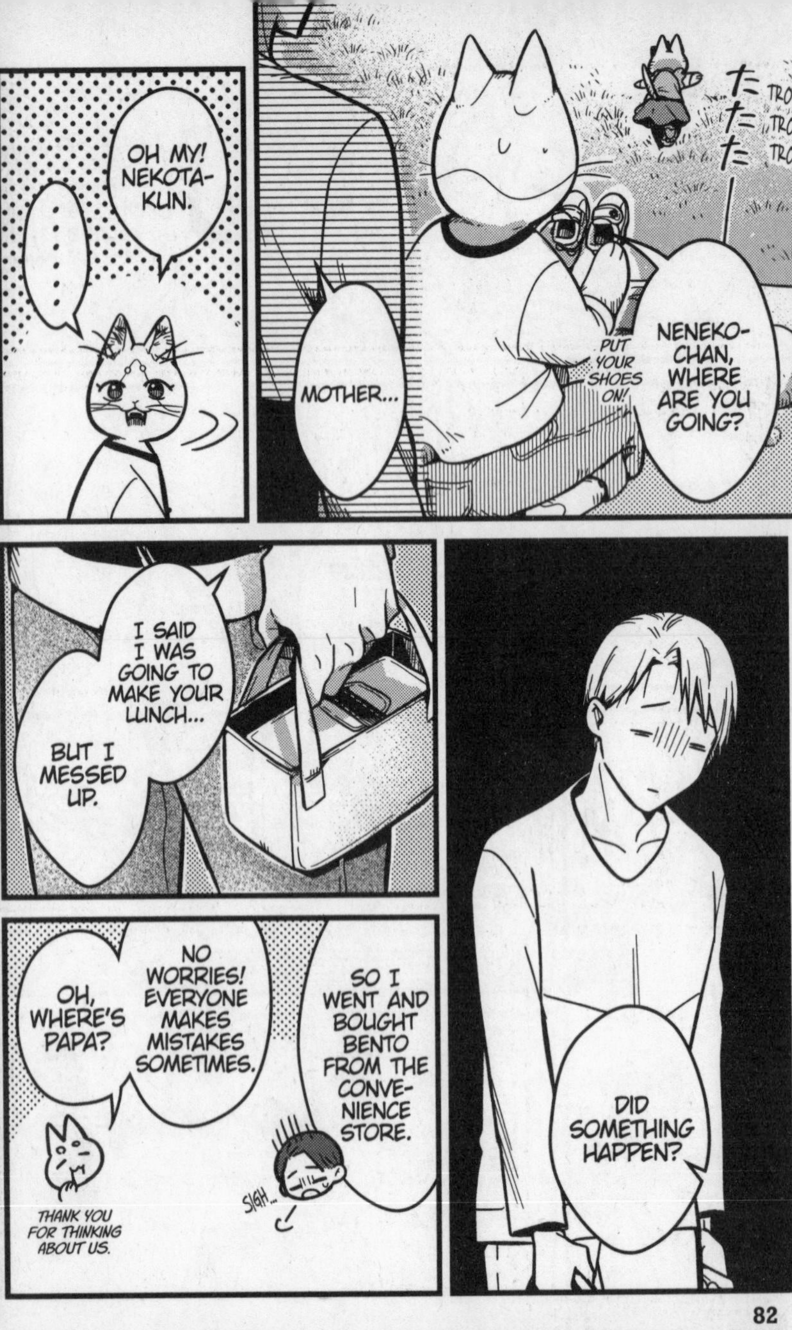
たたた
TROT TROT TROT
NENEKO-CHAN, WHERE ARE YOU GOING?
PUT YOUR SHOES ON!
MOTHER...
OH MY! NEKOTA-KUN.
......
DID SOMETHING HAPPEN?
I SAID I WAS GOING TO MAKE YOUR LUNCH...
BUT I MESSED UP.
SO I WENT AND BOUGHT BENTO FROM THE CONVENIENCE STORE.
SIGH...
NO WORRIES! EVERYONE MAKES MISTAKES SOMETIMES.
OH, WHERE'S PAPA?
THANK YOU FOR THINKING ABOUT US.

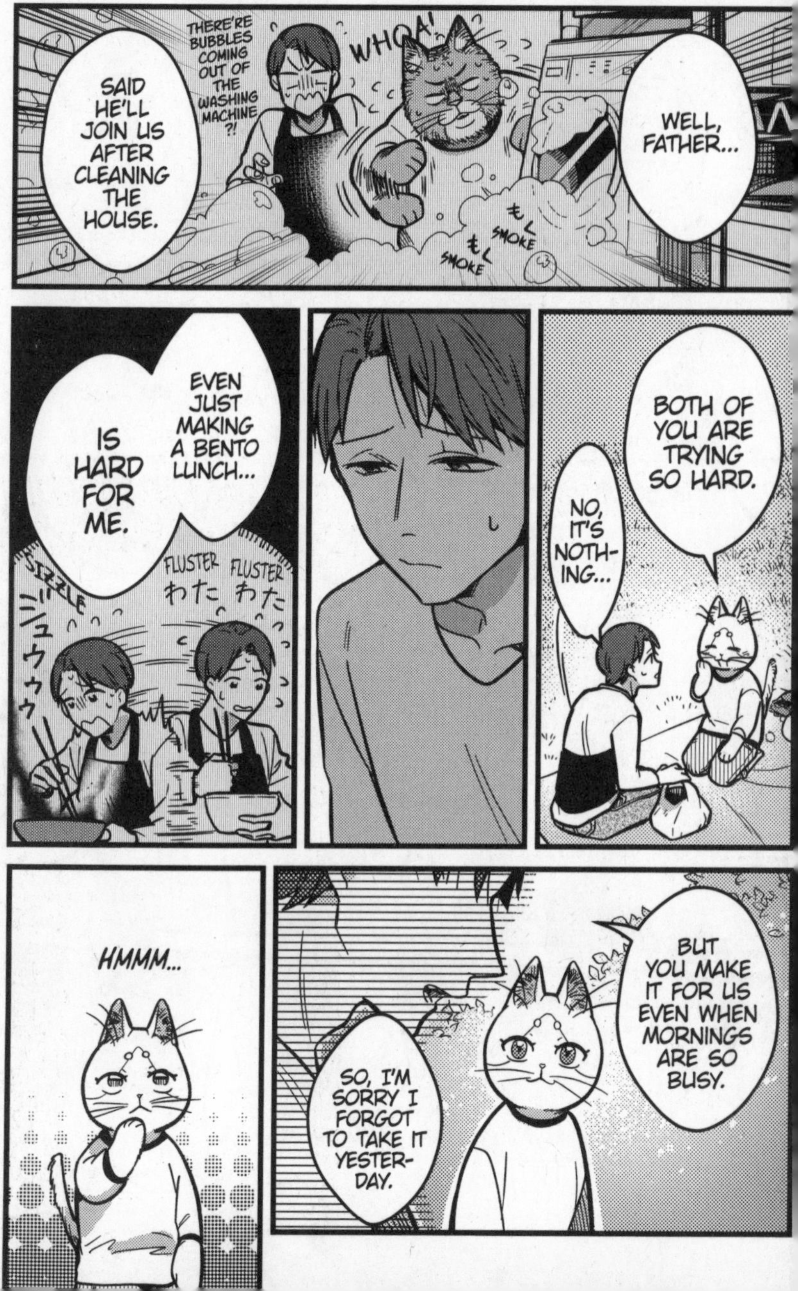
WELL, FATHER...
SAID HE'LL JOIN US AFTER CLEANING THE HOUSE.
WHOA!
THERE'RE BUBBLES COMING OUT OF THE WASHING MACHINE?!
もく SMOKE
もく SMOKE
BOTH OF YOU ARE TRYING SO HARD.
NO, IT'S NOTHING...
EVEN JUST MAKING A BENTO LUNCH...
IS HARD FOR ME.
FLUSTER FLUSTER
わた わた
SIZZLE
ジュウウウ
BUT YOU MAKE IT FOR US EVEN WHEN MORNINGS ARE SO BUSY.
SO, I'M SORRY I FORGOT TO TAKE IT YESTERDAY.
HMMM...

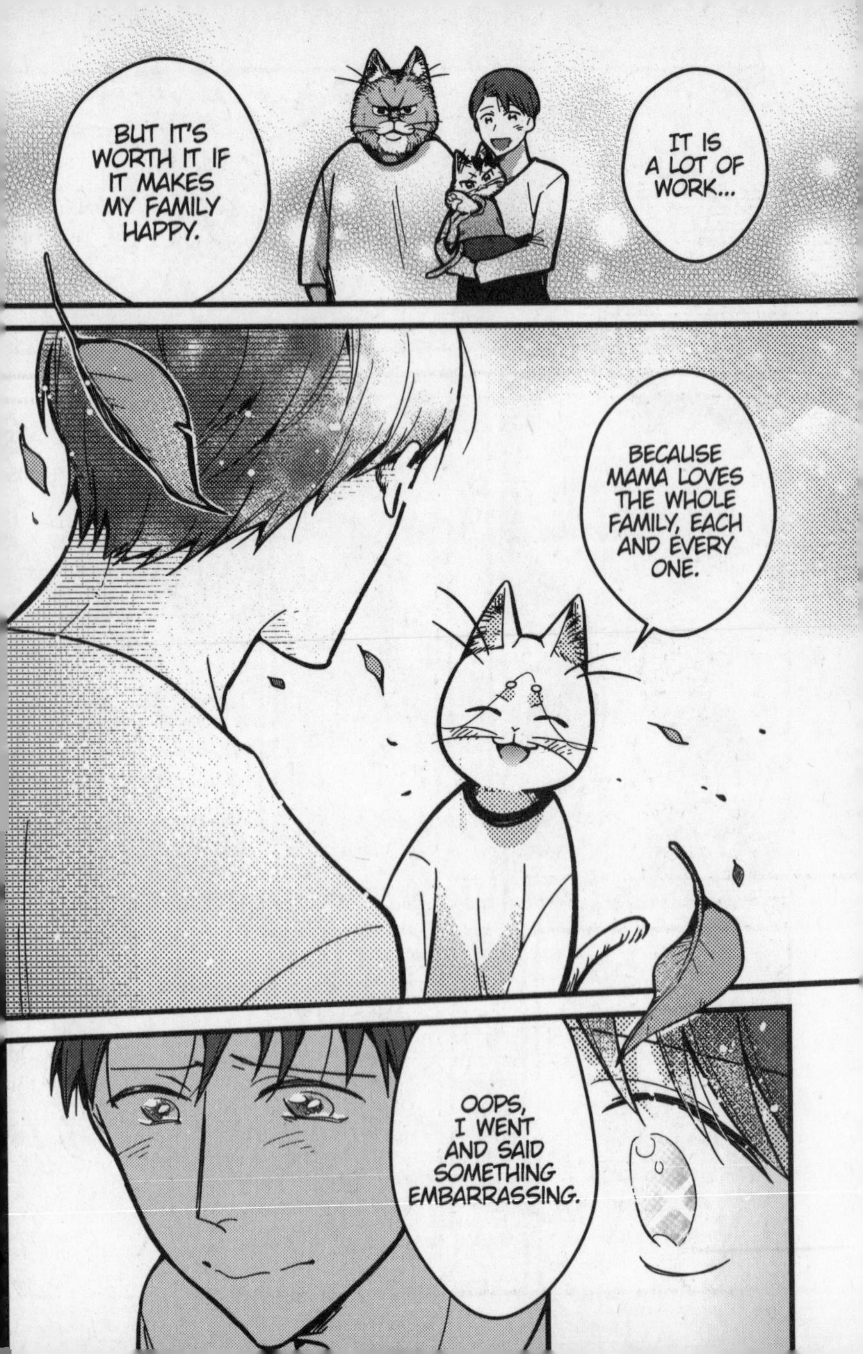
IT IS A LOT OF WORK...
BUT IT'S WORTH IT IF IT MAKES MY FAMILY HAPPY.
BECAUSE MAMA LOVES THE WHOLE FAMILY, EACH AND EVERY ONE.
OOPS, I WENT AND SAID SOMETHING EMBARRASSING.

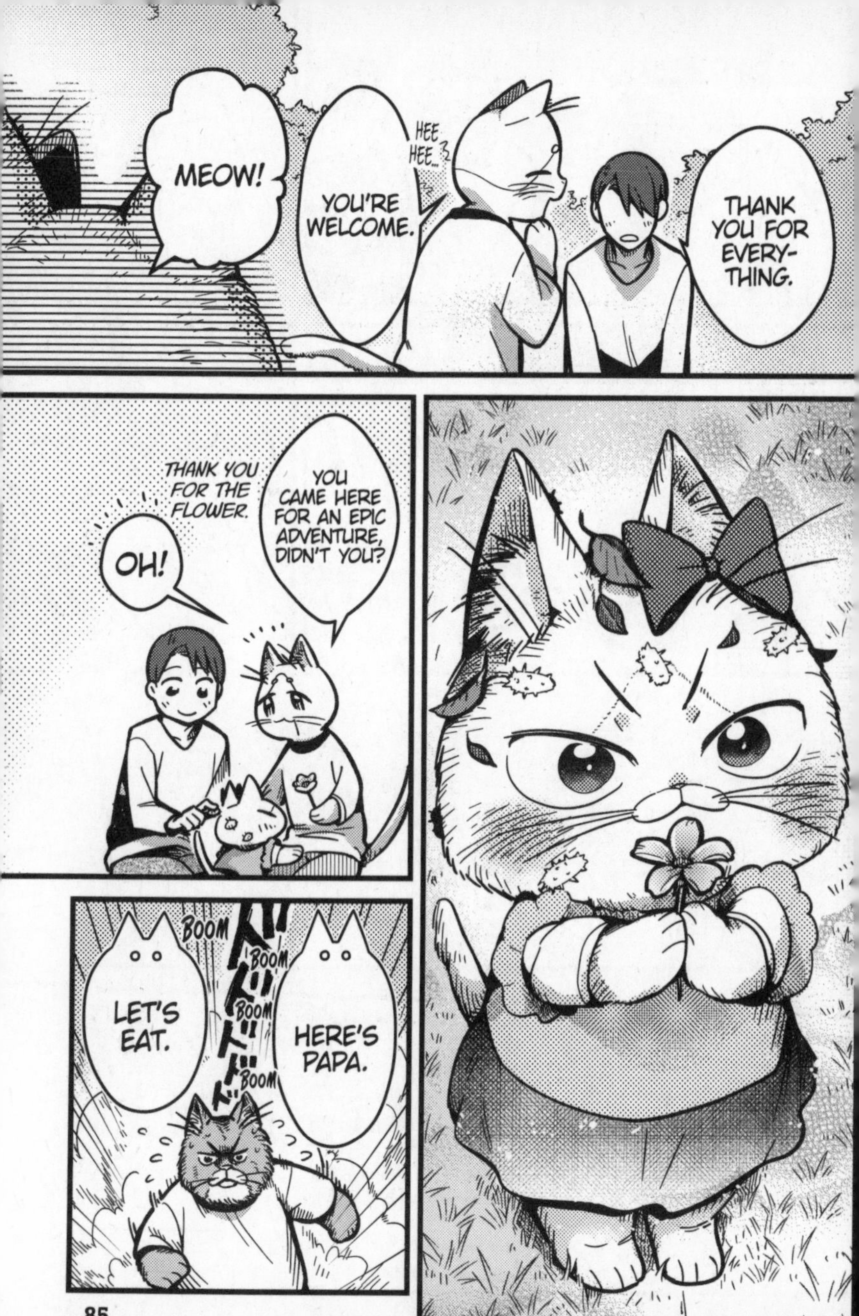
THANK YOU FOR EVERY-THING.
HEE HEE...
YOU'RE WELCOME.
MEOW!
YOU CAME HERE FOR AN EPIC ADVENTURE, DIDN'T YOU?
THANK YOU FOR THE FLOWER.
OH!
HERE'S PAPA.
BOOM BOOM BOOM BOOM
LET'S EAT.

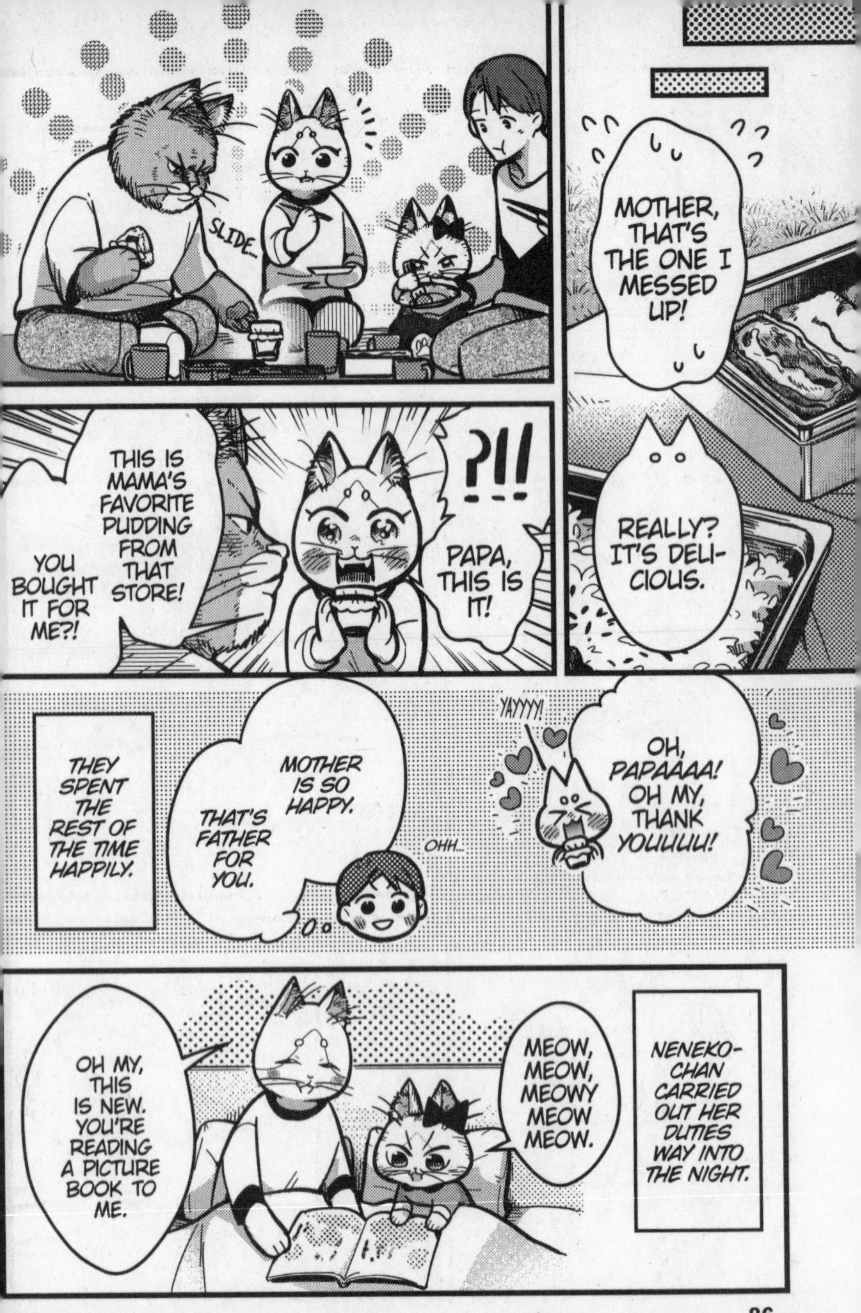
MOTHER, THAT'S THE ONE I MESSED UP!
REALLY? IT'S DELICIOUS.
SLIDE...
?!!
PAPA, THIS IS IT!
THIS IS MAMA'S FAVORITE PUDDING FROM THAT STORE!
YOU BOUGHT IT FOR ME?!
YAYYYY!
OH, PAPAAAA! OH MY, THANK YOUUUUU!
OHH...
MOTHER IS SO HAPPY.
THAT'S FATHER FOR YOU.
THEY SPENT THE REST OF THE TIME HAPPILY.
NENEKO-CHAN CARRIED OUT HER DUTIES WAY INTO THE NIGHT.
MEOW, MEOW, MEOWY MEOW MEOW.
OH MY, THIS IS NEW. YOU'RE READING A PICTURE BOOK TO ME.

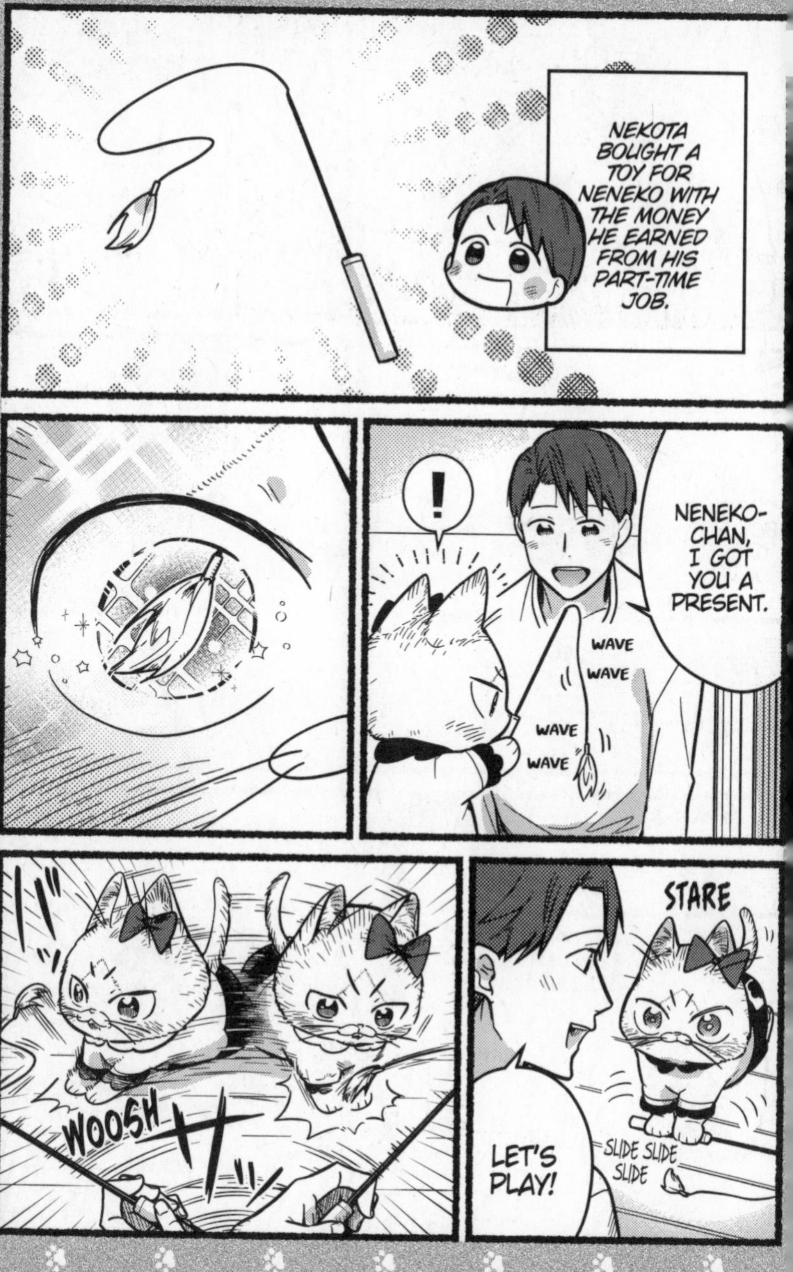
NEKOTA BOUGHT A TOY FOR NENEKO WITH THE MONEY HE EARNED FROM HIS PART-TIME JOB.
NENEKO-CHAN, I GOT YOU A PRESENT.
!
WAVE WAVE
WAVE WAVE
STARE
SLIDE SLIDE SLIDE SLIDE
LET'S PLAY!
WOOSH

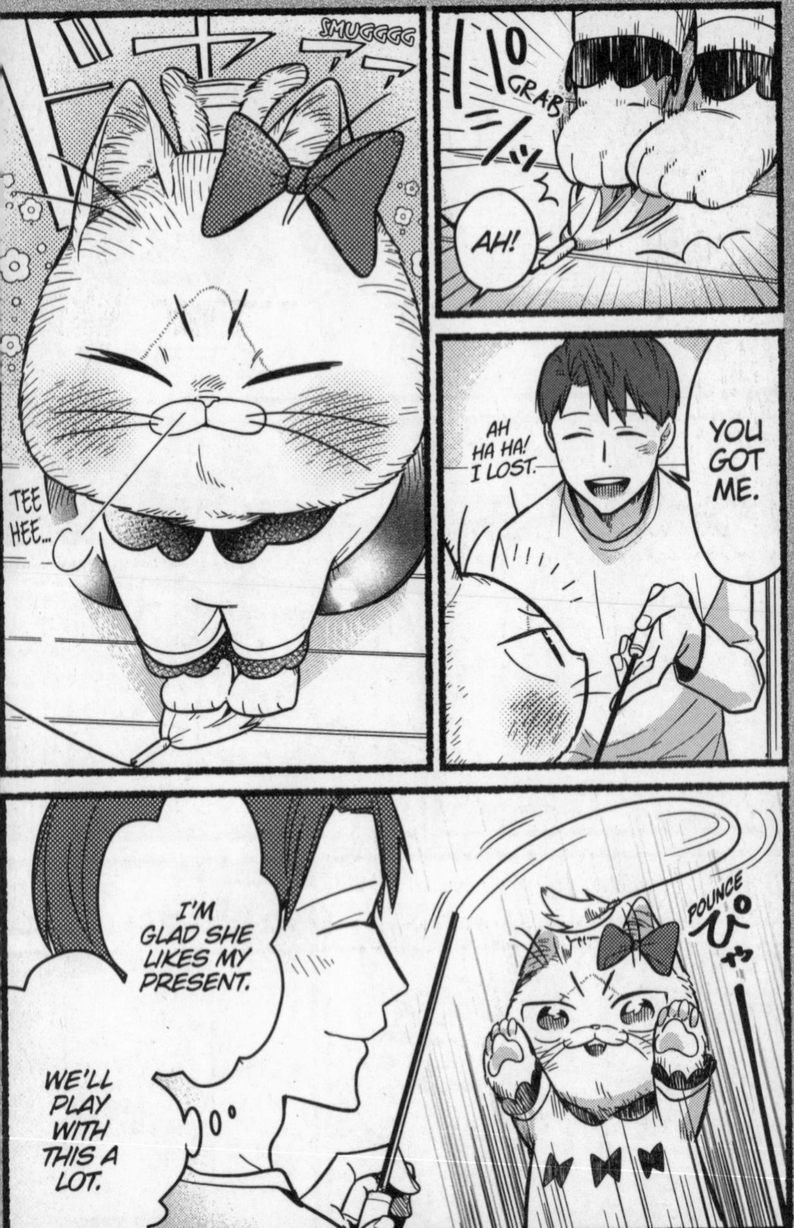
GRAB
AH!
YOU GOT ME.
AH HA HA! I LOST.
SMUGGGG
TEE HEE...
POUNCE
I'M GLAD SHE LIKES MY PRESENT.
WE'LL PLAY WITH THIS A LOT.

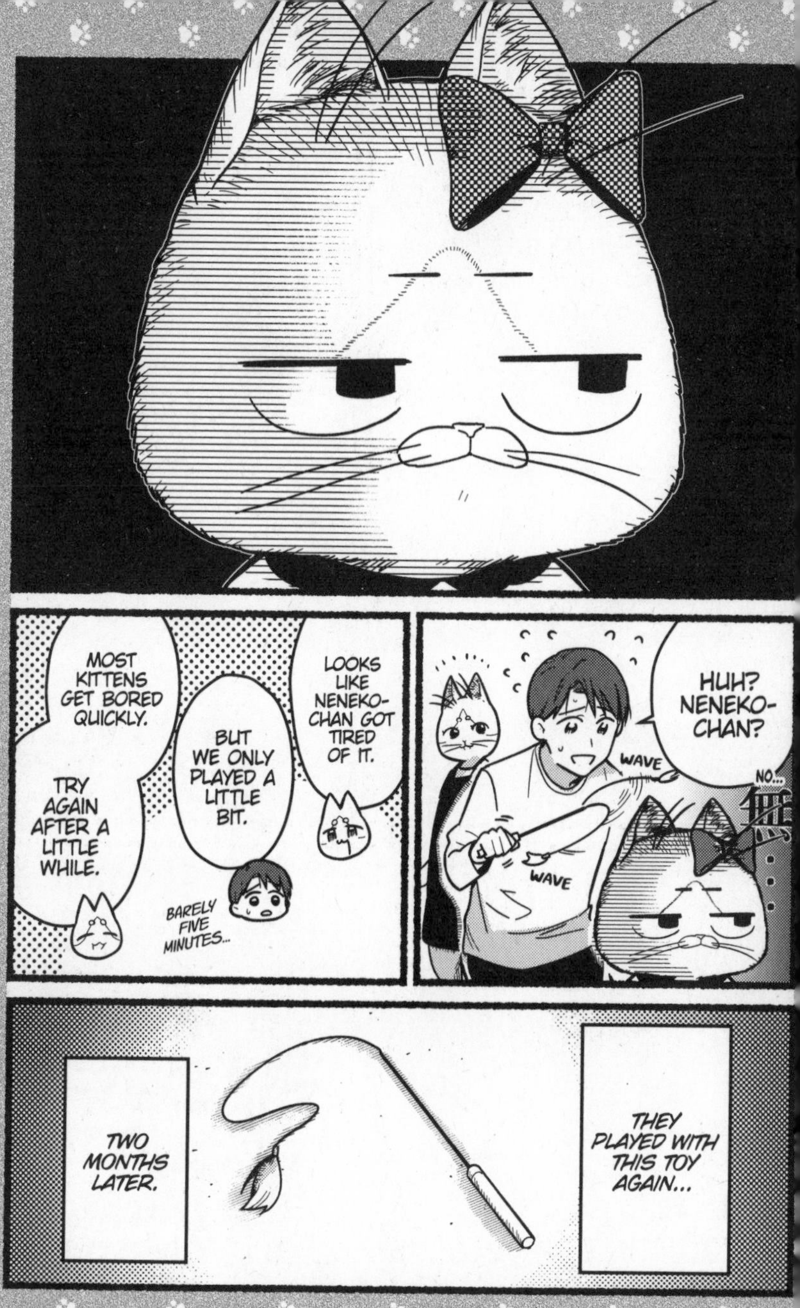
HUH? NENEKO-CHAN?
WAVE
NO...
WAVE
LOOKS LIKE NENEKO-CHAN GOT TIRED OF IT.
BUT WE ONLY PLAYED A LITTLE BIT.
MOST KITTENS GET BORED QUICKLY.
TRY AGAIN AFTER A LITTLE WHILE.
BARELY FIVE MINUTES...
THEY PLAYED WITH THIS TOY AGAIN...
TWO MONTHS LATER.

My: Sister, the Cat

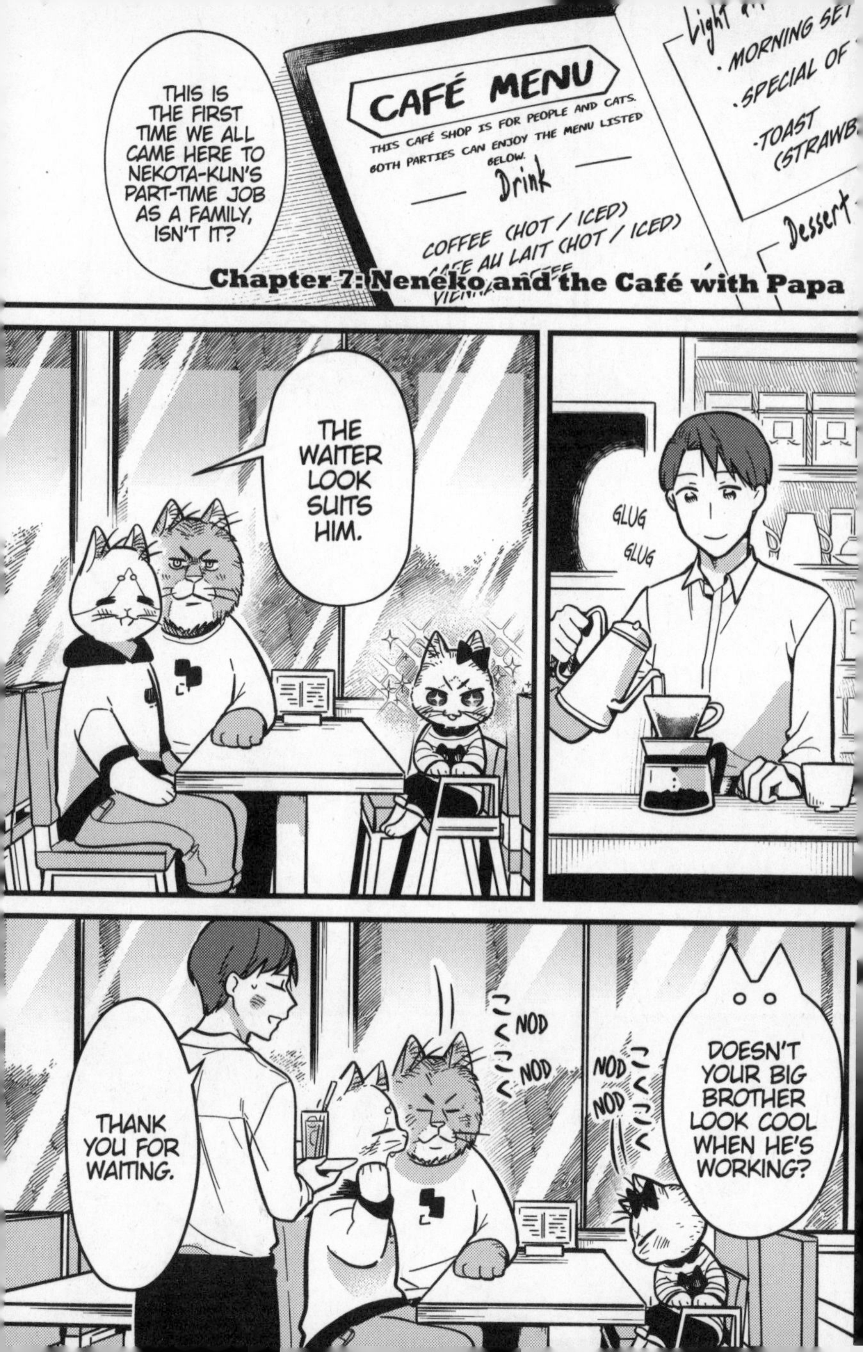
MORNING SET
Dessert
CAFÉ MENU
THIS CAFÉ SHOP IS FOR PEOPLE AND CATS. BOTH PARTIES CAN ENJOY THE MENU LISTED BELOW.
Drink
COFFEE (HOT / ICED)
THIS IS THE FIRST TIME WE ALL CAME HERE TO NEKOTA-KUN'S PART-TIME JOB AS A FAMILY, ISN'T IT?
Chapter 7: Neneko and the Café with Papa
GLUG GLUG
THE WAITER LOOK SUITS HIM.
DOESN'T YOUR BIG BROTHER LOOK COOL WHEN HE'S WORKING?
NOD NOD
NOD NOD
THANK YOU FOR WAITING.

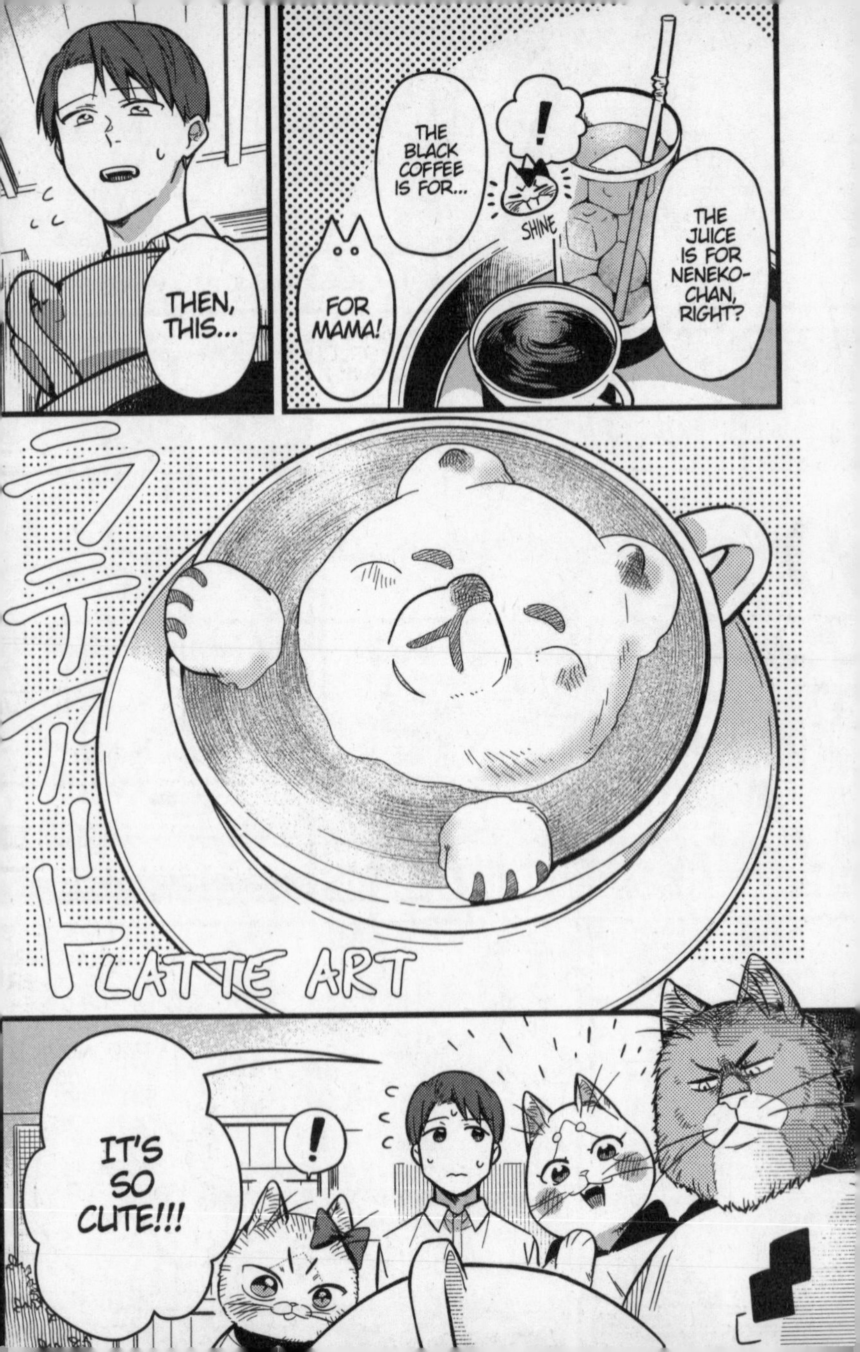
THE JUICE IS FOR NENEKO-CHAN, RIGHT?
!
SHINE
THE BLACK COFFEE IS FOR...
FOR MAMA!
THEN, THIS...
ラテアート
LATTE ART
!
IT'S SO CUTE!!!

I SEE...

I'M GLAD TO HEAR THAT.

AMAZING! PAPA LIKES HIS DRINK, TOO.

I THOUGHT MOTHER ORDERED THIS...

DID YOU MAKE THIS, NEKOTA-KUN?

YEAH, I'M STILL LEARNING HOW.

OH

WOW

SEVERAL DAYS LATER...

OKAY, I'M OFF.

I'M READY TO LEAVE.

29 SUN	30 MON	31 TU
Nekota-kun works	Mama is going out!	Come back and clean

SLAM

NOD NOD

NENEKO-CHAN, YOUR BIG BROTHER IS TIRED BECAUSE HE HAD WORK...

SO PLAY WITH PAPA, OKAY?

WHEN NEKOTA-KUN WAKES UP, MICROWAVE SOMETHING FOR HIM TO EAT.

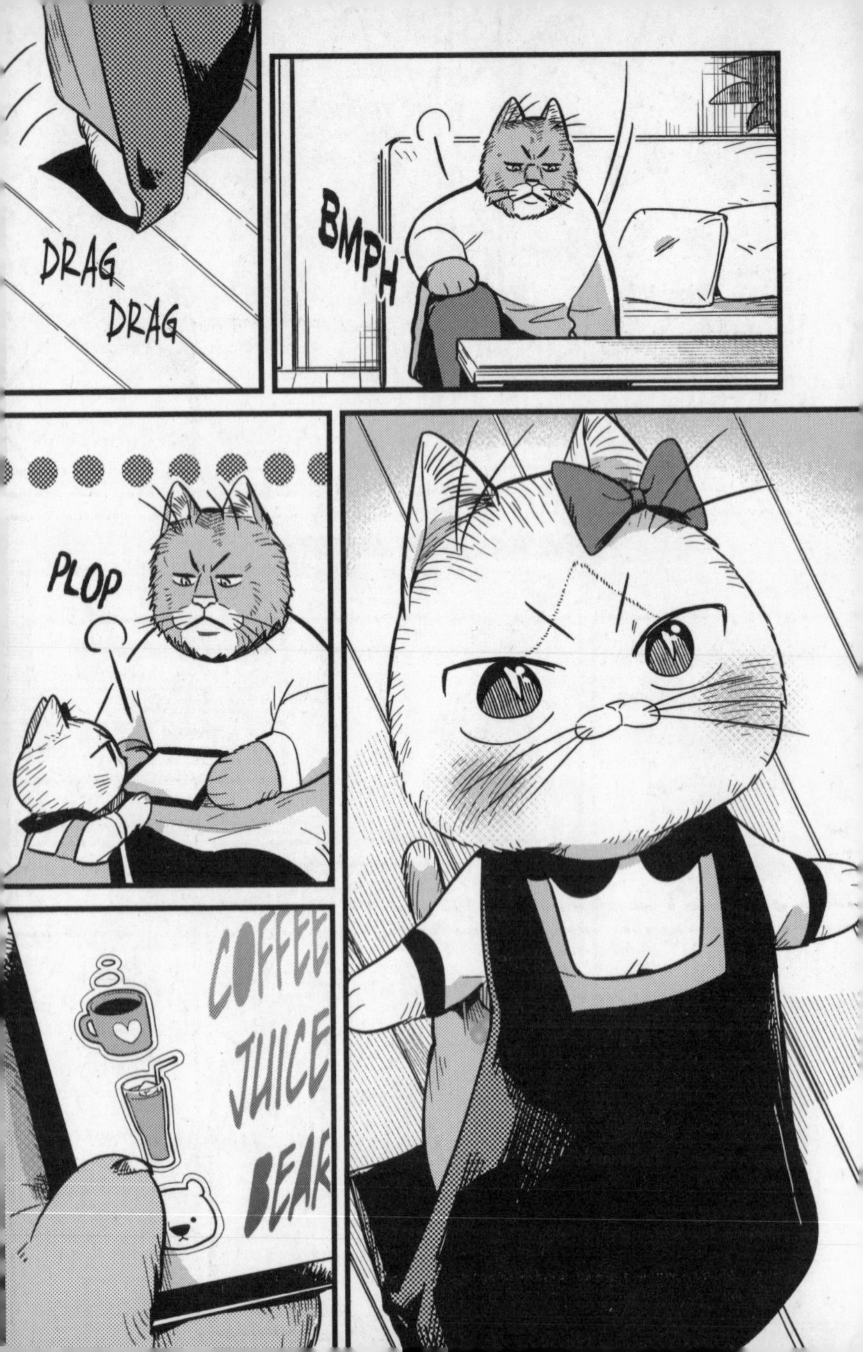
BMPH
DRAG
DRAG
PLOP
COFFEE
JUICE
BEAR

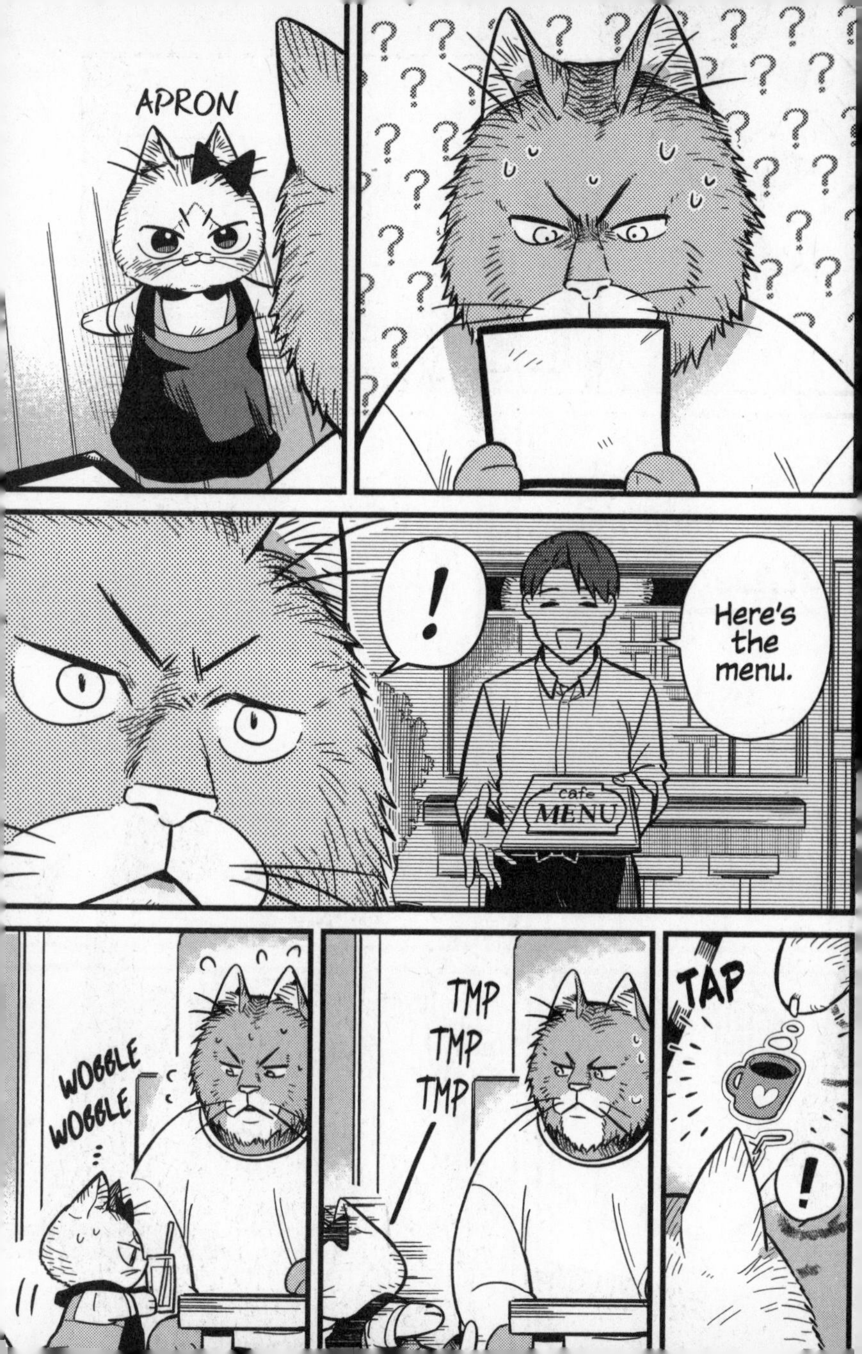
APRON
Here's the menu.
!
cafe
MENU
TAP
!
TMP
TMP
TMP
WOBBLE
WOBBLE

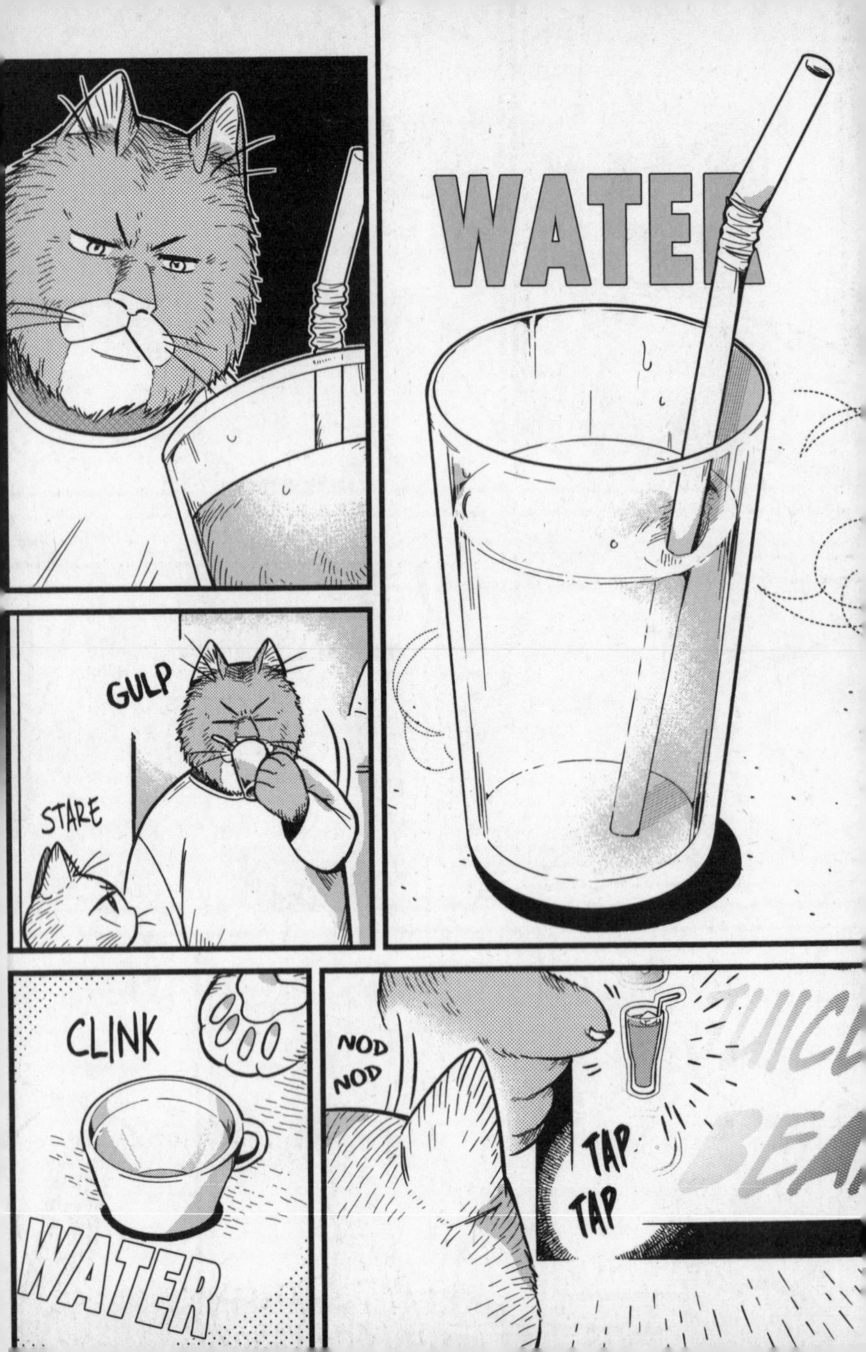
WATER
GULP
STARE
TAP
TAP
NOD
NOD
CLINK
WATER

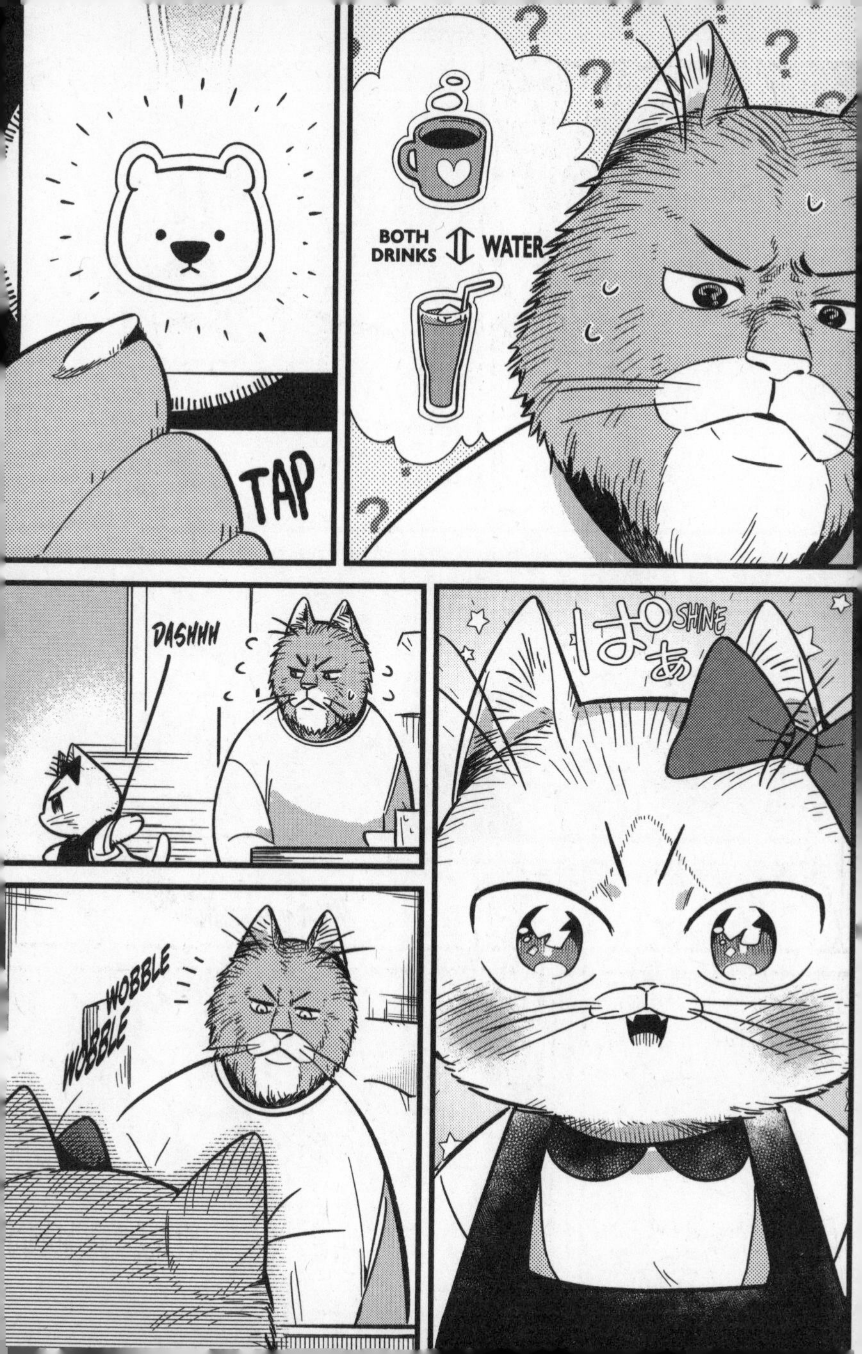
BOTH DRINKS
WATER
TAP
はぁ
SHINE
DASHHH
WOBBLE WOBBLE

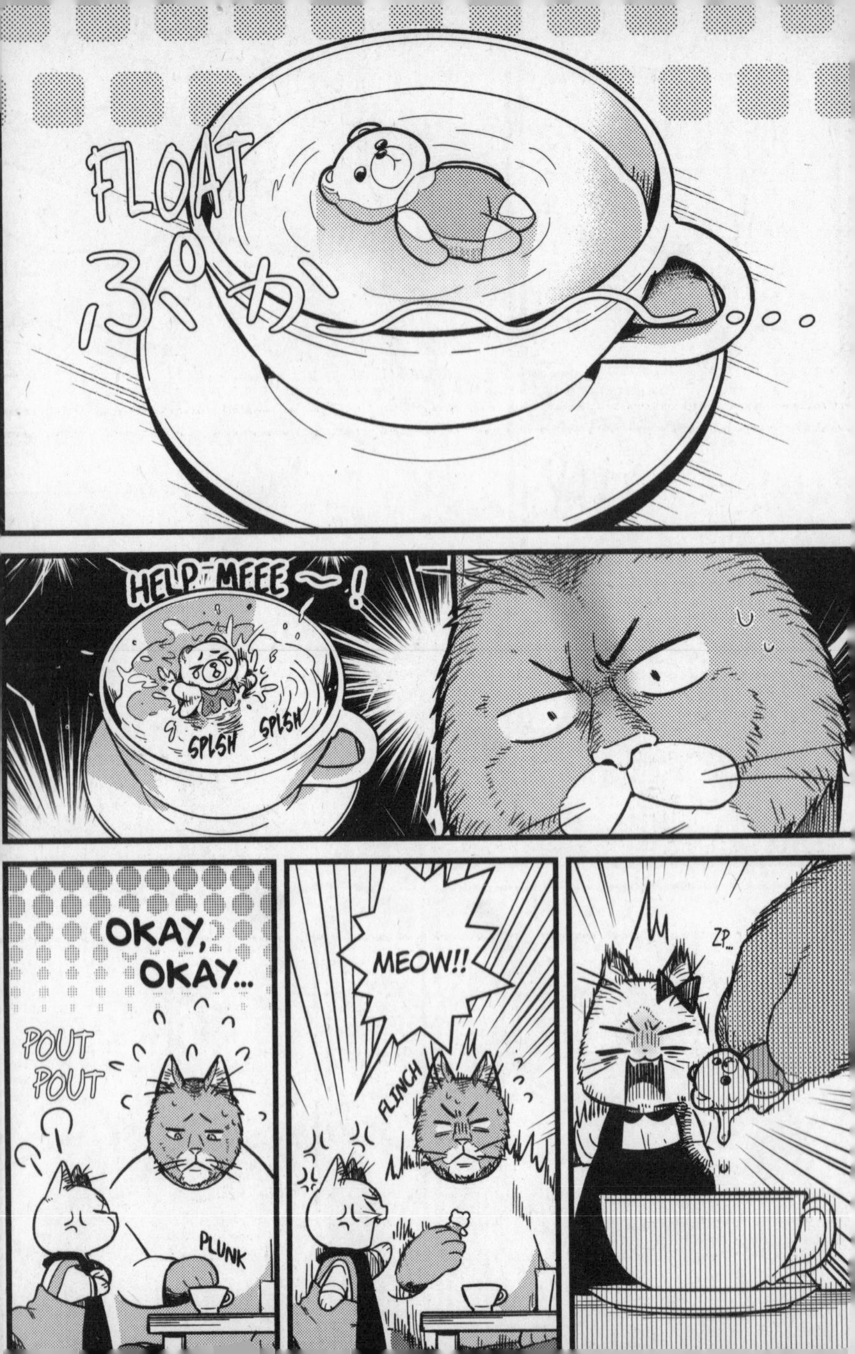
FLOAT
ぷか
HELP MEEE~!
SPLSH
SPLSH
ZP...
MEOW!!
FLINCH
OKAY, OKAY...
POUT POUT
PLUNK

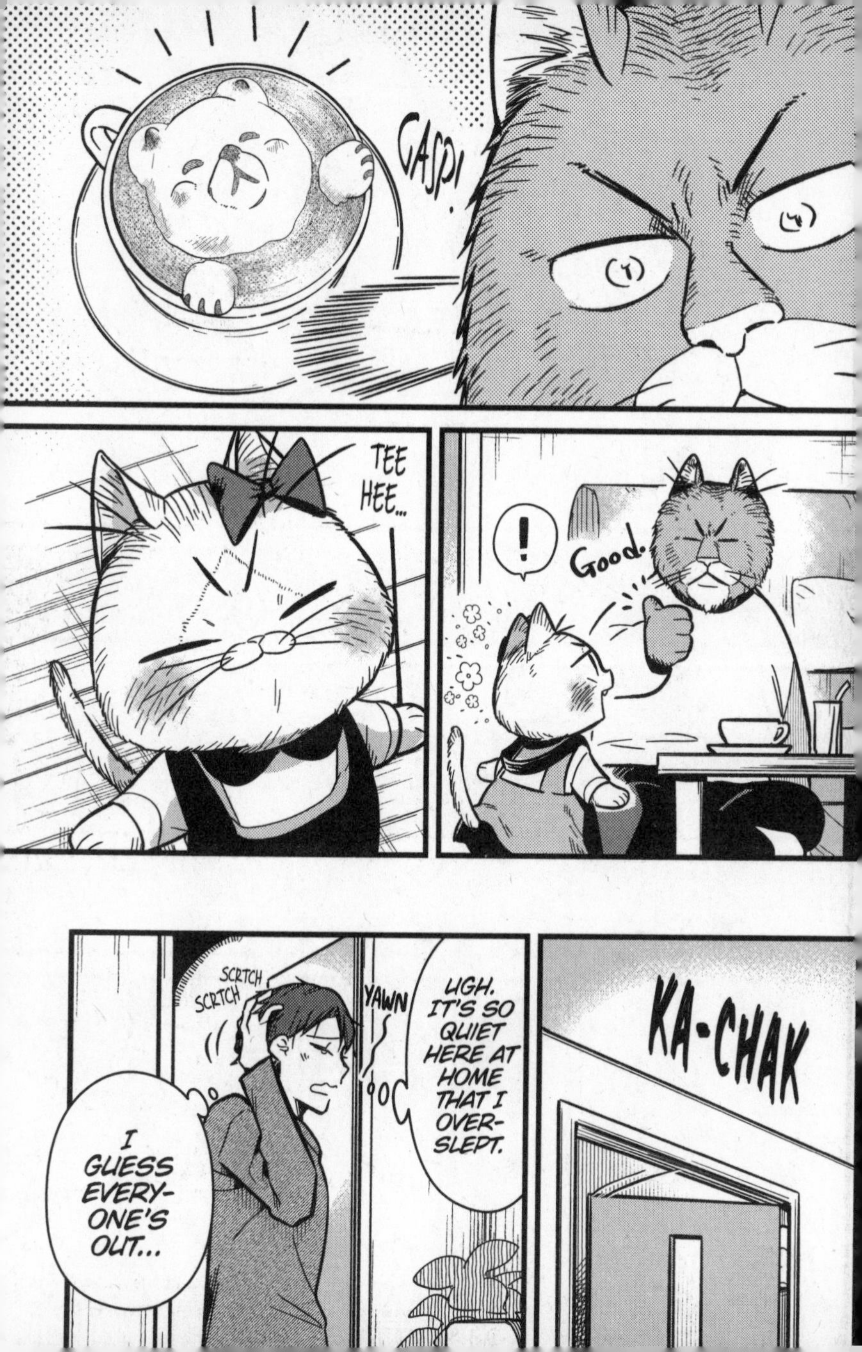
GASP!
!
Good.
TEE HEE...
KA-CHAK
SCRTCH SCRTCH
YAWN
UGH. IT'S SO QUIET HERE AT HOME THAT I OVER-SLEPT.
I GUESS EVERY-ONE'S OUT...

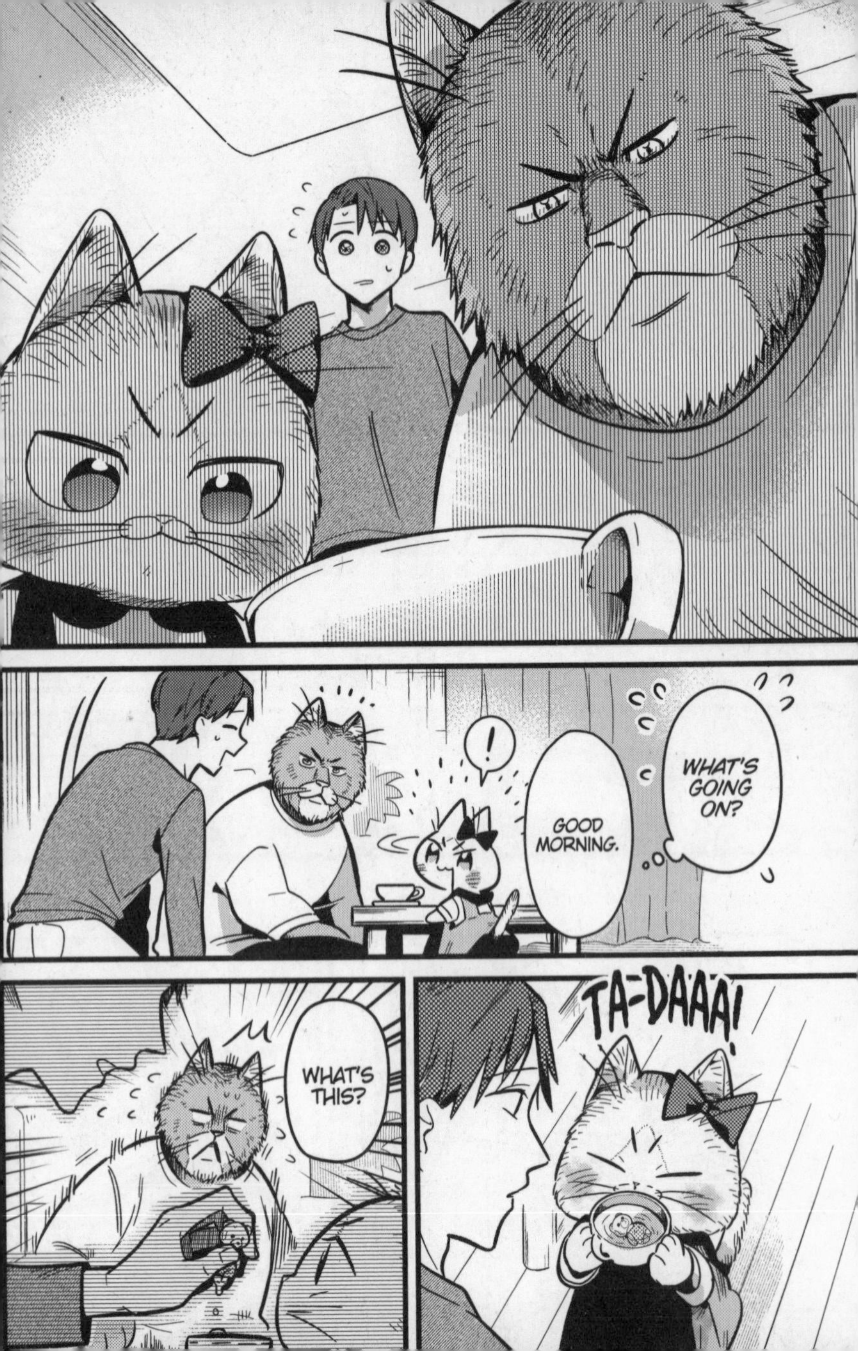
WHAT'S GOING ON?
GOOD MORNING.
!
TA-DAAA!
WHAT'S THIS?

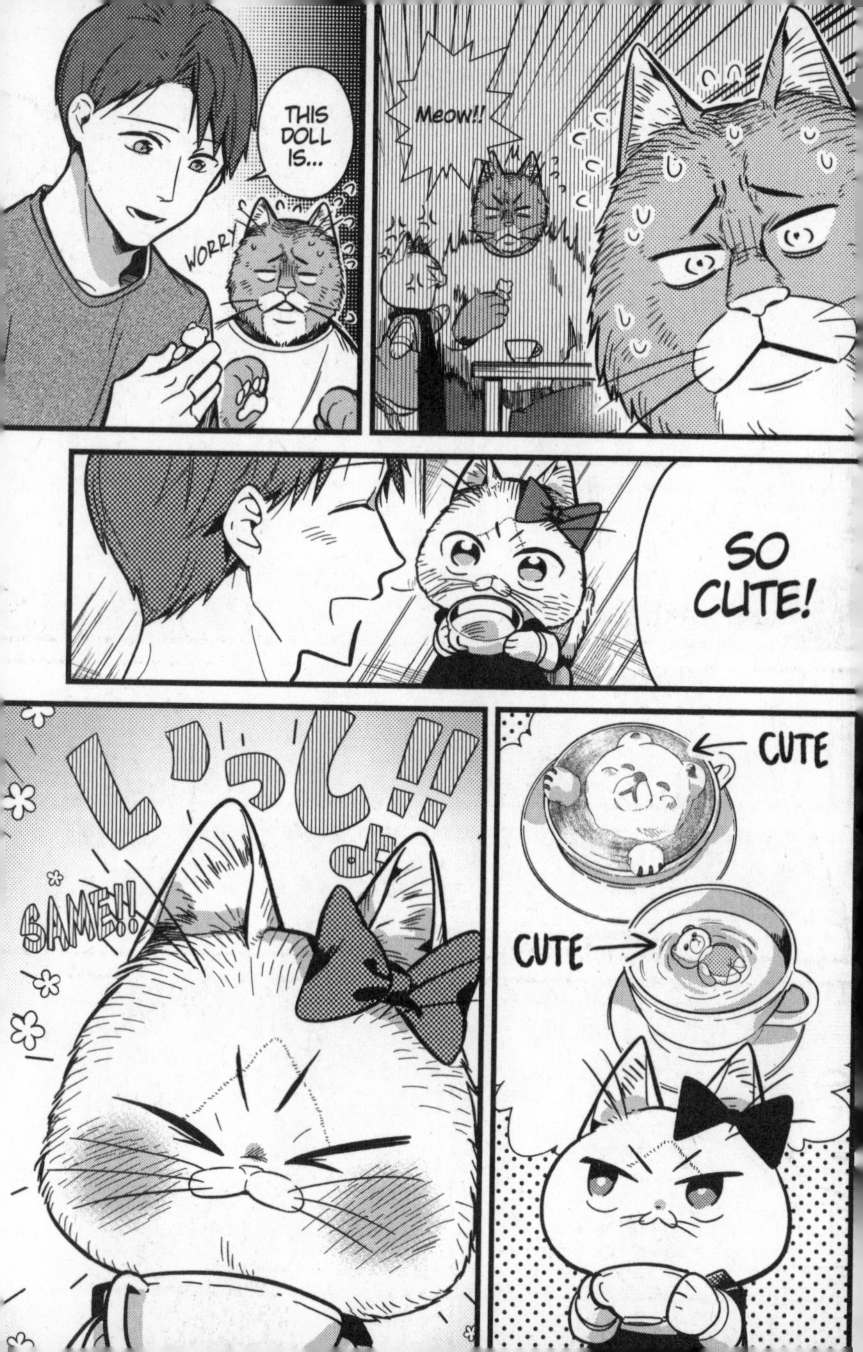
Meow!!
THIS DOLL IS...
WORRY
SO CUTE!
CUTE
CUTE
しっし!!
SAME!!

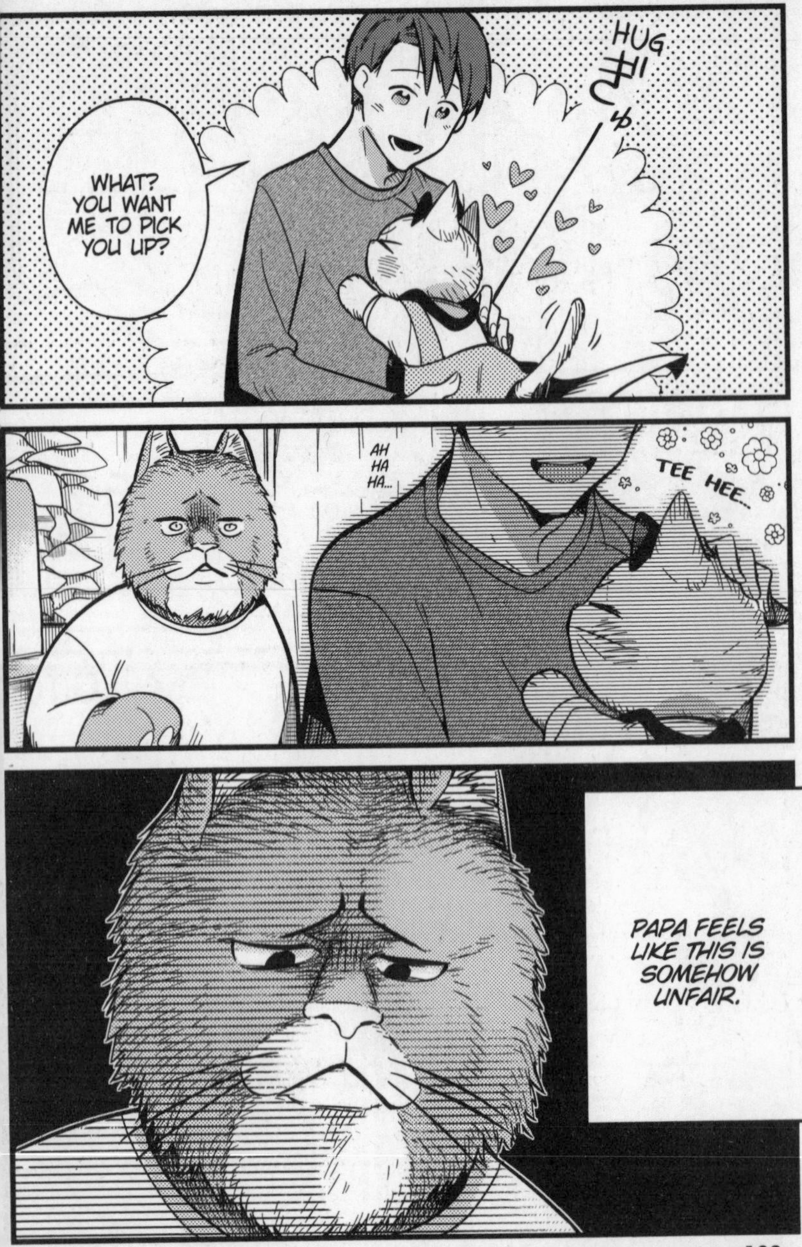
HUG
ぎゅ
WHAT? YOU WANT ME TO PICK YOU UP?
TEE HEE...
AH HA HA...
PAPA FEELS LIKE THIS IS SOMEHOW UNFAIR.

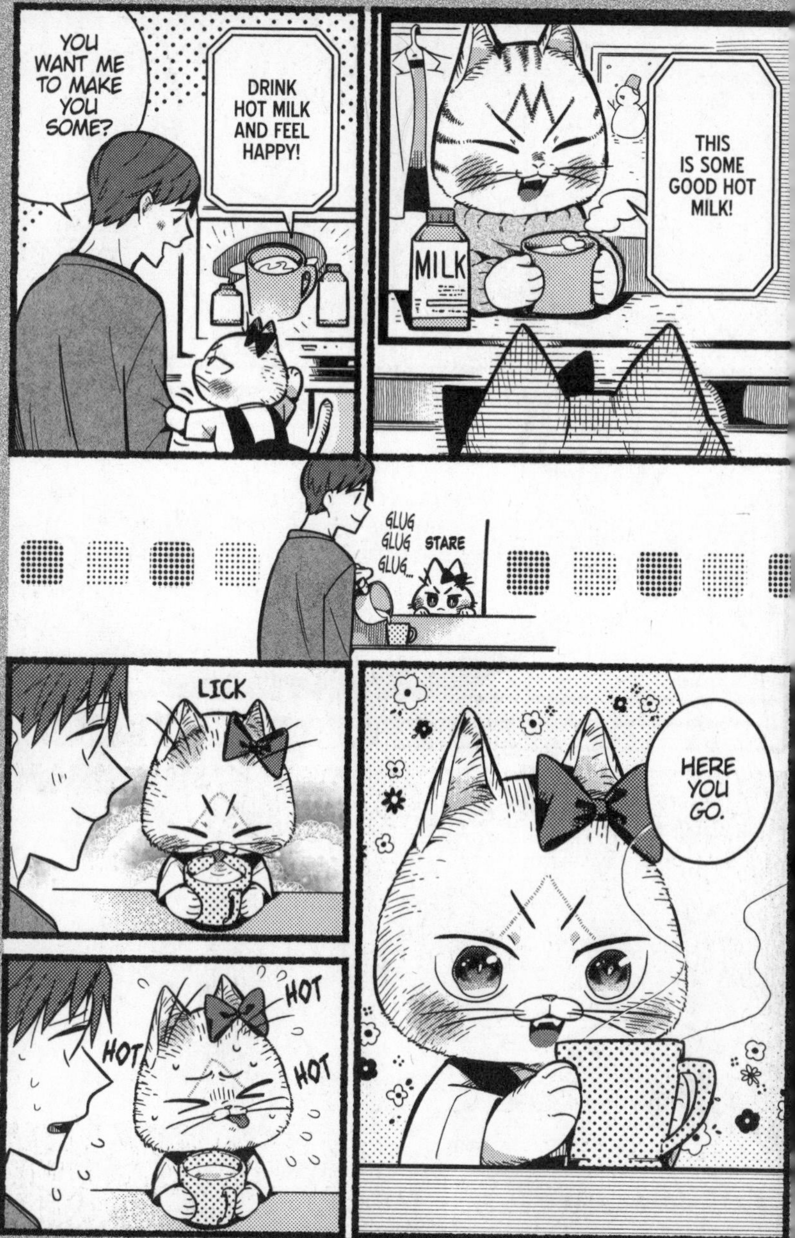
THIS IS SOME GOOD HOT MILK!
MILK
DRINK HOT MILK AND FEEL HAPPY!
YOU WANT ME TO MAKE YOU SOME?
STARE
GLUG GLUG GLUG...
HERE YOU GO.
LICK
HOT
HOT
HOT

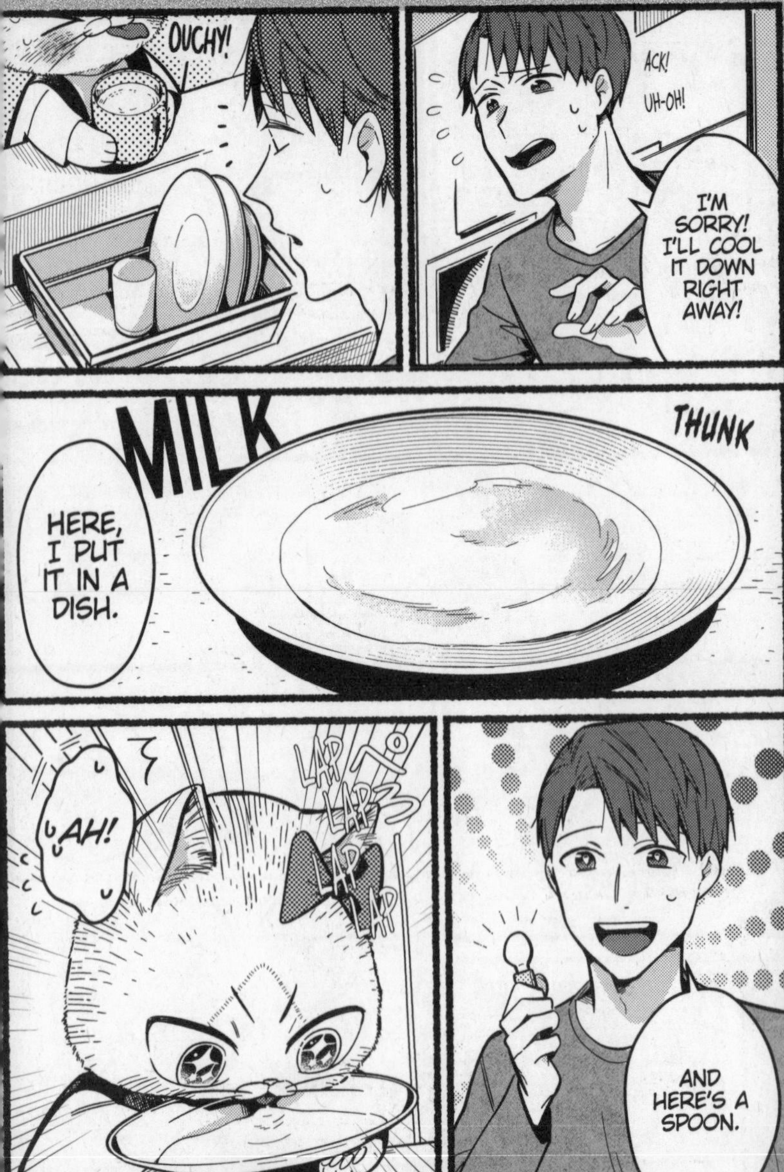
ACK!
UH-OH!
I'M SORRY! I'LL COOL IT DOWN RIGHT AWAY!
OUCHY!
THUNK
MILK
HERE, I PUT IT IN A DISH.
AND HERE'S A SPOON.
AH!
LAP LAP LAP LAP

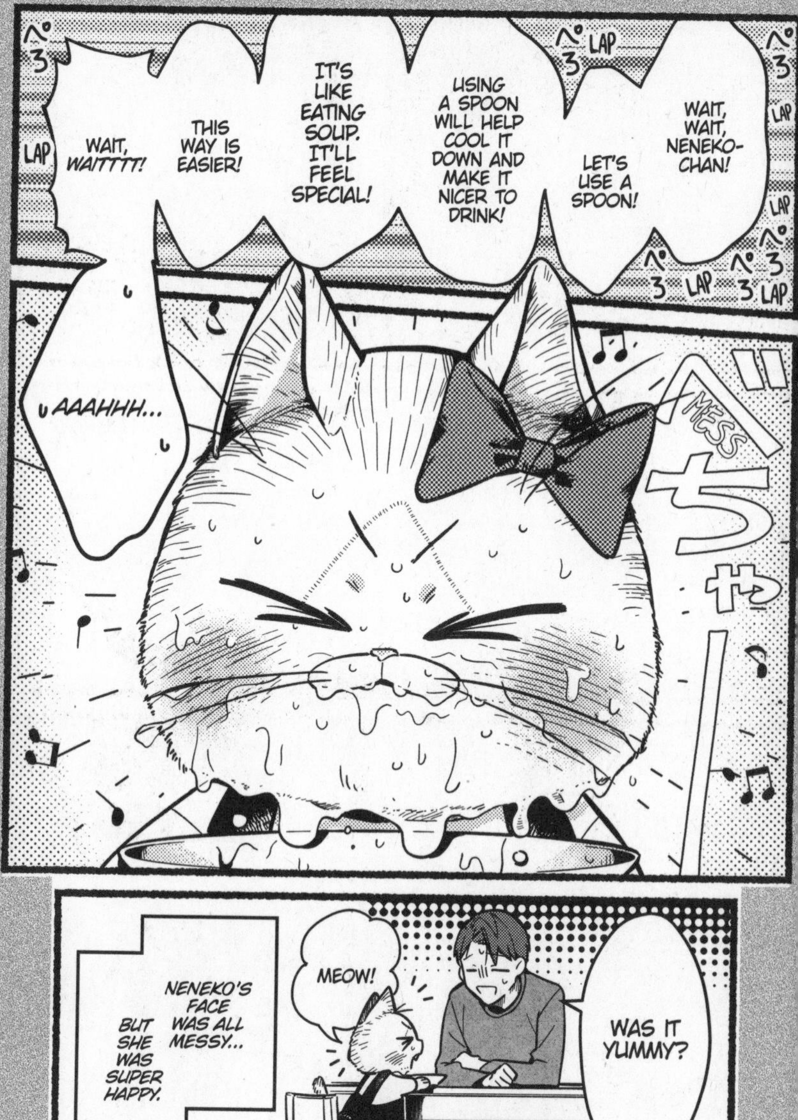
LAP
WAIT, WAIT, NENEKO-CHAN!
LET'S USE A SPOON!
USING A SPOON WILL HELP COOL IT DOWN AND MAKE IT NICER TO DRINK!
IT'S LIKE EATING SOUP. IT'LL FEEL SPECIAL!
THIS WAY IS EASIER!
WAIT, WAITTTT!
LAP
LAP
LAP
MESS
AAAHHH...
WAS IT YUMMY?
MEOW!
NENEKO'S FACE WAS ALL MESSY...
BUT SHE WAS SUPER HAPPY.

My
Sister,
the
Cat

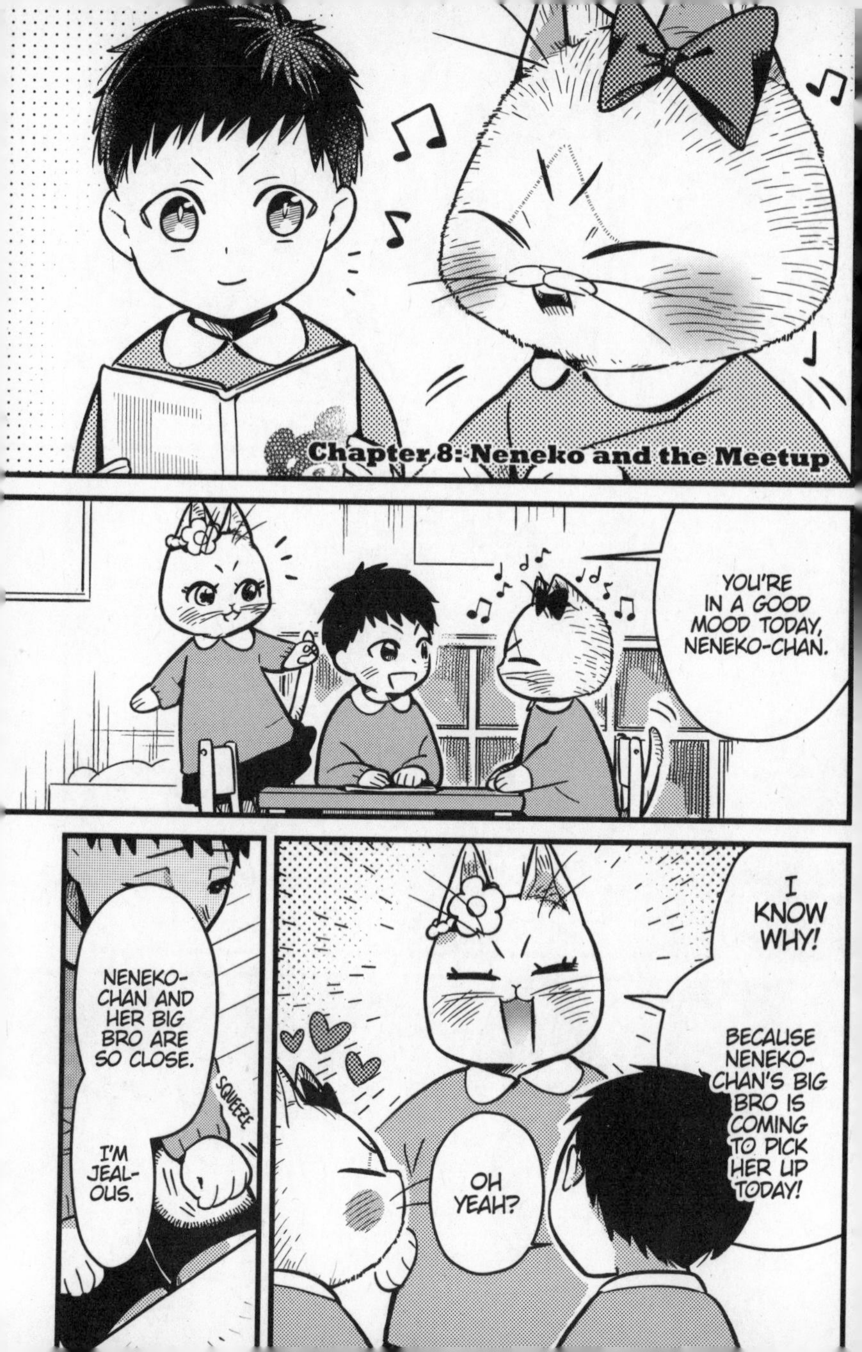
Chapter 8: Neneko and the Meetup
YOU'RE IN A GOOD MOOD TODAY, NENEKO-CHAN.
I KNOW WHY!
BECAUSE NENEKO-CHAN'S BIG BRO IS COMING TO PICK HER UP TODAY!
OH YEAH?
NENEKO-CHAN AND HER BIG BRO ARE SO CLOSE.
SQUEEZE
I'M JEAL-OUS.

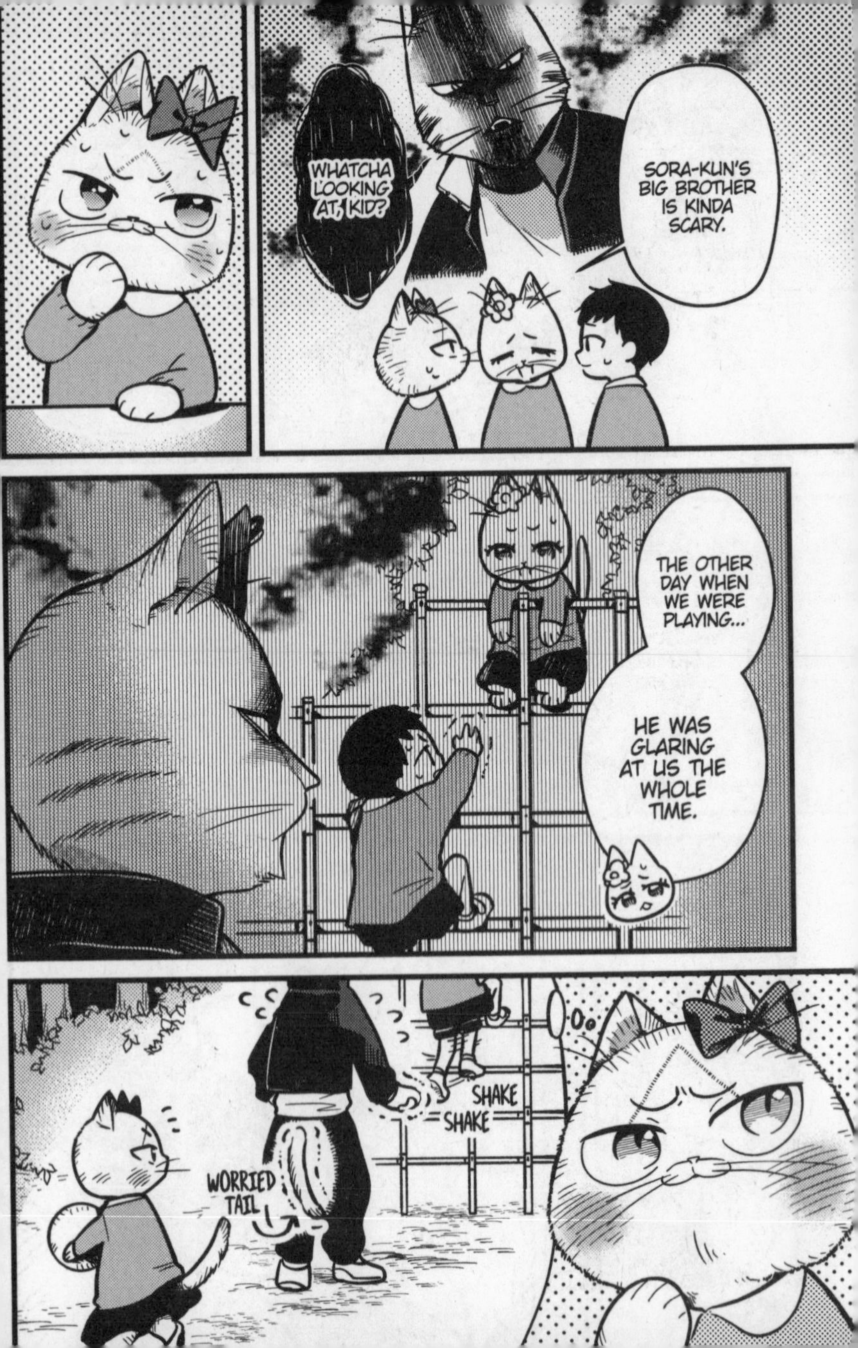
SORA-KUN'S BIG BROTHER IS KINDA SCARY.
WHATCHA LOOKING AT, KID?
THE OTHER DAY WHEN WE WERE PLAYING...
HE WAS GLARING AT US THE WHOLE TIME.
SHAKE
SHAKE
WORRIED TAIL

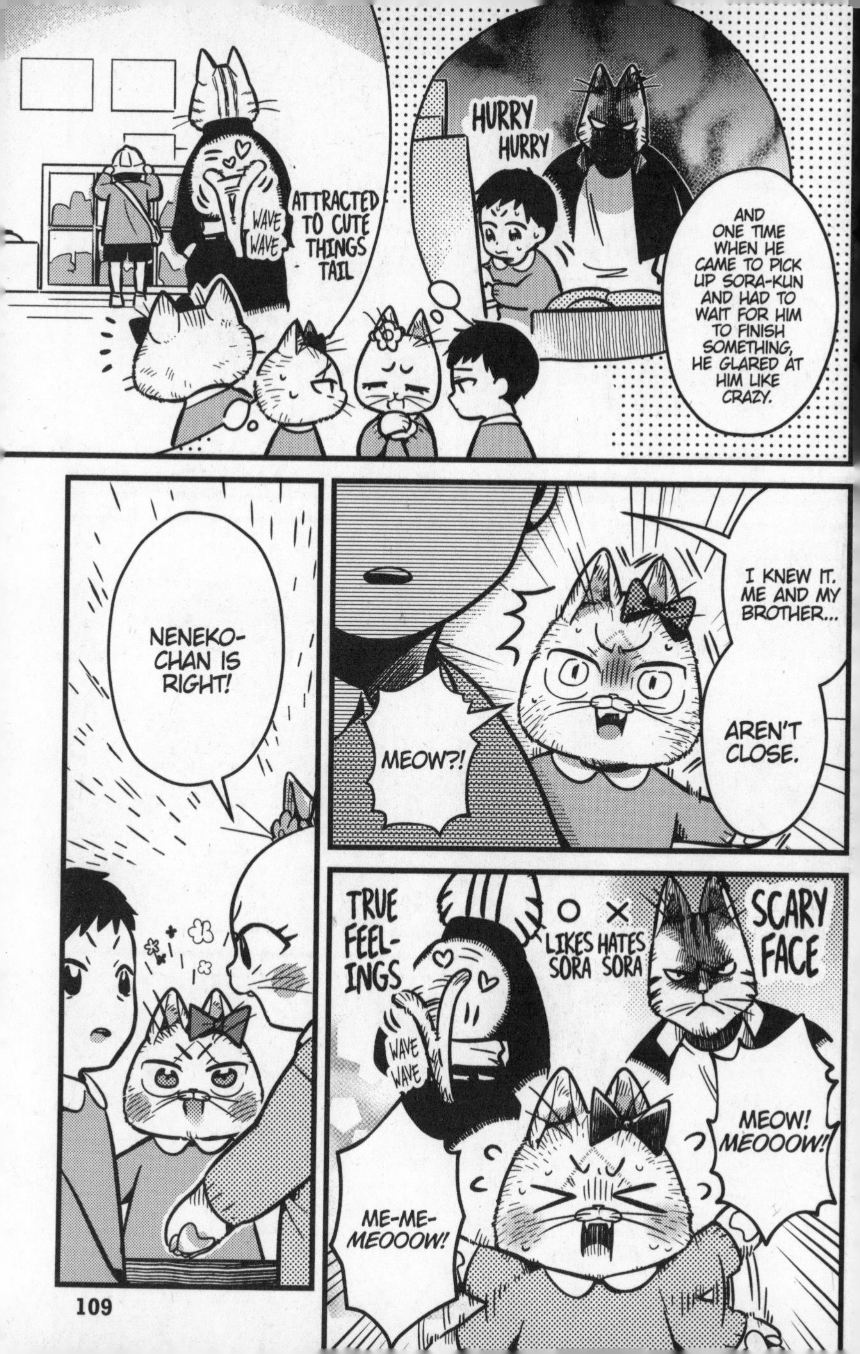
AND ONE TIME WHEN HE CAME TO PICK UP SORA-KUN AND HAD TO WAIT FOR HIM TO FINISH SOMETHING, HE GLARED AT HIM LIKE CRAZY.
HURRY HURRY
ATTRACTED TO CUTE THINGS TAIL
WAVE WAVE
I KNEW IT. ME AND MY BROTHER...
AREN'T CLOSE.
MEOW?!
SCARY FACE
MEOW! MEOOOW!
HATES SORA
LIKES SORA
TRUE FEEL-INGS
WAVE WAVE
ME-ME-MEOOOW!
NENEKO-CHAN IS RIGHT!

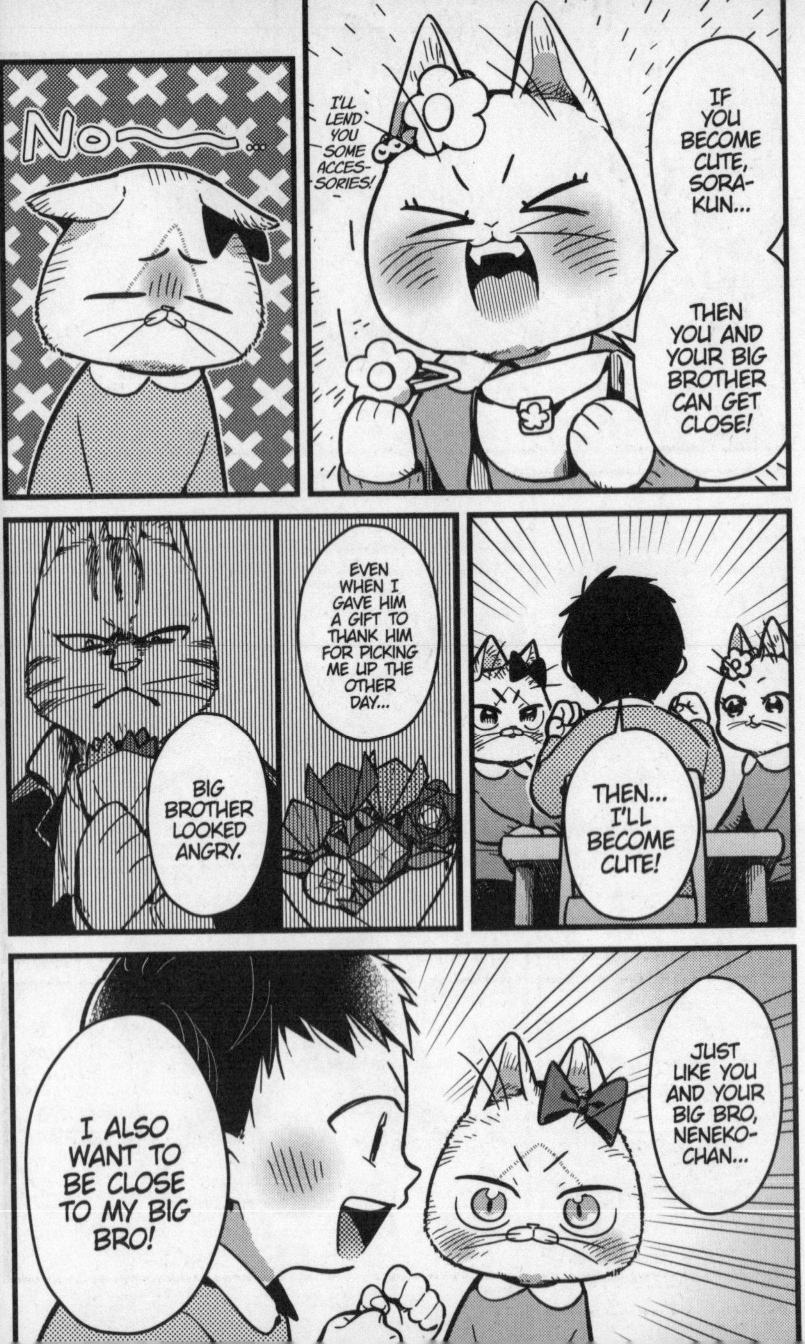
IF YOU BECOME CUTE, SORA-KUN...
I'LL LEND YOU SOME ACCES-SORIES!
THEN YOU AND YOUR BIG BROTHER CAN GET CLOSE!
No——...
THEN... I'LL BECOME CUTE!
EVEN WHEN I GAVE HIM A GIFT TO THANK HIM FOR PICKING ME UP THE OTHER DAY...
BIG BROTHER LOOKED ANGRY.
JUST LIKE YOU AND YOUR BIG BRO, NENEKO-CHAN...
I ALSO WANT TO BE CLOSE TO MY BIG BRO!

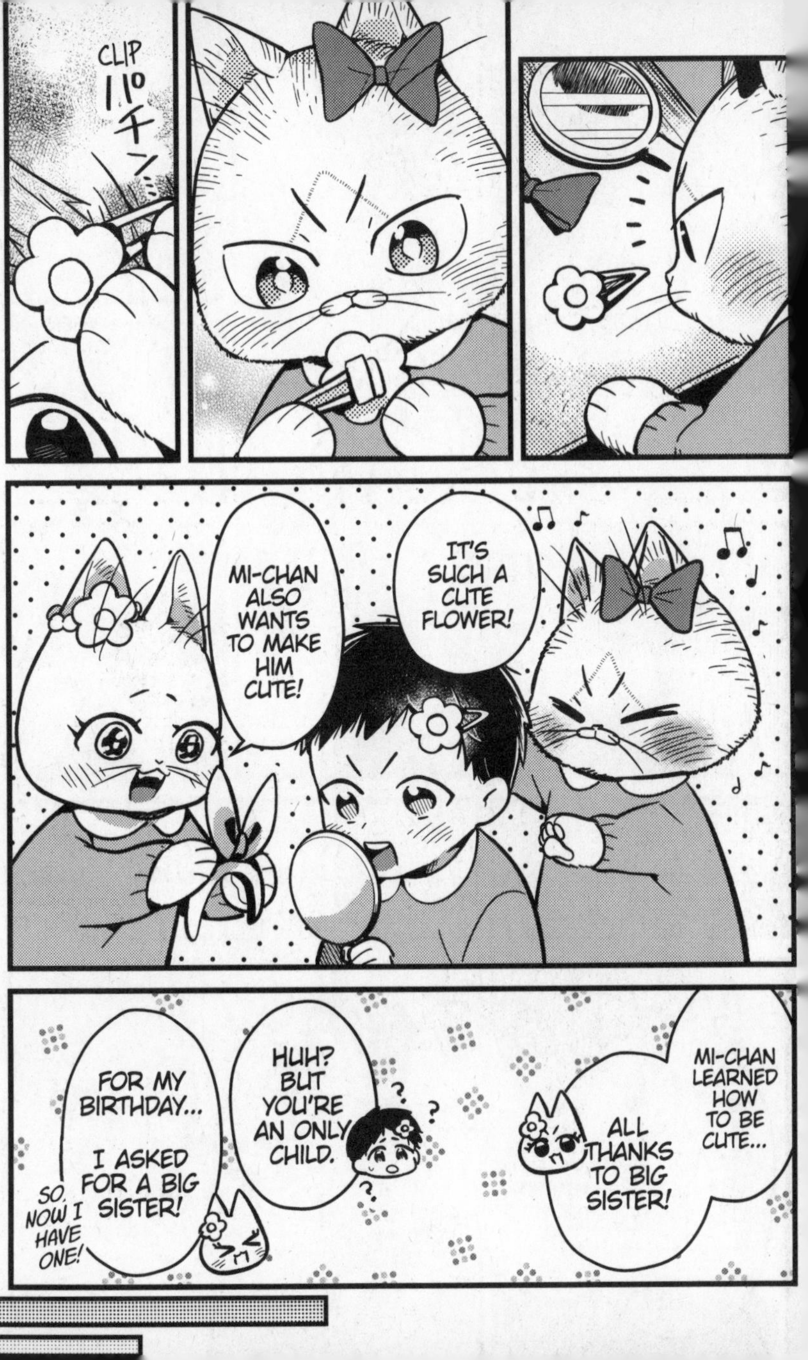
CLIP
パチン
IT'S SUCH A CUTE FLOWER!
MI-CHAN ALSO WANTS TO MAKE HIM CUTE!
MI-CHAN LEARNED HOW TO BE CUTE...
ALL THANKS TO BIG SISTER!
HUH? BUT YOU'RE AN ONLY CHILD.
FOR MY BIRTHDAY...
I ASKED FOR A BIG SISTER!
SO, NOW I HAVE ONE!

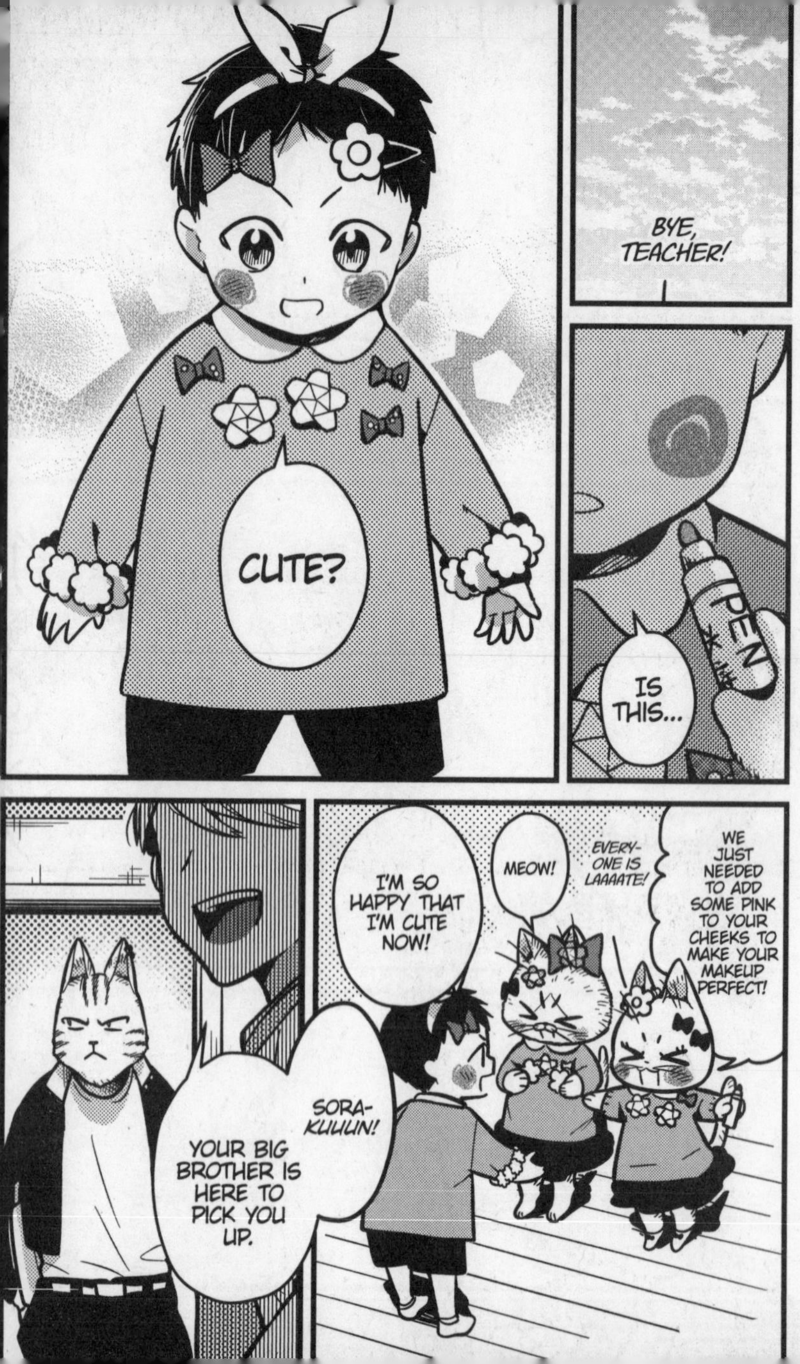
BYE, TEACHER!
PEN
IS THIS...
CUTE?
WE JUST NEEDED TO ADD SOME PINK TO YOUR CHEEKS TO MAKE YOUR MAKEUP PERFECT!
EVERY-ONE IS LAAAATE!
MEOW!
I'M SO HAPPY THAT I'M CUTE NOW!
SORA-KUUUN!
YOUR BIG BROTHER IS HERE TO PICK YOU UP.

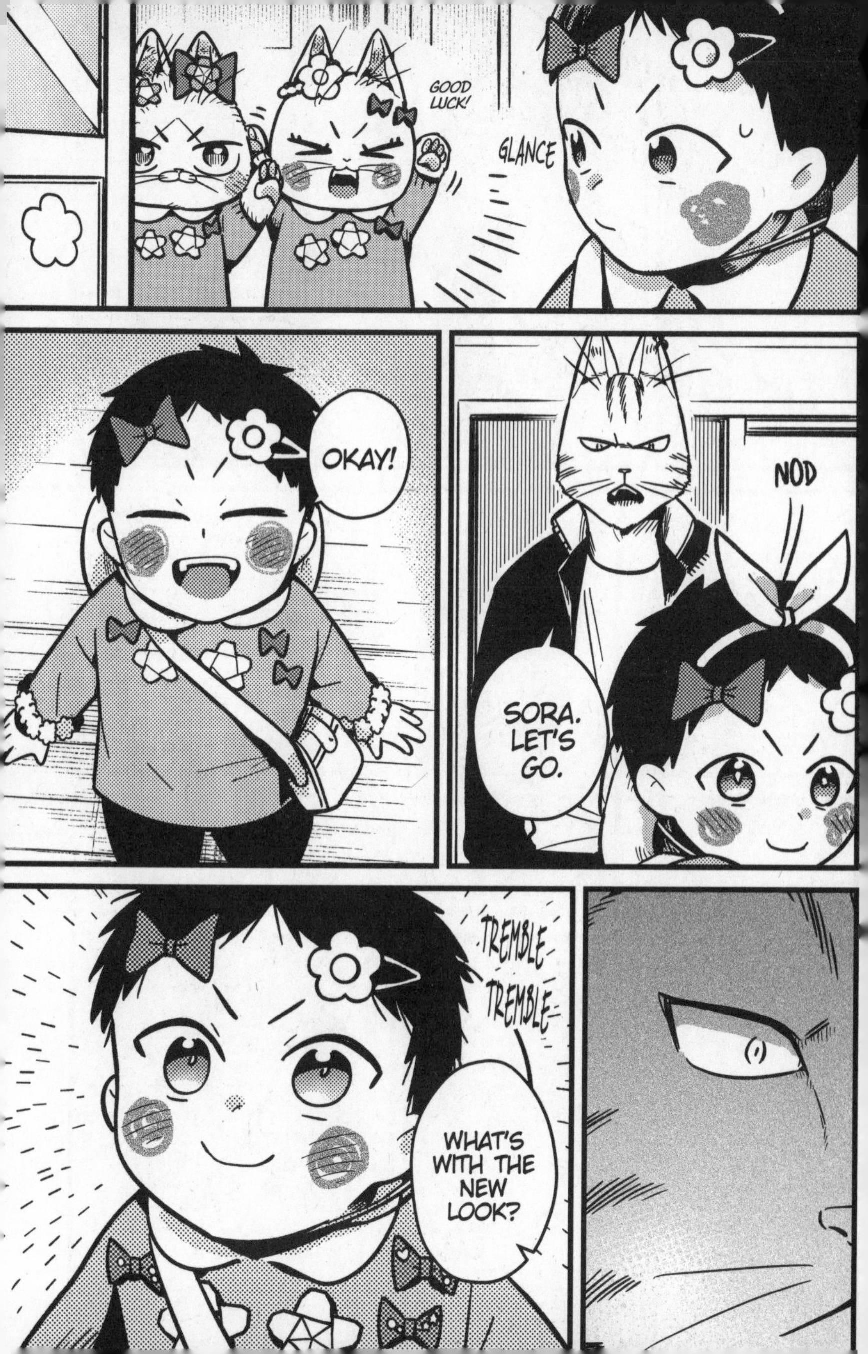
GOOD LUCK!
GLANCE
NOD
SORA. LET'S GO.
OKAY!
TREMBLE
TREMBLE
WHAT'S WITH THE NEW LOOK?

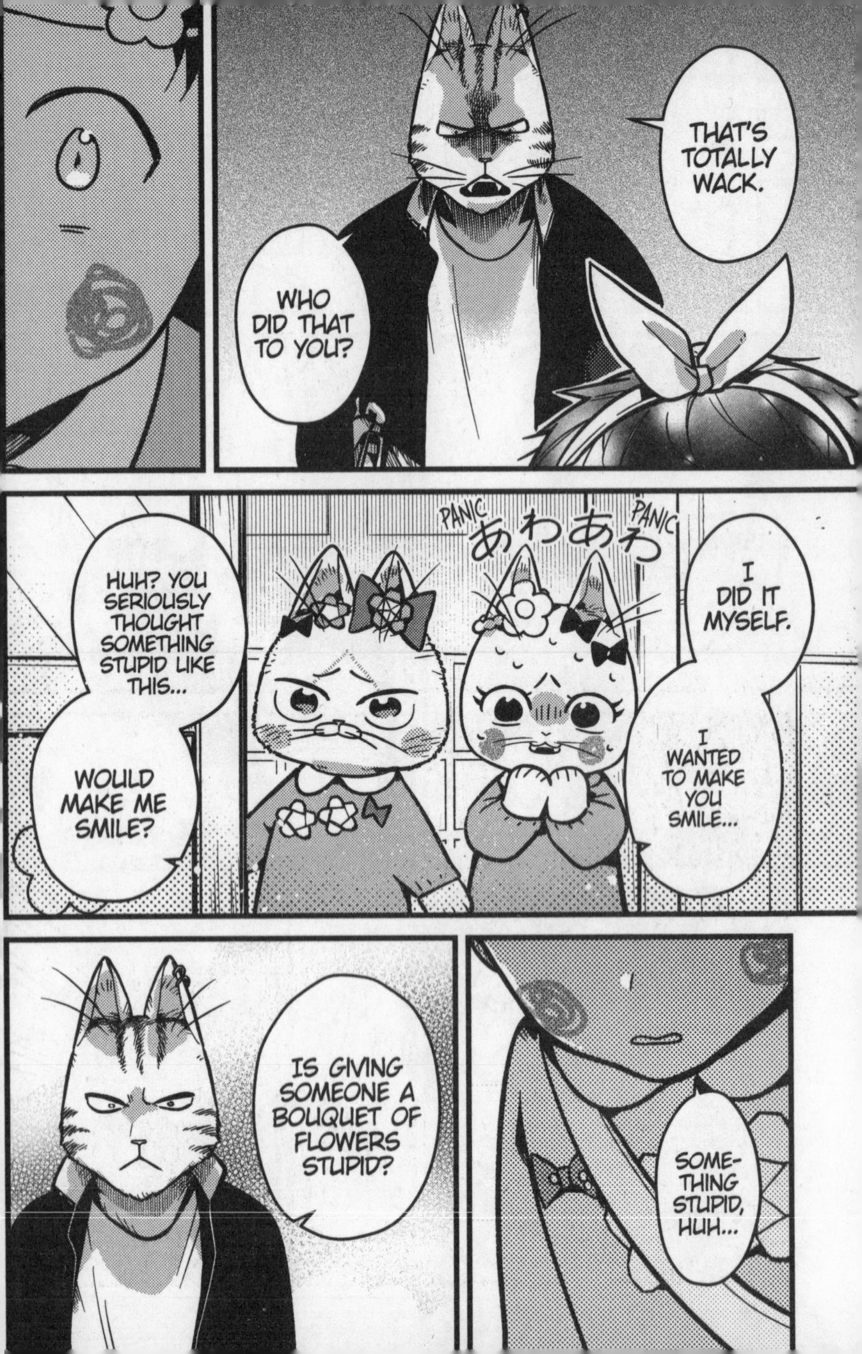
THAT'S TOTALLY WACK.
WHO DID THAT TO YOU?
PANIC あわあわ PANIC
I DID IT MYSELF.
I WANTED TO MAKE YOU SMILE...
HUH? YOU SERIOUSLY THOUGHT SOMETHING STUPID LIKE THIS...
WOULD MAKE ME SMILE?
SOME-THING STUPID, HUH...
IS GIVING SOMEONE A BOUQUET OF FLOWERS STUPID?

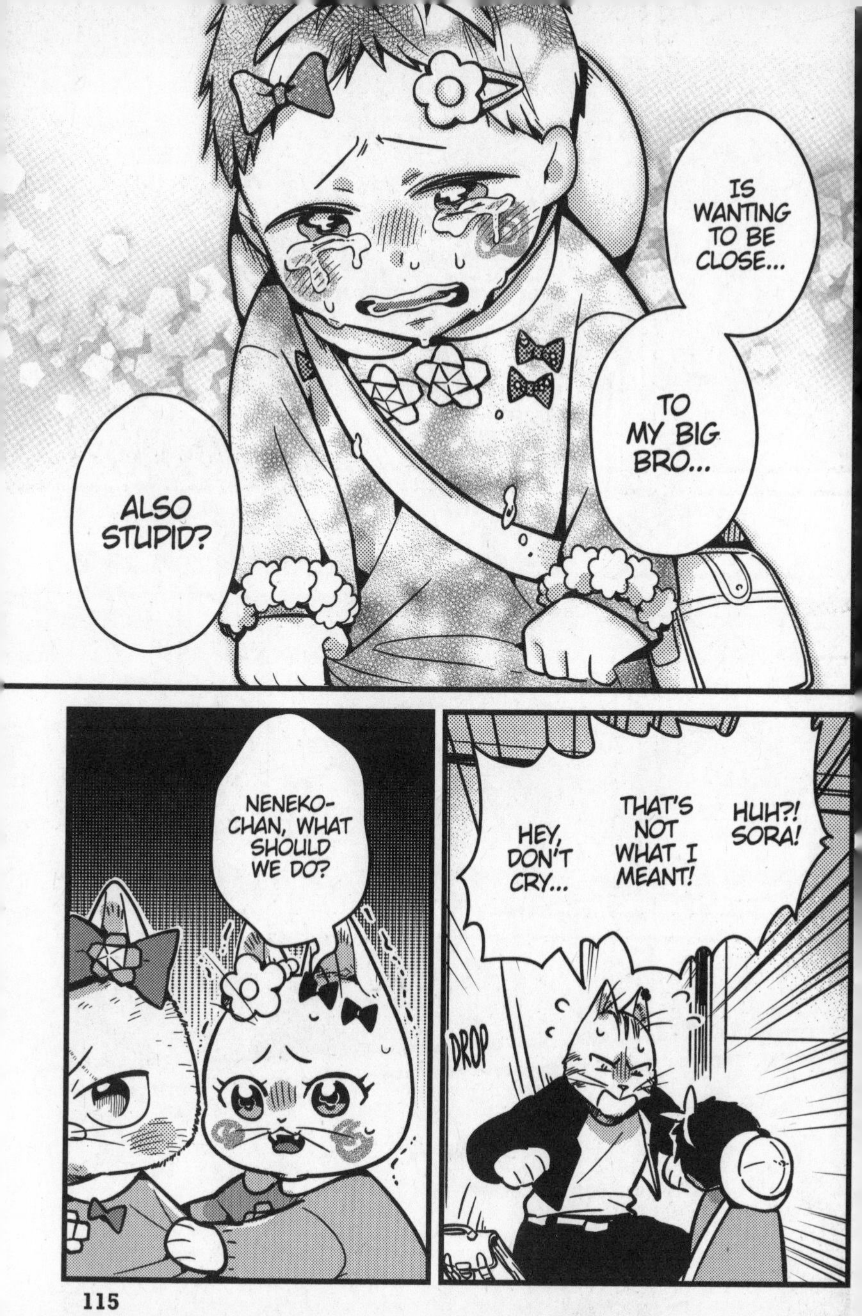
IS WANTING TO BE CLOSE...
TO MY BIG BRO...
ALSO STUPID?
HUH?! SORA!
THAT'S NOT WHAT I MEANT!
HEY, DON'T CRY...
DROP
NENEKO-CHAN, WHAT SHOULD WE DO?

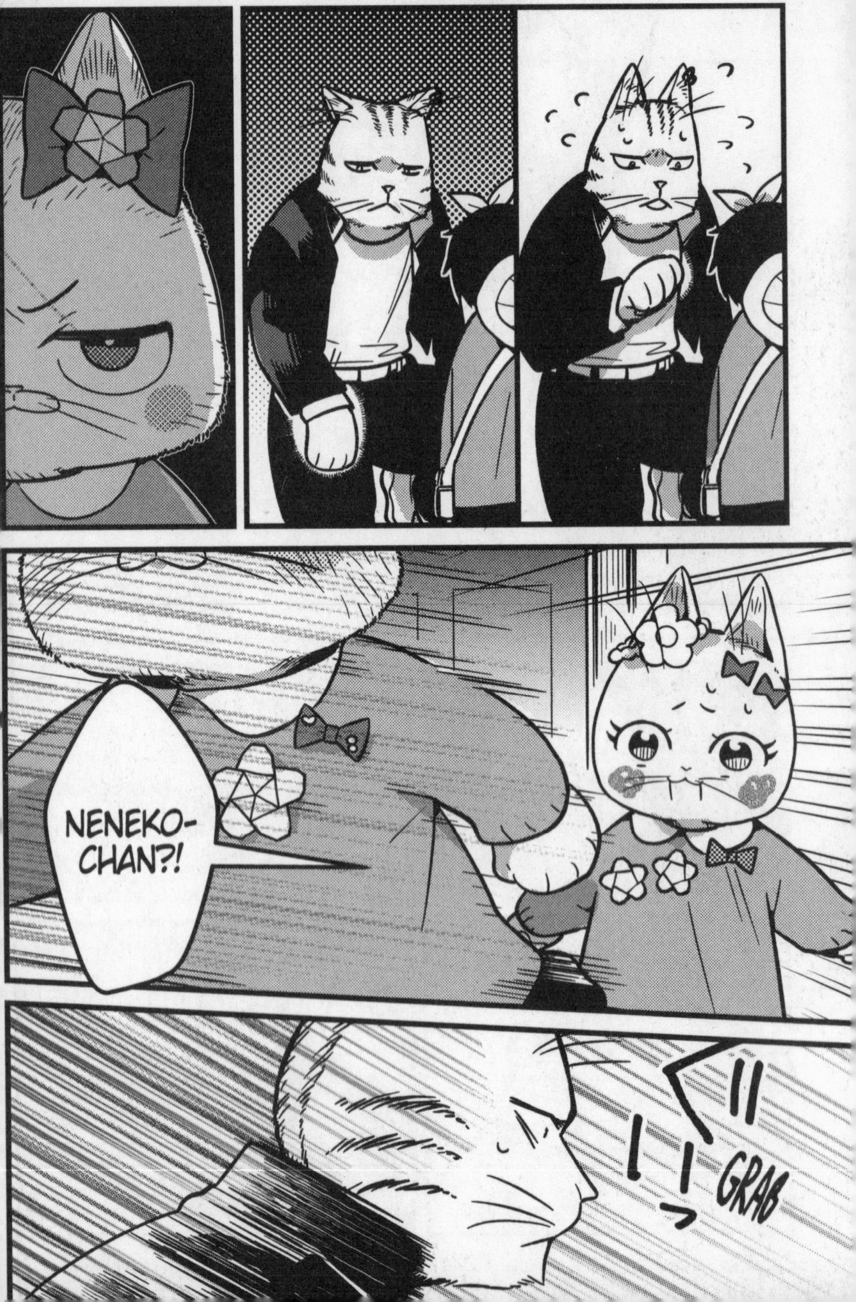
NENEKO-
CHAN?!
GRAB

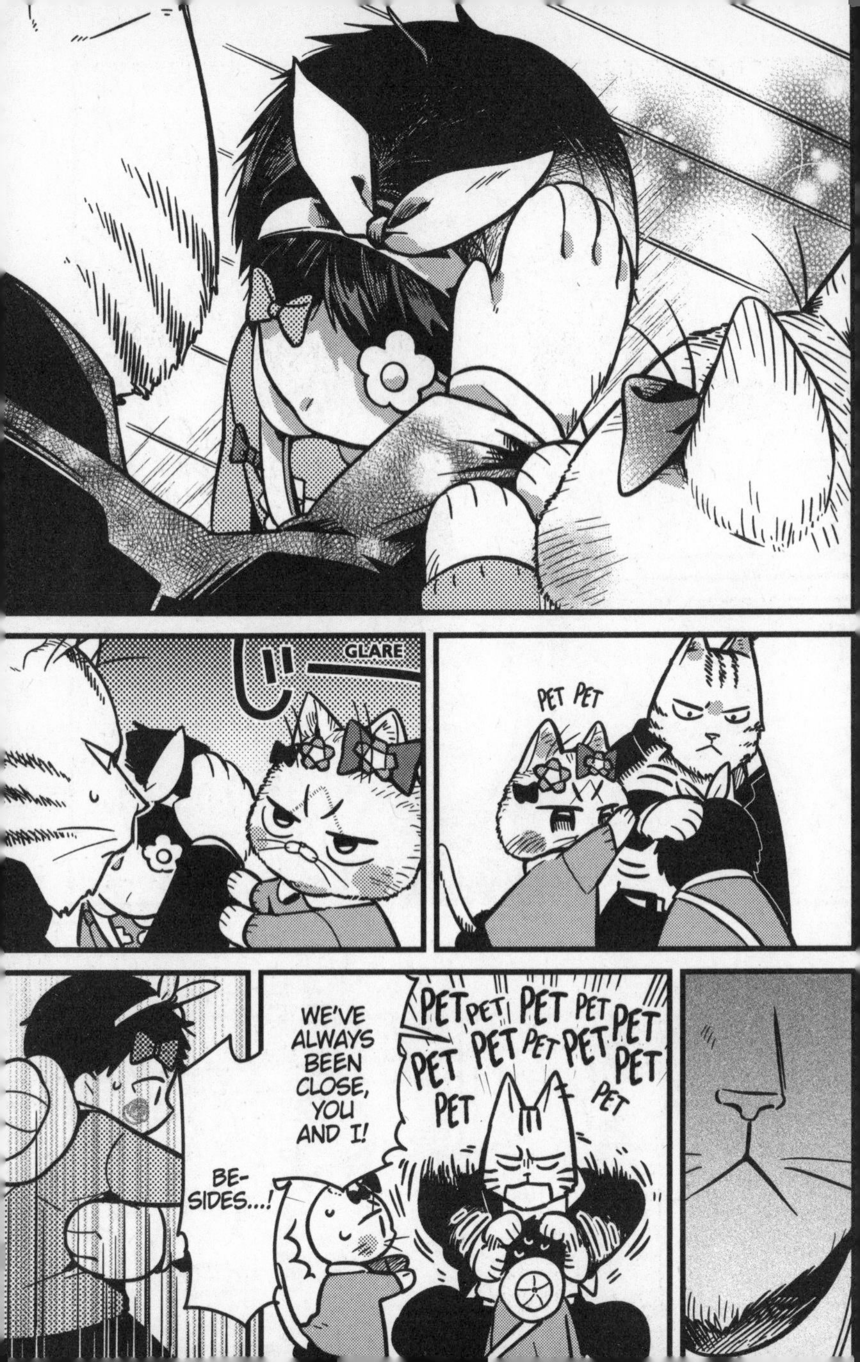
PET PET
GLARE
PET PET PET PET PET PET PET PET PET PET PET PET
WE'VE ALWAYS BEEN CLOSE, YOU AND I!
BE-SIDES...!

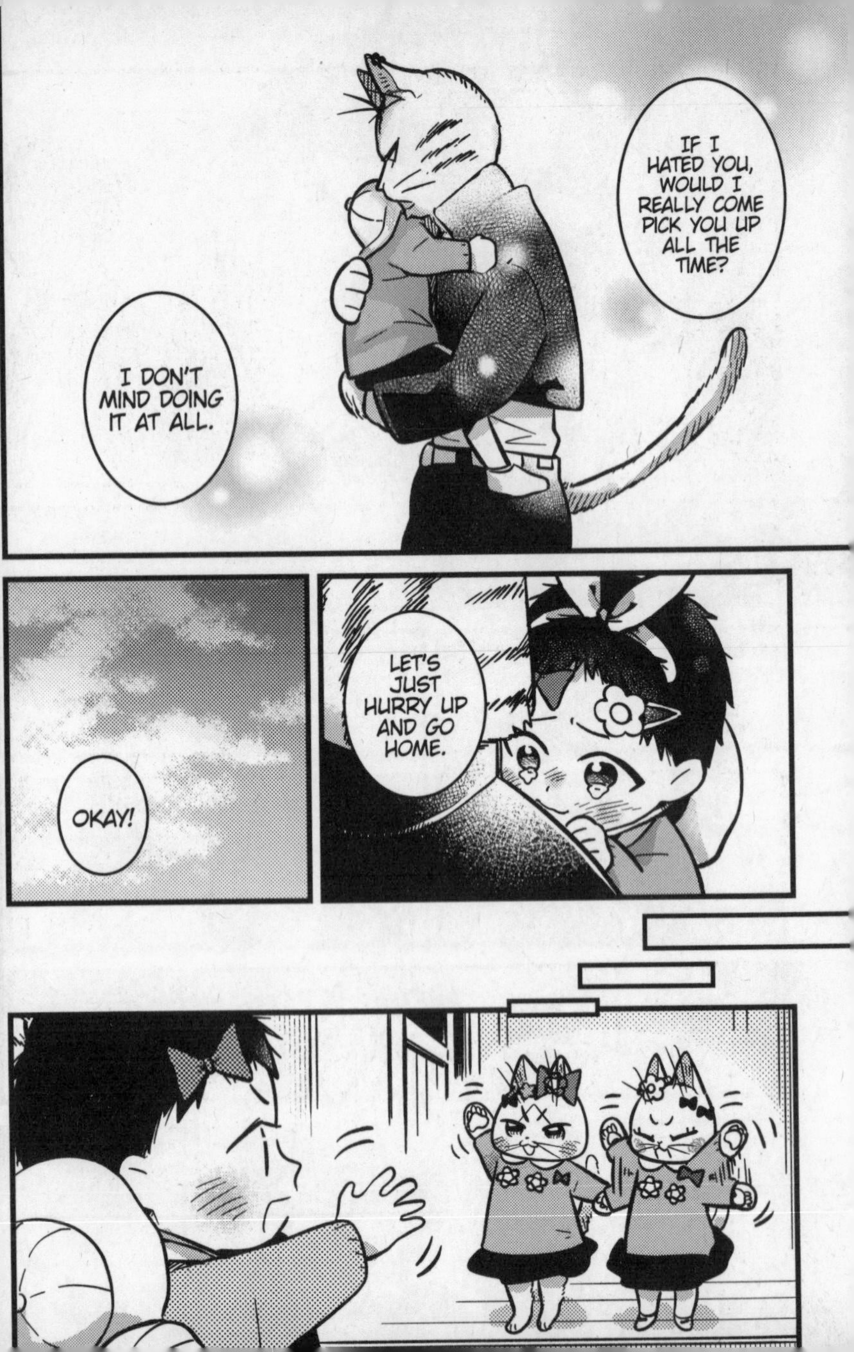
IF I HATED YOU, WOULD I REALLY COME PICK YOU UP ALL THE TIME?
I DON'T MIND DOING IT AT ALL.
LET'S JUST HURRY UP AND GO HOME.
OKAY!

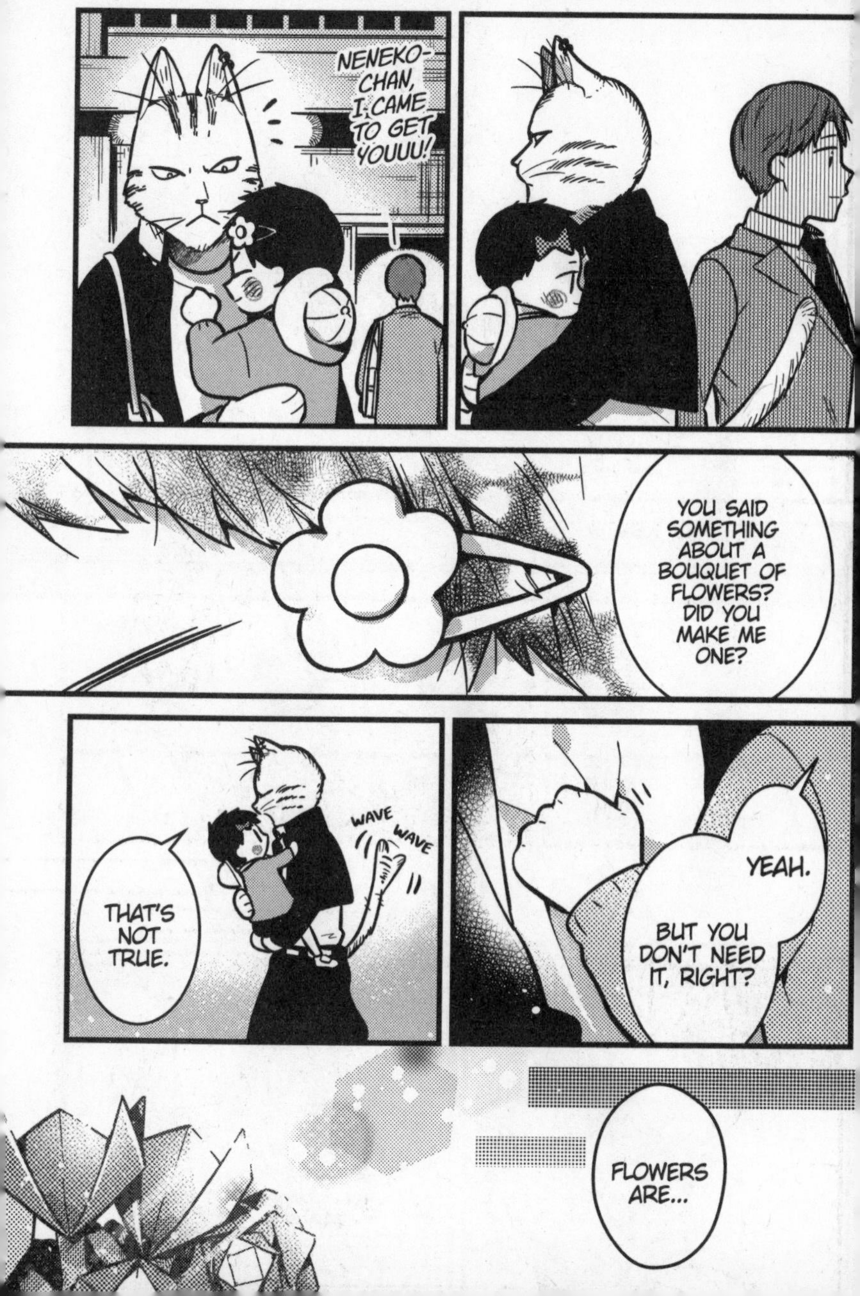
NENEKO-CHAN, I CAME TO GET YOUUU!
YOU SAID SOMETHING ABOUT A BOUQUET OF FLOWERS? DID YOU MAKE ME ONE?
YEAH.
BUT YOU DON'T NEED IT, RIGHT?
WAVE WAVE
THAT'S NOT TRUE.
FLOWERS ARE...

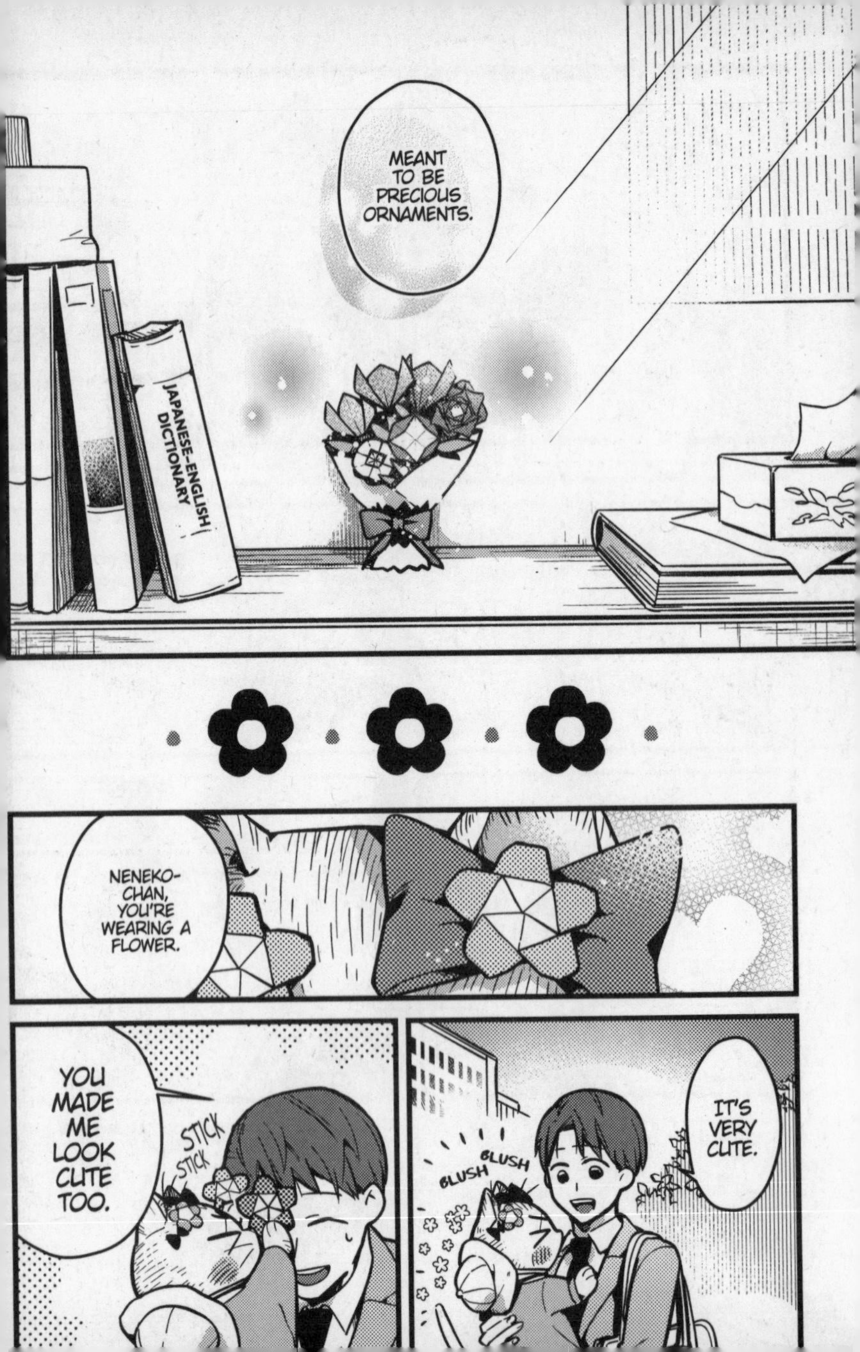
MEANT TO BE PRECIOUS ORNAMENTS.
JAPANESE-ENGLISH DICTIONARY
NENEKO-CHAN, YOU'RE WEARING A FLOWER.
IT'S VERY CUTE.
BLUSH BLUSH
YOU MADE ME LOOK CUTE TOO.
STICK STICK

Extra 8

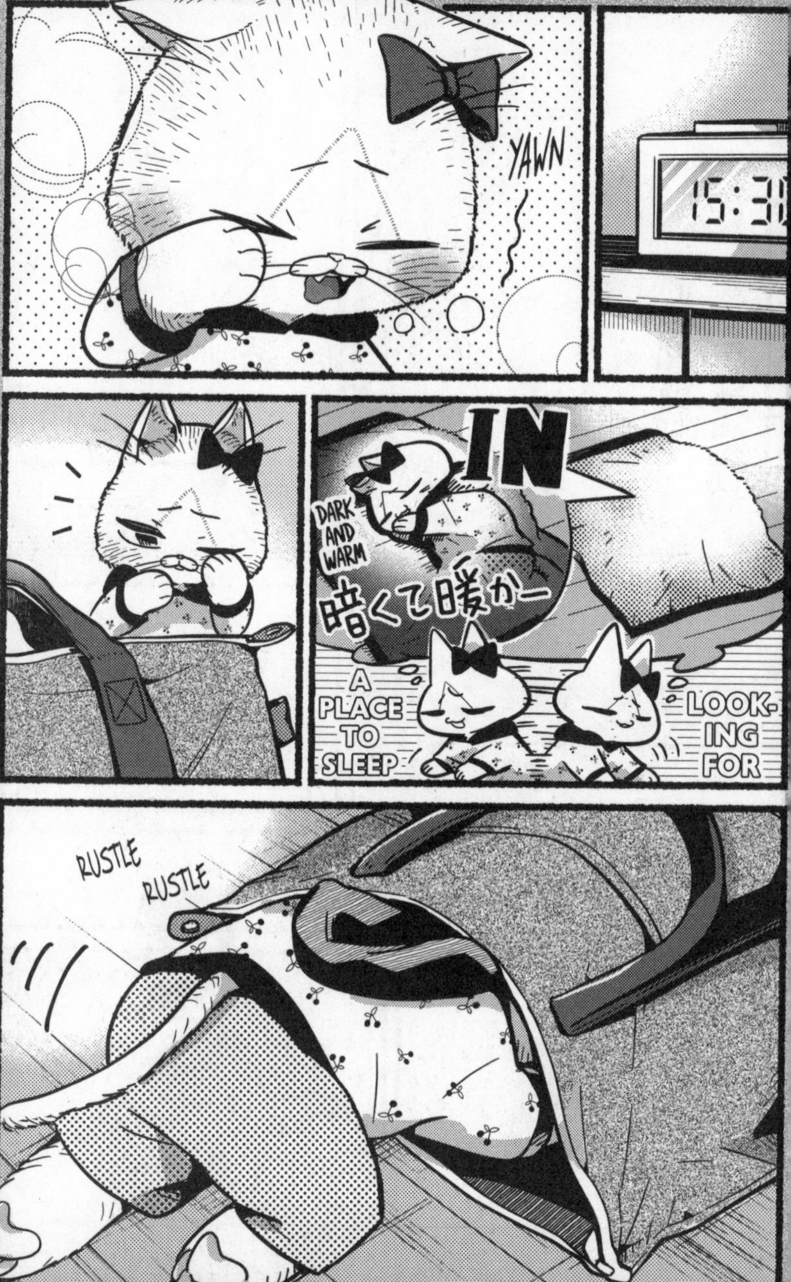
YAWN
IN
DARK AND WARM
暗くて暖かー
LOOK-ING FOR
A PLACE TO SLEEP
RUSTLE
RUSTLE

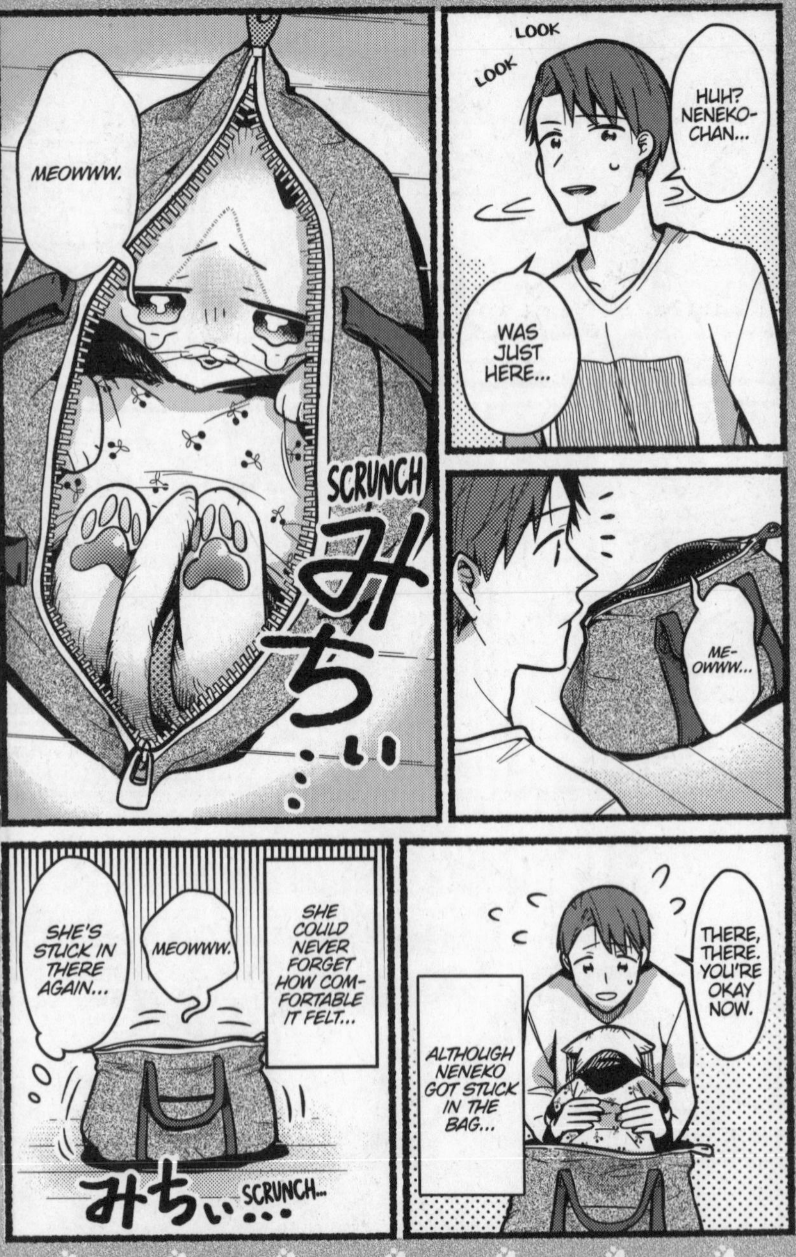
LOOK
LOOK
HUH? NENEKO-CHAN...
WAS JUST HERE...
ME-OWWW...
MEOWWW.
SCRUNCH
みちぃ...
THERE, THERE. YOU'RE OKAY NOW.
ALTHOUGH NENEKO GOT STUCK IN THE BAG...
SHE COULD NEVER FORGET HOW COMFORTABLE IT FELT...
MEOWWW.
SHE'S STUCK IN THERE AGAIN...
みちぃ...
SCRUNCH...

Chapter 9: Neneko and the Celebrities

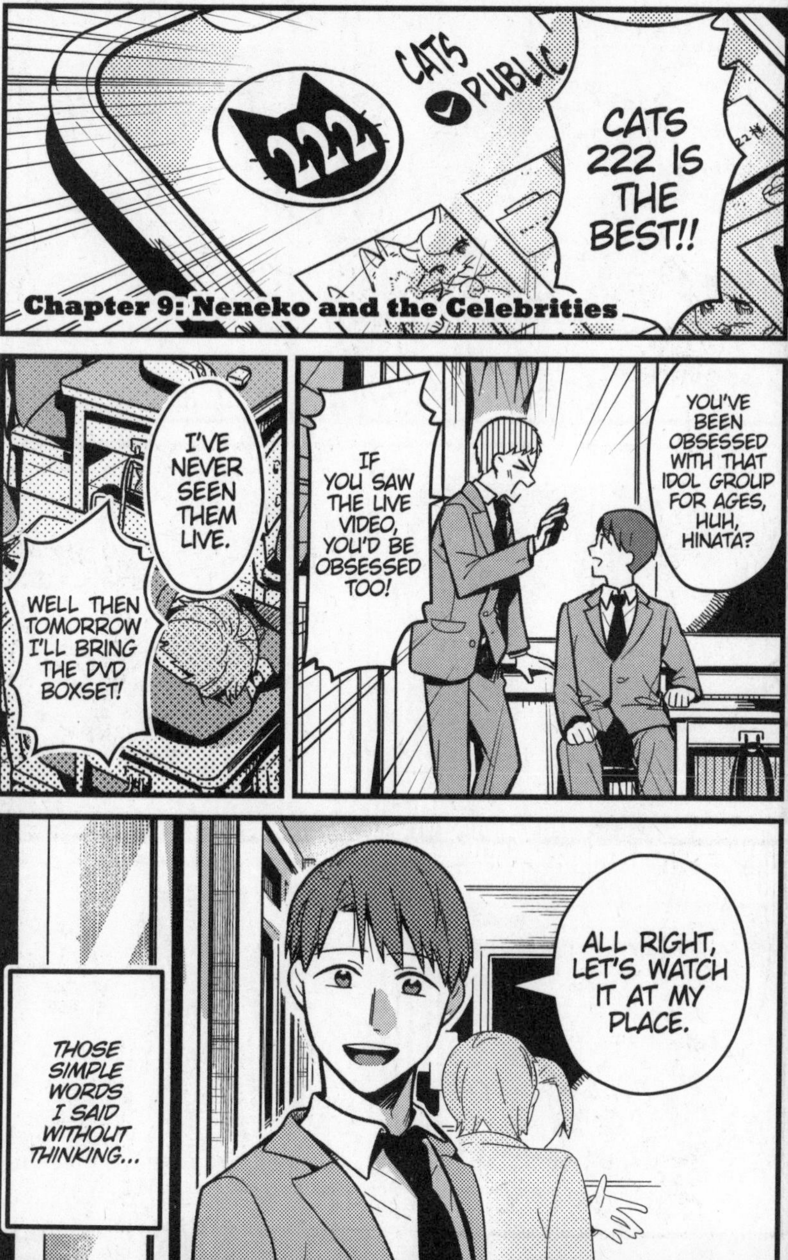
CATS
PUBLIC
222
CATS 222 IS THE BEST!!
YOU'VE BEEN OBSESSED WITH THAT IDOL GROUP FOR AGES, HUH, HINATA?
IF YOU SAW THE LIVE VIDEO, YOU'D BE OBSESSED TOO!
I'VE NEVER SEEN THEM LIVE.
WELL THEN TOMORROW I'LL BRING THE DVD BOXSET!
ALL RIGHT, LET'S WATCH IT AT MY PLACE.
THOSE SIMPLE WORDS I SAID WITHOUT THINKING...

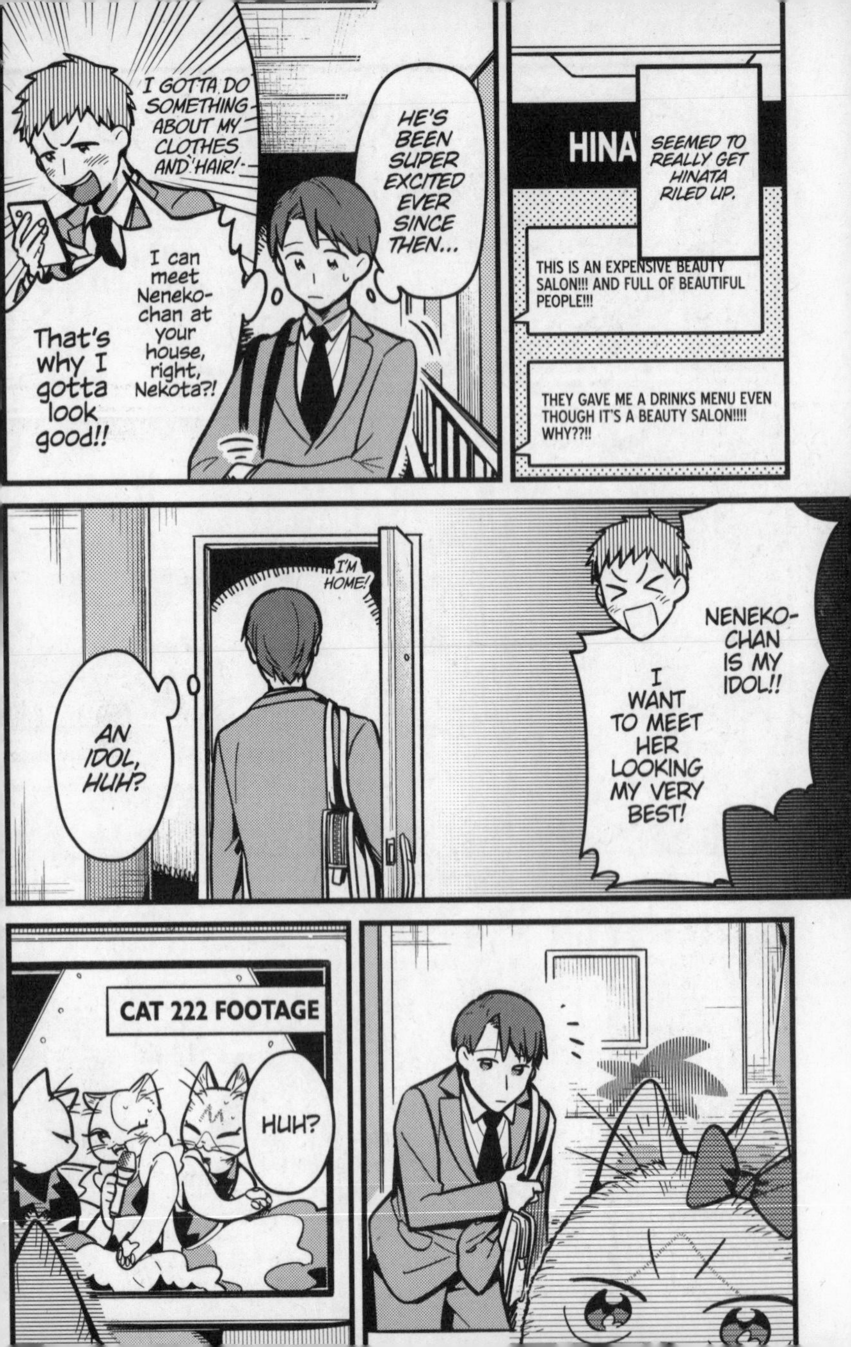
SEEMED TO REALLY GET HINATA RILED UP.
THIS IS AN EXPENSIVE BEAUTY SALON!!! AND FULL OF BEAUTIFUL PEOPLE!!!
THEY GAVE ME A DRINKS MENU EVEN THOUGH IT'S A BEAUTY SALON!!!! WHY??!!
HE'S BEEN SUPER EXCITED EVER SINCE THEN...
I GOTTA DO SOMETHING ABOUT MY CLOTHES AND HAIR!
I can meet Neneko-chan at your house, right, Nekota?!
That's why I gotta look good!!
NENEKO-CHAN IS MY IDOL!!
I WANT TO MEET HER LOOKING MY VERY BEST!
I'M HOME!
AN IDOL, HUH?
CAT 222 FOOTAGE
HUH?

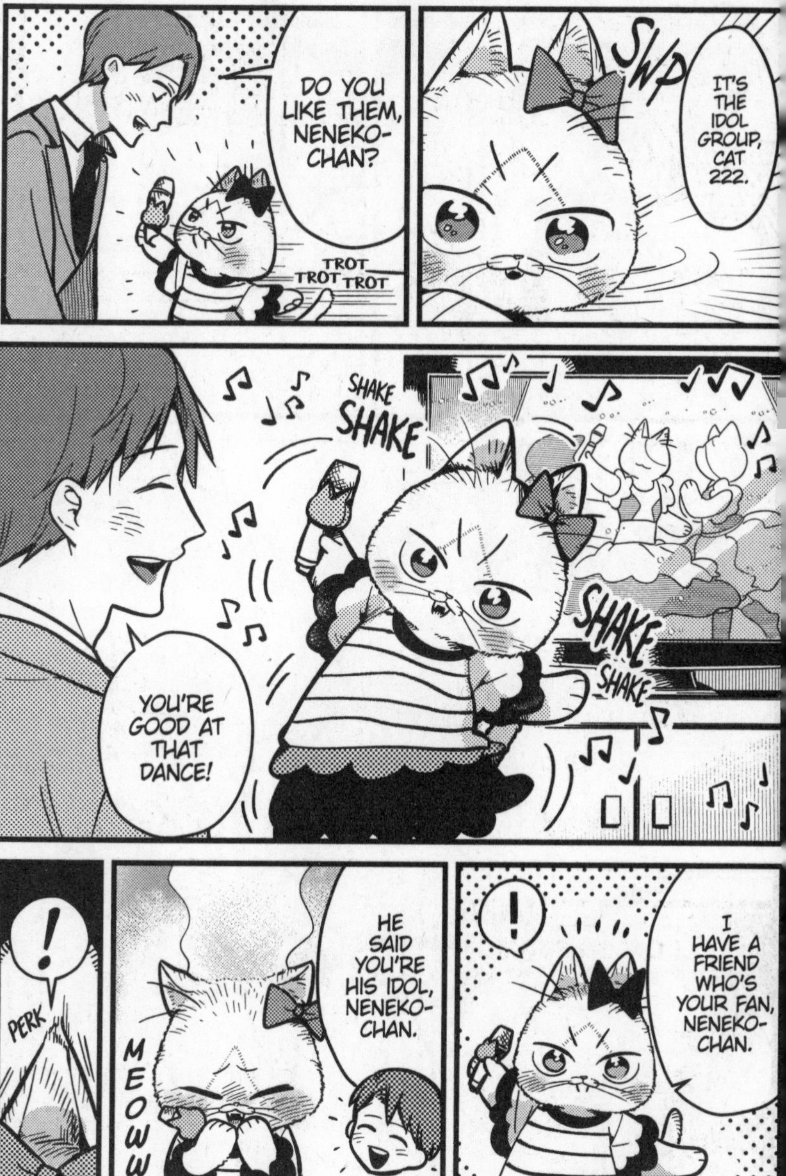
SWP
IT'S THE IDOL GROUP, CAT 222.
DO YOU LIKE THEM, NENEKO-CHAN?
TROT TROT TROT
SHAKE SHAKE
YOU'RE GOOD AT THAT DANCE!
SHAKE SHAKE
I HAVE A FRIEND WHO'S YOUR FAN, NENEKO-CHAN.
!
HE SAID YOU'RE HIS IDOL, NENEKO-CHAN.
MEOWW!
!
PERK

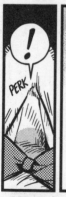

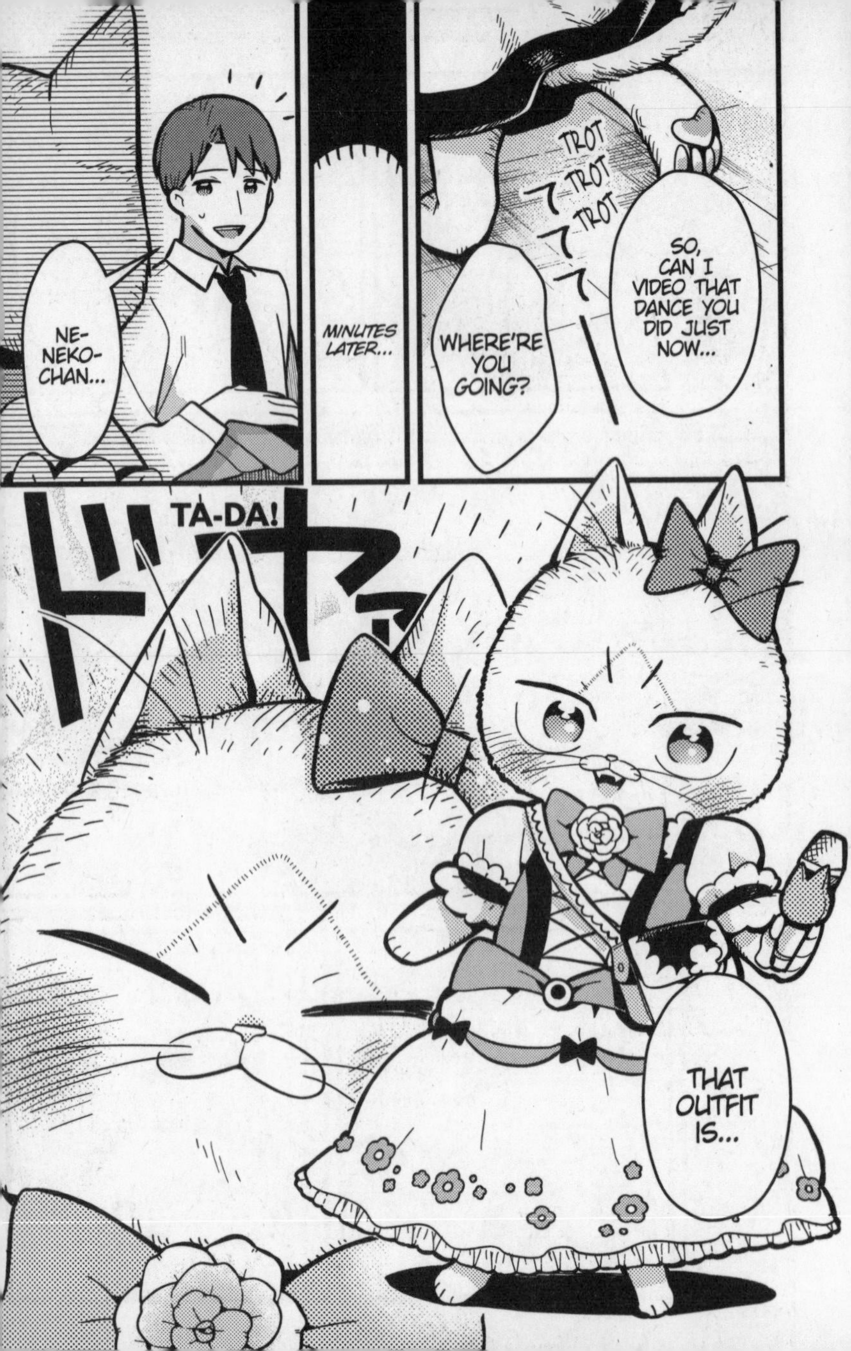
TROT TROT TROT
SO, CAN I VIDEO THAT DANCE YOU DID JUST NOW...
WHERE'RE YOU GOING?
MINUTES LATER...
NE-NEKO-CHAN...
TA-DA!
ドヤァ
THAT OUTFIT IS...

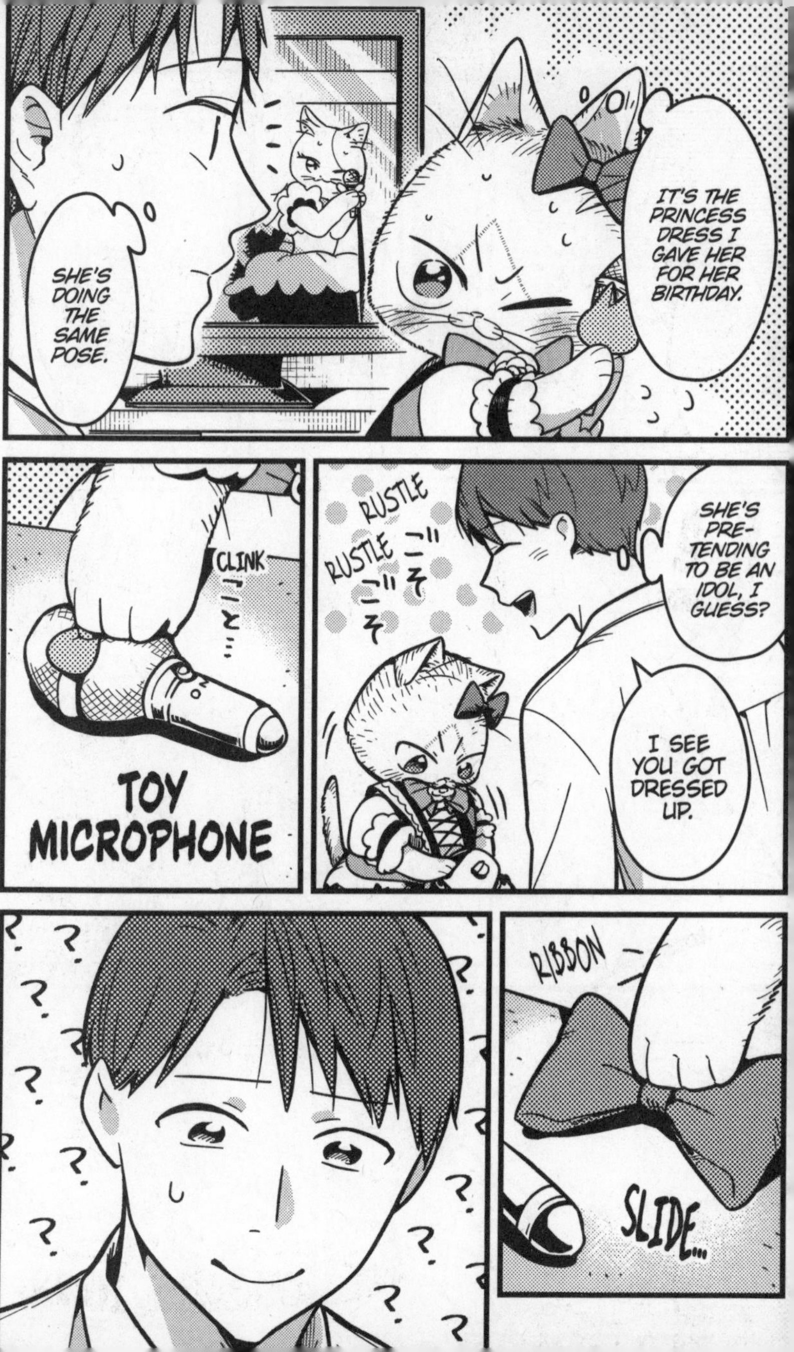
IT'S THE PRINCESS DRESS I GAVE HER FOR HER BIRTHDAY.
SHE'S DOING THE SAME POSE.
RUSTLE
RUSTLE
ごそごそ
SHE'S PRE-TENDING TO BE AN IDOL, I GUESS?
I SEE YOU GOT DRESSED UP.
CLINK
ごと…
TOY MICROPHONE
RIBBON
SLIDE...

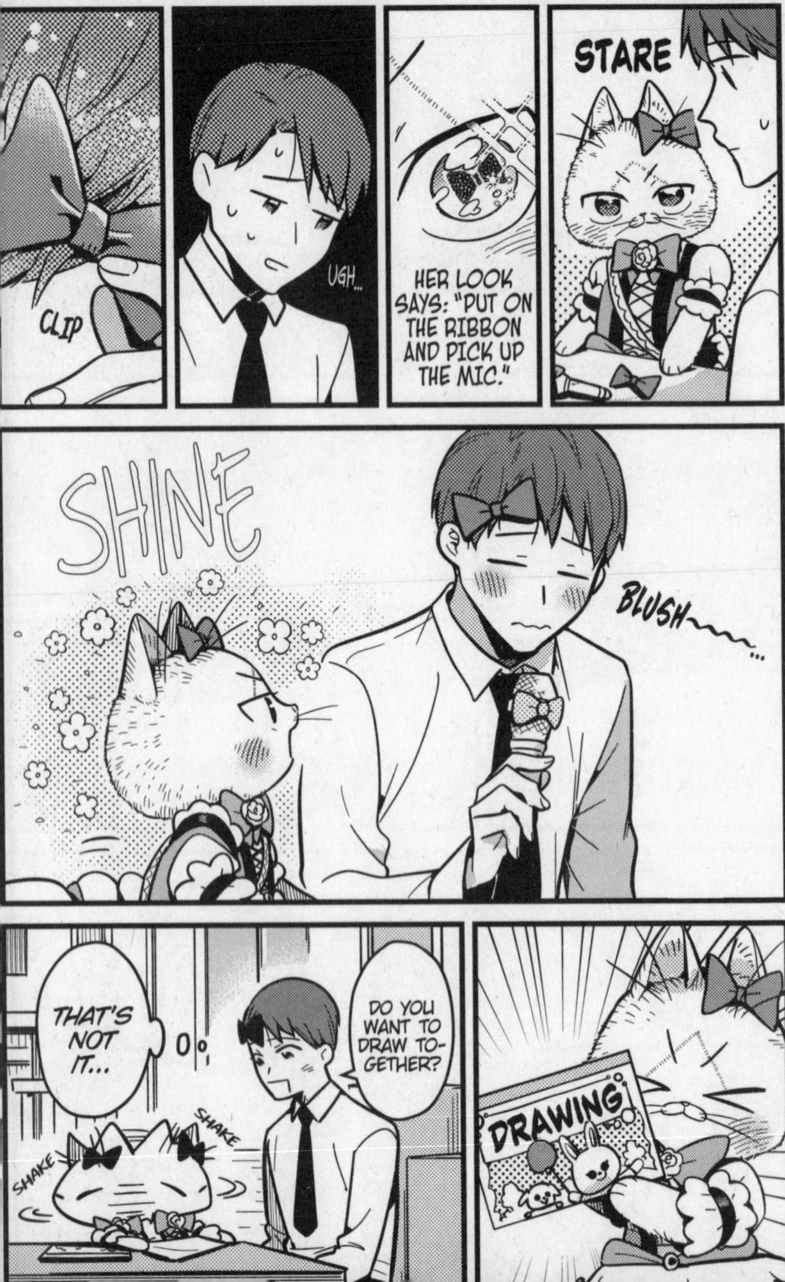
STARE
HER LOOK SAYS: "PUT ON THE RIBBON AND PICK UP THE MIC."
UGH...
CLIP
BLUSH~~~...
SHINE
DRAWING
DO YOU WANT TO DRAW TO-GETHER?
THAT'S NOT IT...
SHAKE
SHAKE

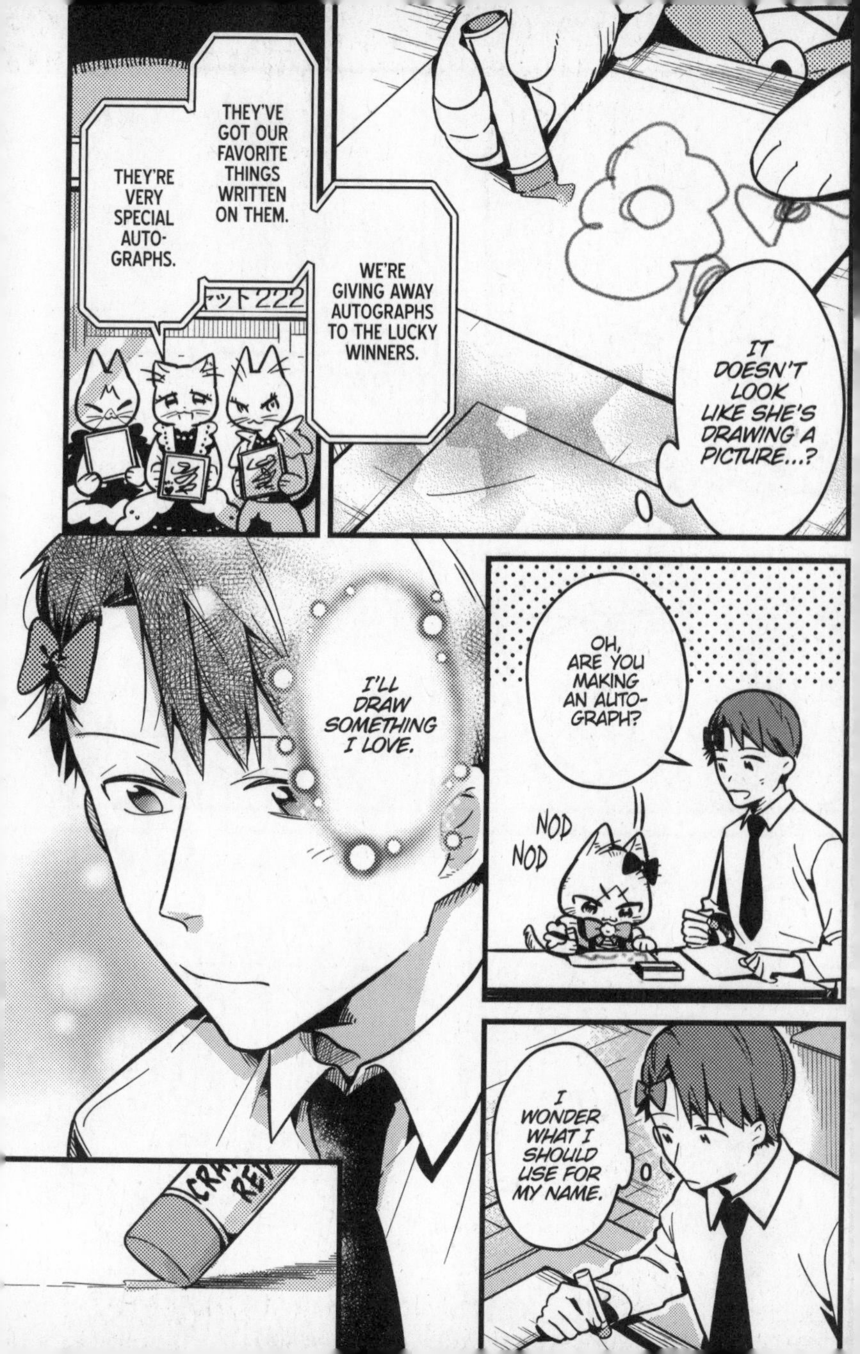
IT DOESN'T LOOK LIKE SHE'S DRAWING A PICTURE...?
WE'RE GIVING AWAY AUTOGRAPHS TO THE LUCKY WINNERS.
THEY'VE GOT OUR FAVORITE THINGS WRITTEN ON THEM.
THEY'RE VERY SPECIAL AUTO-GRAPHS.
OH, ARE YOU MAKING AN AUTO-GRAPH?
NOD NOD
I WONDER WHAT I SHOULD USE FOR MY NAME.
I'LL DRAW SOMETHING I LOVE.

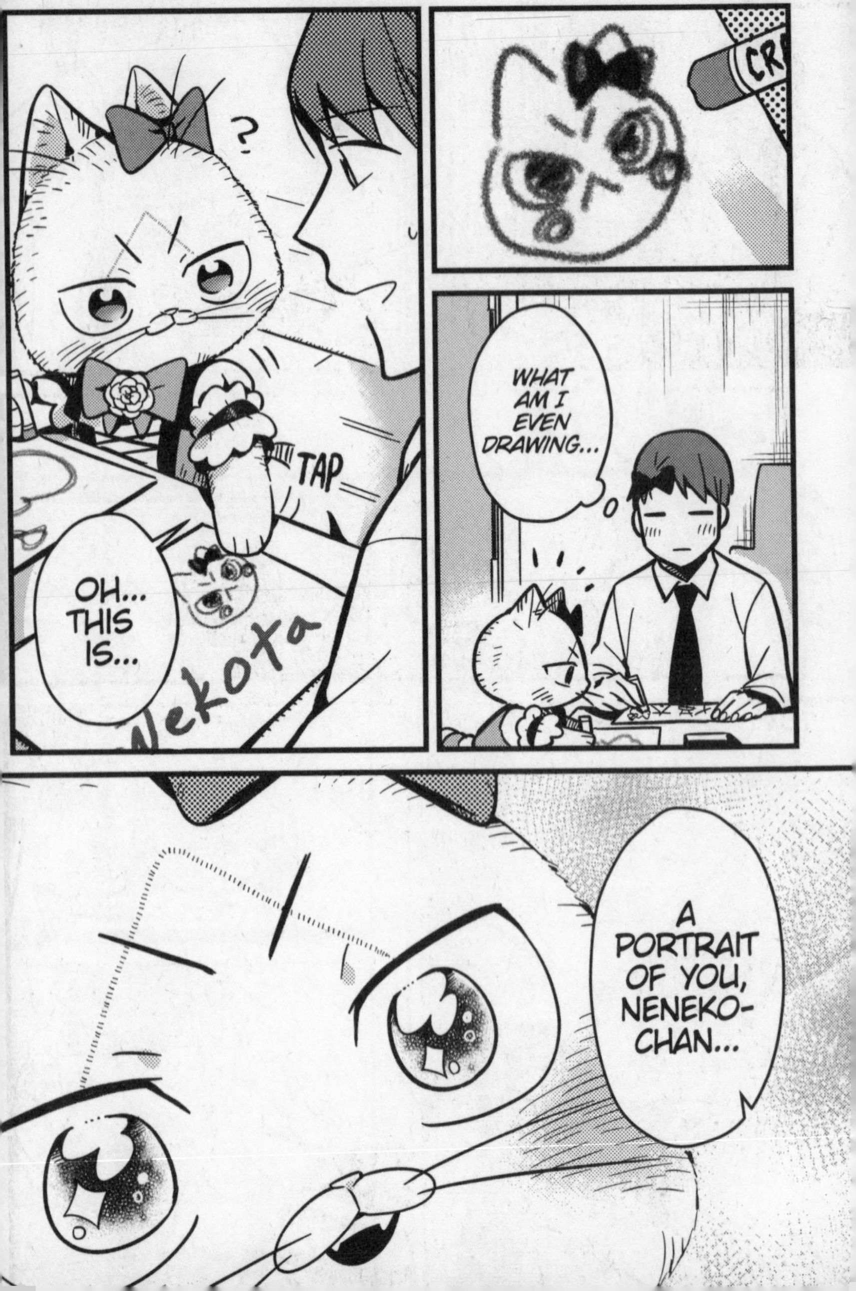
CR
WHAT AM I EVEN DRAWING...
?
TAP
OH... THIS IS...
Nekota
A PORTRAIT OF YOU, NENEKO-CHAN...

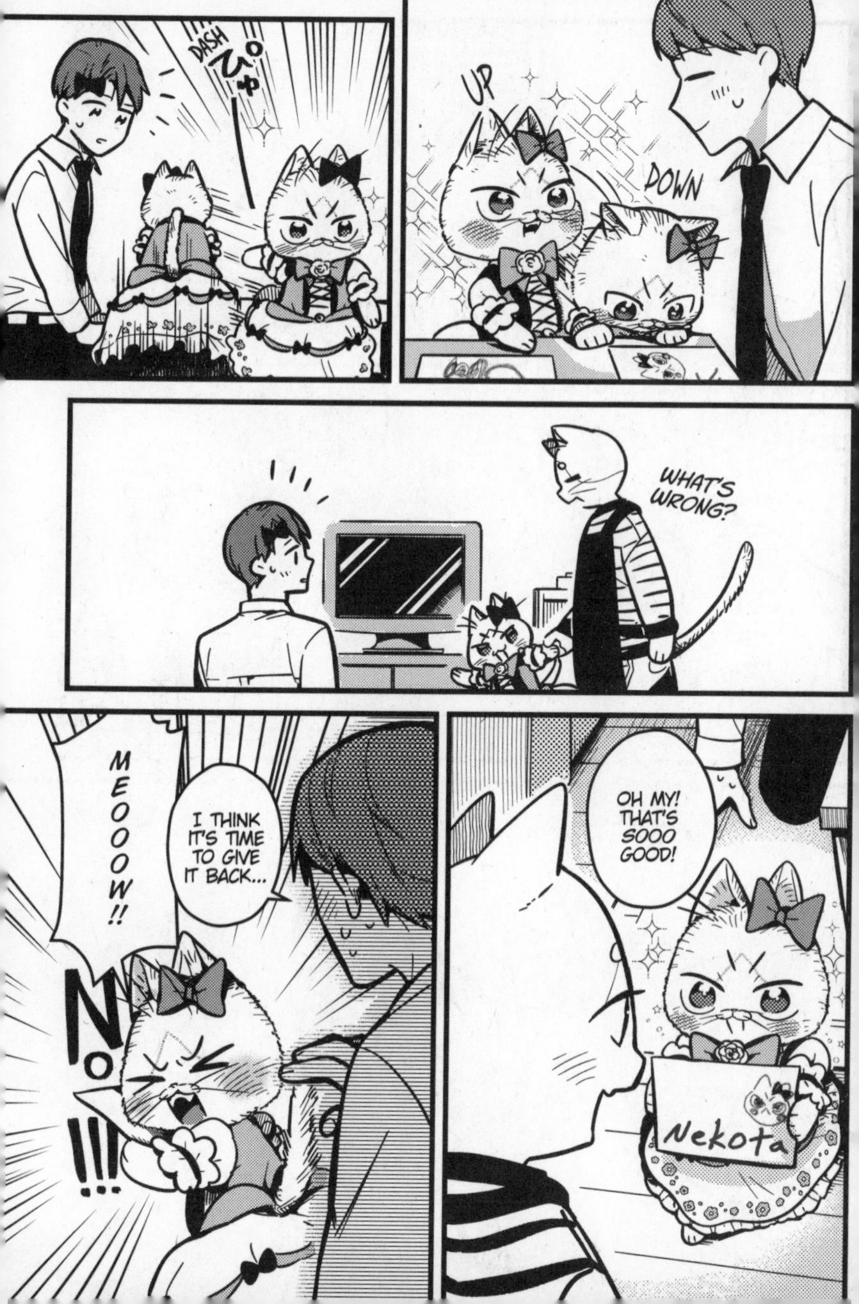
UP
DOWN
DASH
ぴゅ
WHAT'S WRONG?
OH MY! THAT'S SOOO GOOD!
Nekota
I THINK IT'S TIME TO GIVE IT BACK...
MEOOOOW!!
NO!!!!

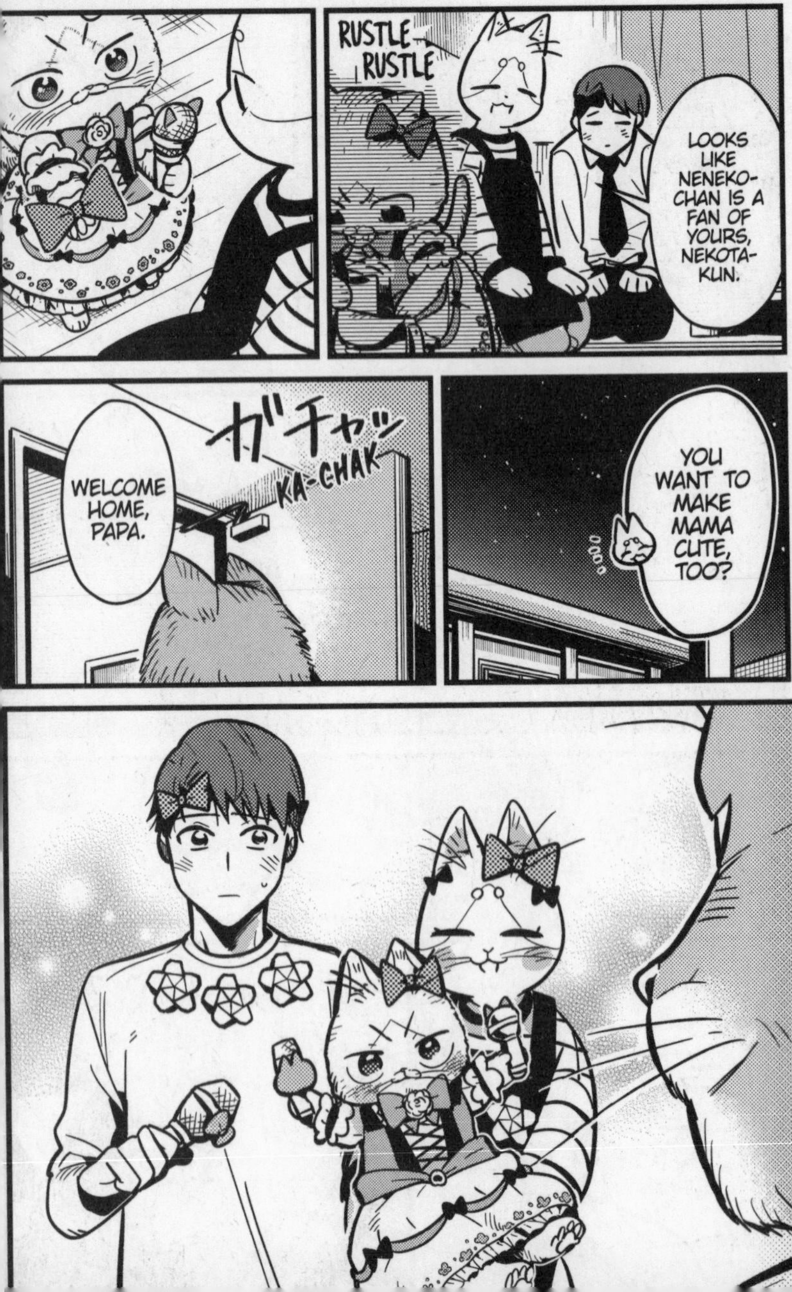
LOOKS LIKE NENEKO-CHAN IS A FAN OF YOURS, NEKOTA-KUN.
RUSTLE RUSTLE
YOU WANT TO MAKE MAMA CUTE, TOO?
ガチャッ
KA-CHAK
WELCOME HOME, PAPA.

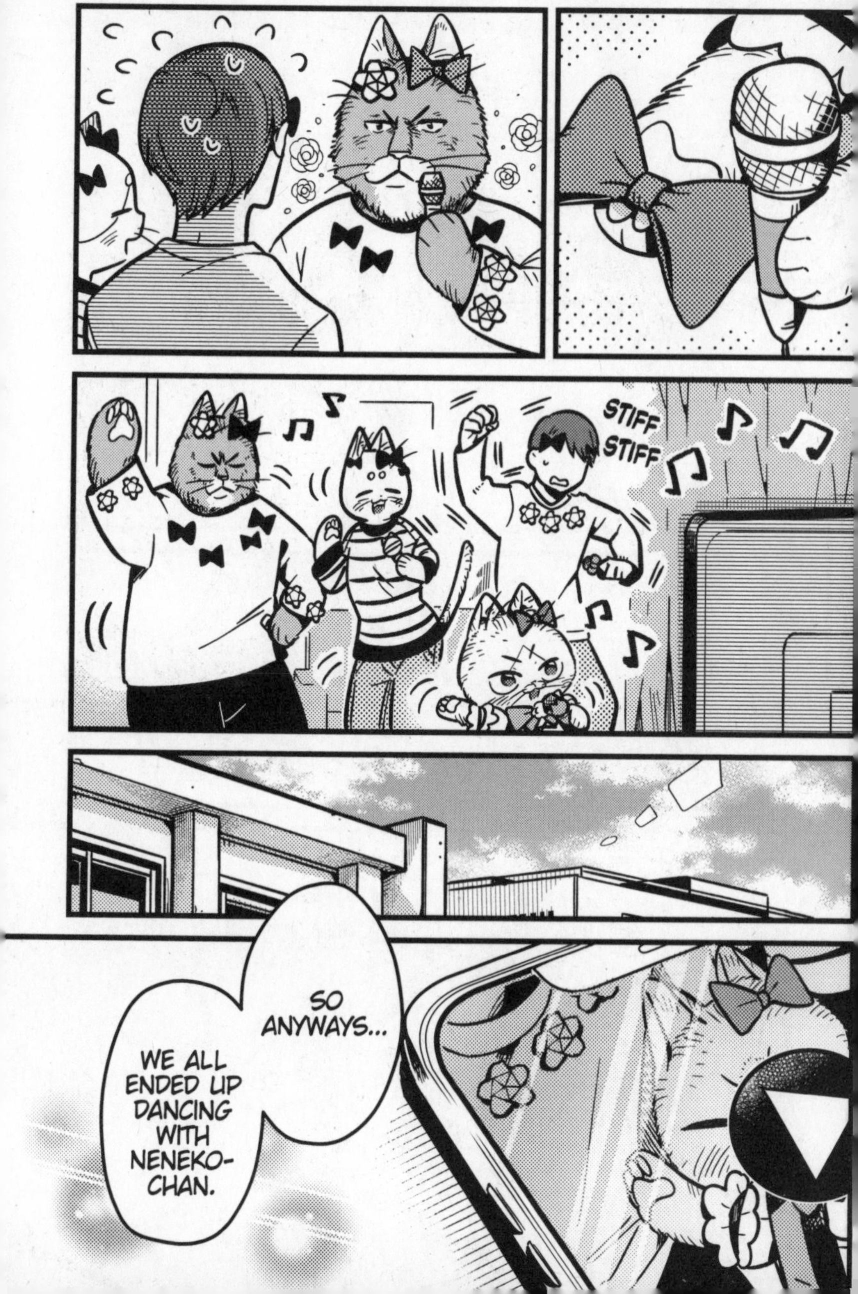
STIFF
STIFF
SO ANYWAYS...
WE ALL ENDED UP DANCING WITH NENEKO-CHAN.

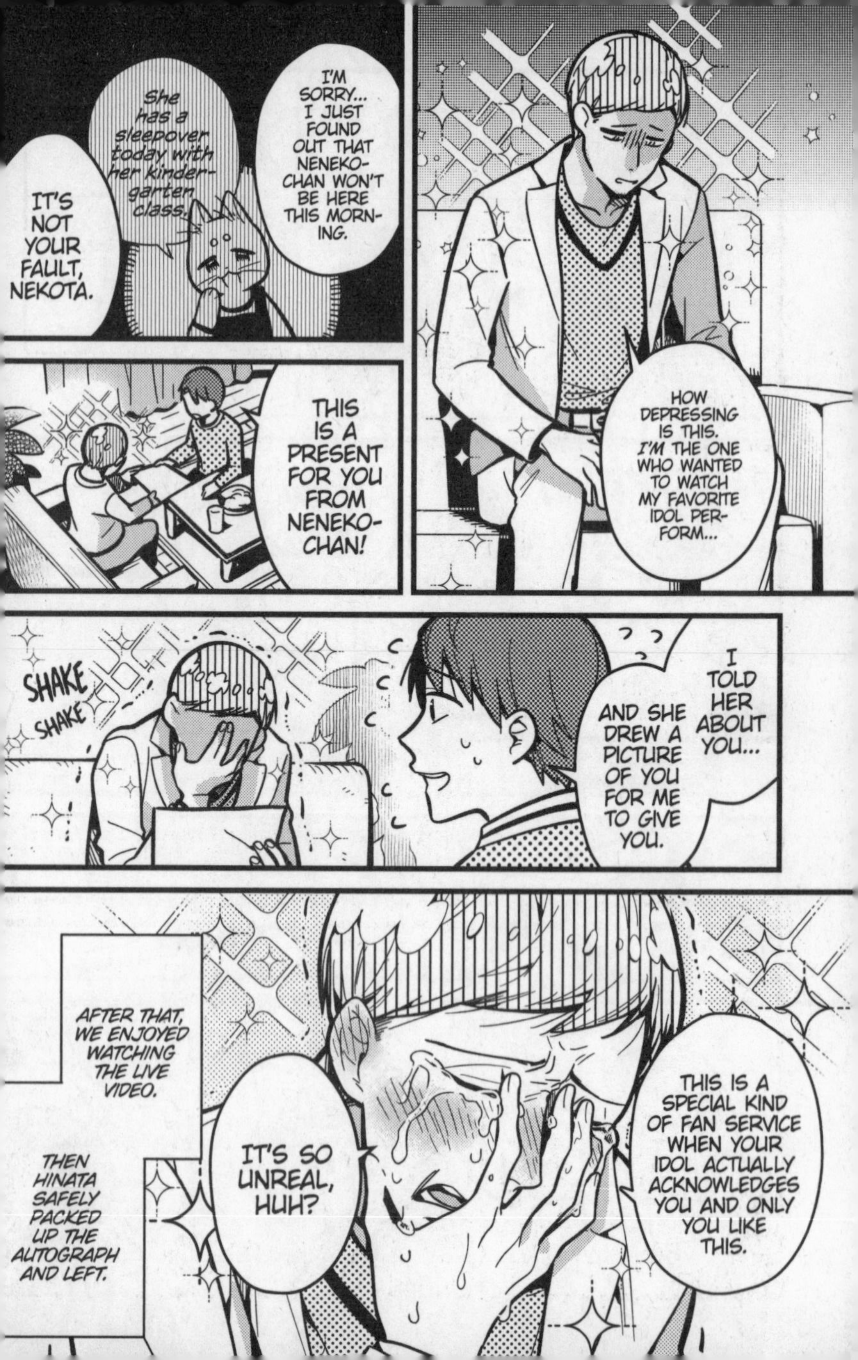
HOW DEPRESSING IS THIS. I'M THE ONE WHO WANTED TO WATCH MY FAVORITE IDOL PERFORM...
I'M SORRY... I JUST FOUND OUT THAT NENEKO-CHAN WON'T BE HERE THIS MORNING.
She has a sleepover today with her kindergarten class.
IT'S NOT YOUR FAULT, NEKOTA.
THIS IS A PRESENT FOR YOU FROM NENEKO-CHAN!
I TOLD HER ABOUT YOU...
AND SHE DREW A PICTURE OF YOU FOR ME TO GIVE YOU.
SHAKE
SHAKE
THIS IS A SPECIAL KIND OF FAN SERVICE WHEN YOUR IDOL ACTUALLY ACKNOWLEDGES YOU AND ONLY YOU LIKE THIS.
IT'S SO UNREAL, HUH?
AFTER THAT, WE ENJOYED WATCHING THE LIVE VIDEO.
THEN HINATA SAFELY PACKED UP THE AUTOGRAPH AND LEFT.

Extra 9

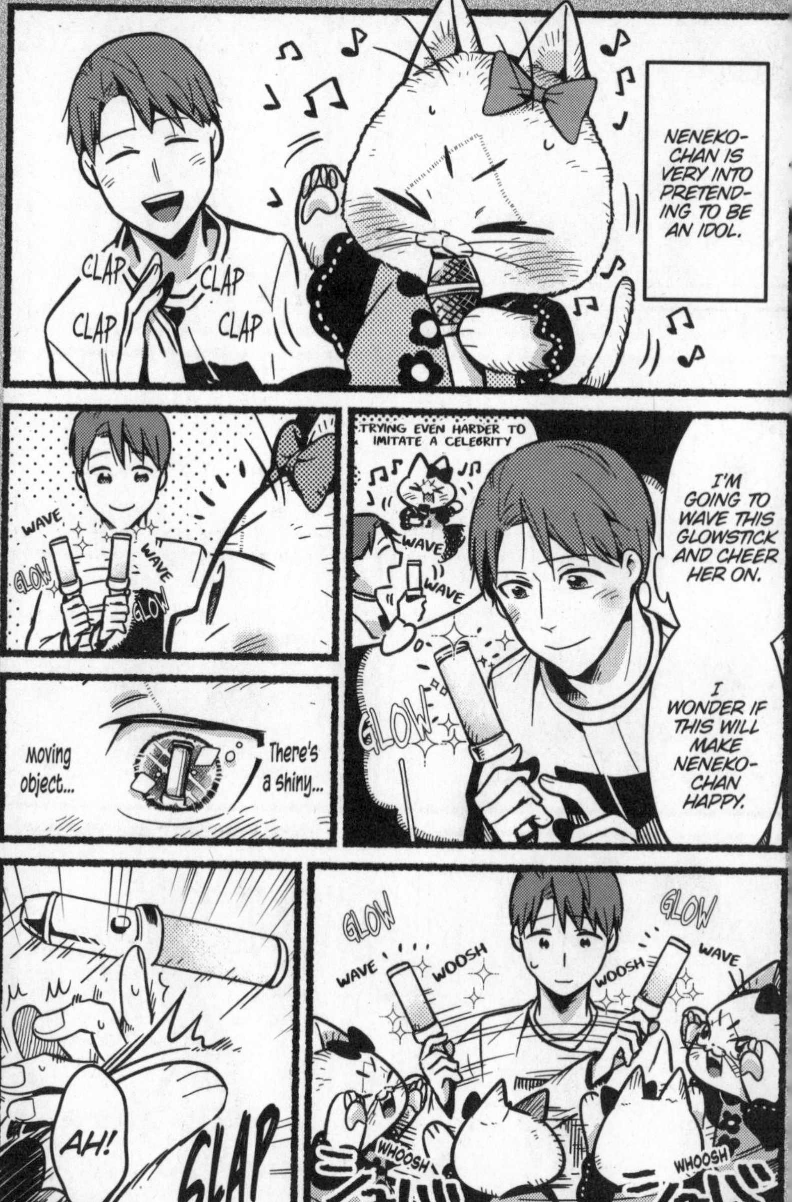
NENEKO-CHAN IS VERY INTO PRETENDING TO BE AN IDOL.
CLAP
CLAP
CLAP
CLAP
I'M GOING TO WAVE THIS GLOWSTICK AND CHEER HER ON.
TRYING EVEN HARDER TO IMITATE A CELEBRITY
WAVE
WAVE
GLOW
I WONDER IF THIS WILL MAKE NENEKO-CHAN HAPPY.
WAVE
WAVE
GLOW
GLOW
There's a shiny...
Moving object...
GLOW
GLOW
WAVE
WOOSH
WOOSH
WAVE
WHOOSH
WHOOSH
AH!
SLAP

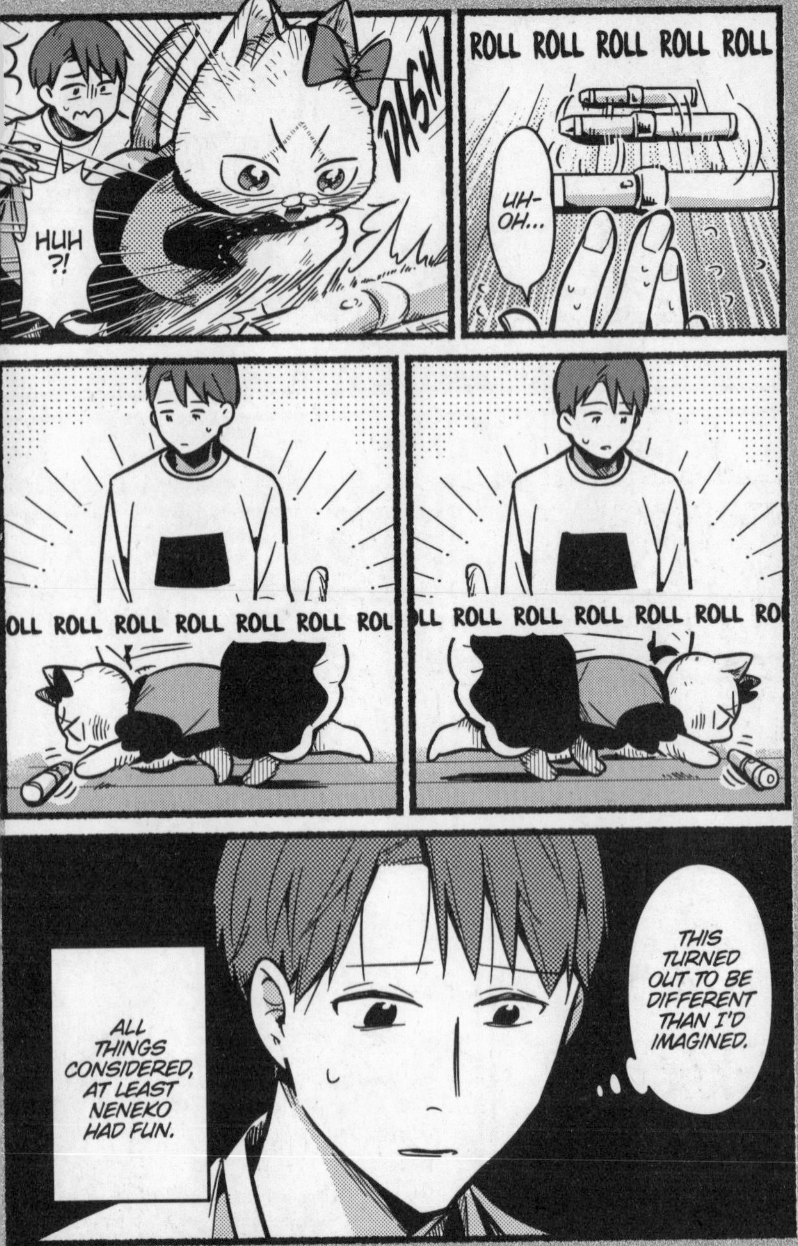
ROLL ROLL ROLL ROLL ROLL
UH-OH...
DASH
HUH ?!
ROLL ROLL ROLL ROLL ROLL
ROLL ROLL ROLL ROLL ROLL
THIS TURNED OUT TO BE DIFFERENT THAN I'D IMAGINED.
ALL THINGS CONSIDERED, AT LEAST NENEKO HAD FUN.

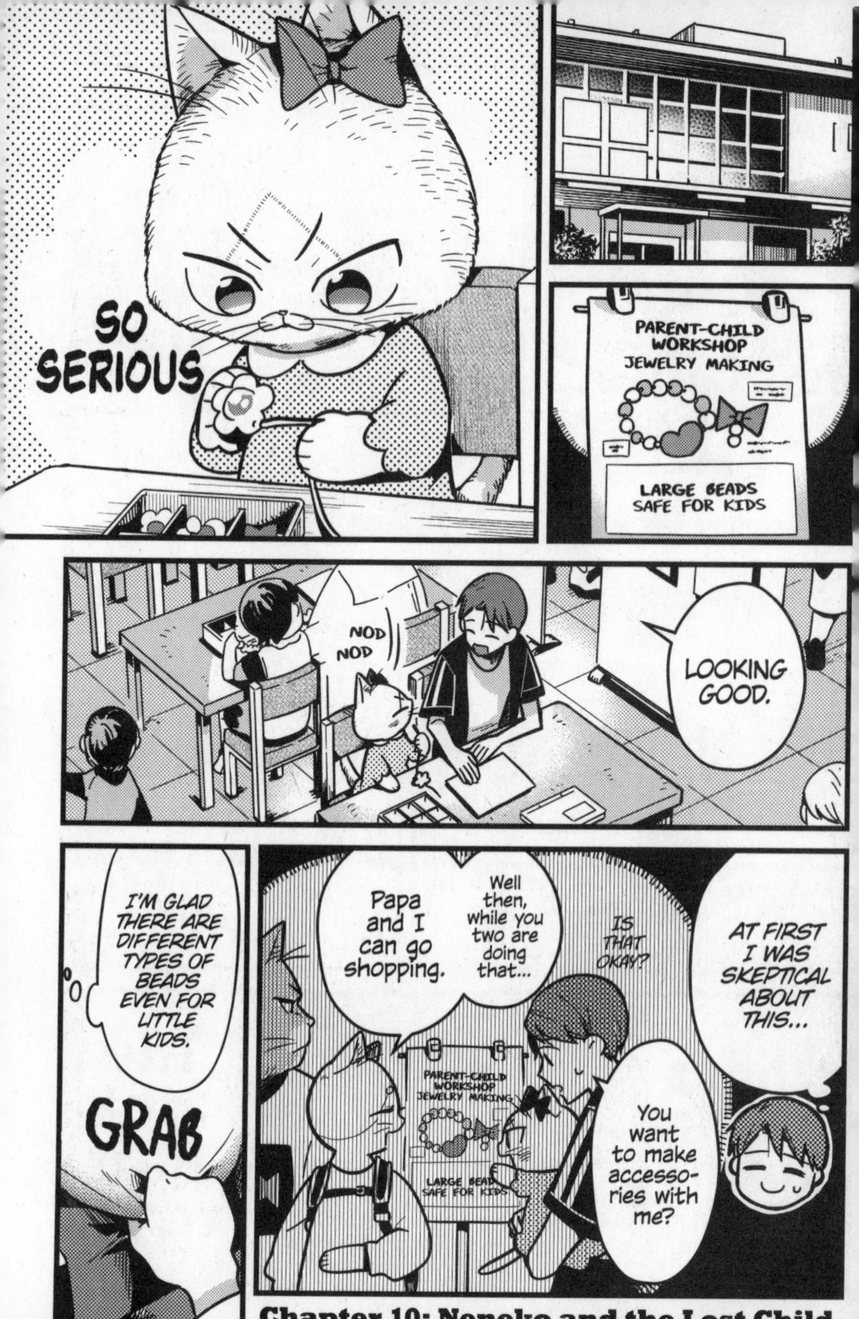
PARENT-CHILD WORKSHOP JEWELRY MAKING
LARGE BEADS SAFE FOR KIDS
SO SERIOUS
LOOKING GOOD.
NOD NOD
AT FIRST I WAS SKEPTICAL ABOUT THIS...
You want to make accessories with me?
IS THAT OKAY?
Well then, while you two are doing that...
Papa and I can go shopping.
PARENT-CHILD WORKSHOP JEWELRY MAKING
LARGE BEAD SAFE FOR KIDS
I'M GLAD THERE ARE DIFFERENT TYPES OF BEADS EVEN FOR LITTLE KIDS.
GRAB

Chapter 10: Neneko and the Lost Child

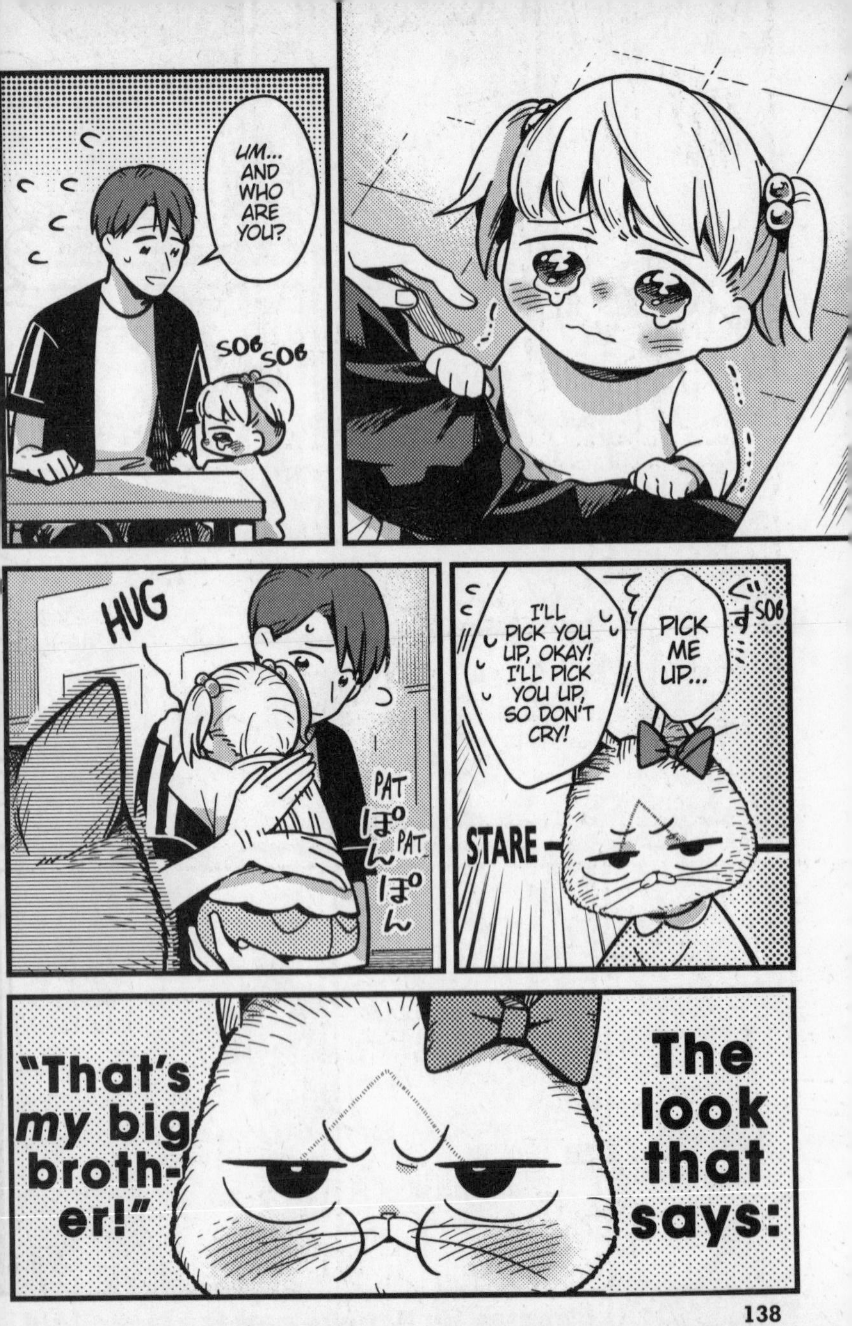
UM... AND WHO ARE YOU?
SOB SOB
PICK ME UP...
ぐす SOB
I'LL PICK YOU UP, OKAY! I'LL PICK YOU UP, SO DON'T CRY!
STARE
HUG
PAT PAT
ぽんぽん
The look that says:
"That's my big broth-er!"

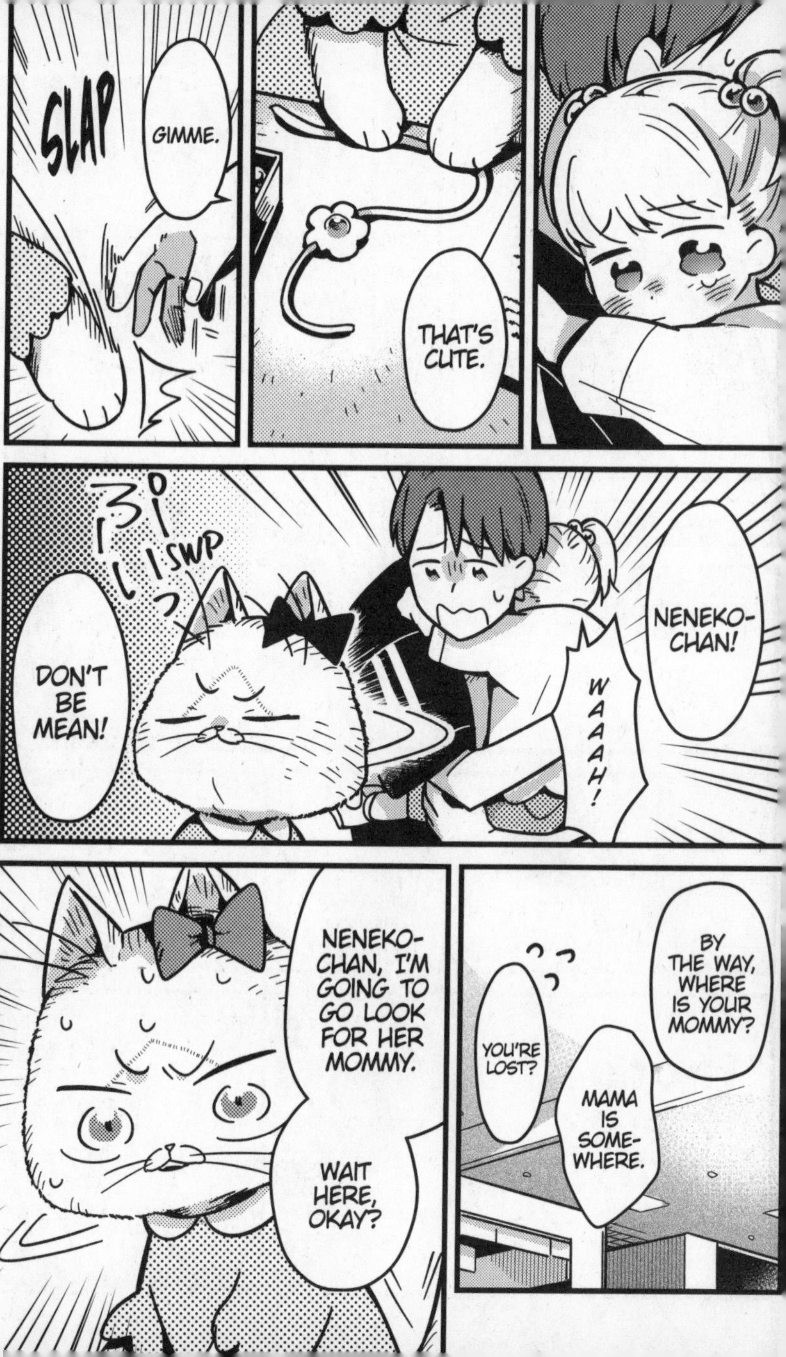
THAT'S CUTE.
SLAP
GIMME.
NENEKO-CHAN!
WAAAAH!
SWP
DON'T BE MEAN!
BY THE WAY, WHERE IS YOUR MOMMY?
MAMA IS SOMEWHERE.
YOU'RE LOST?
NENEKO-CHAN, I'M GOING TO GO LOOK FOR HER MOMMY.
WAIT HERE, OKAY?

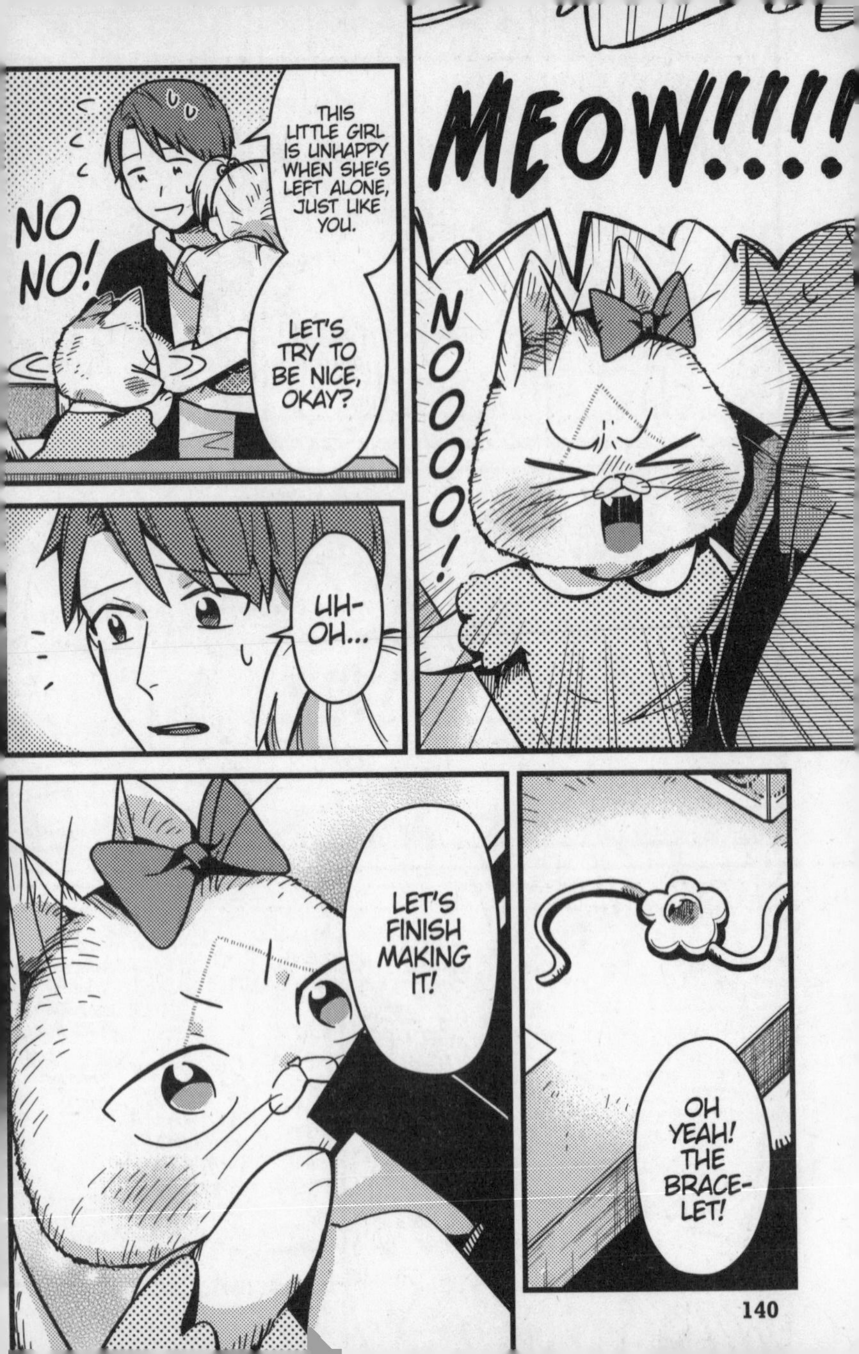
MEOW!!!!....
NOOOOO!
THIS LITTLE GIRL IS UNHAPPY WHEN SHE'S LEFT ALONE, JUST LIKE YOU.
LET'S TRY TO BE NICE, OKAY?
NO NO!
UH-OH...
OH YEAH! THE BRACE-LET!
LET'S FINISH MAKING IT!

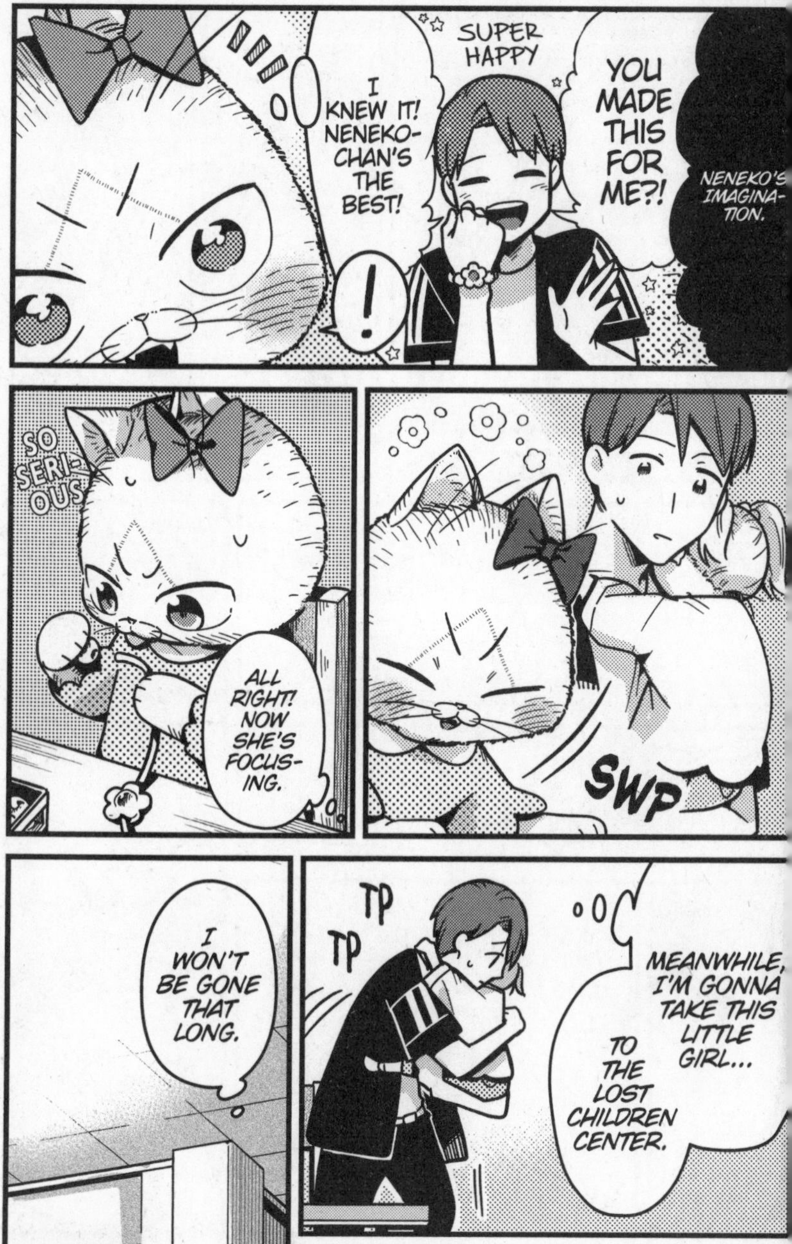
NENEKO'S IMAGINATION.
YOU MADE THIS FOR ME?!
SUPER HAPPY
I KNEW IT! NENEKO-CHAN'S THE BEST!
!
SWP
SO SERIOUS
ALL RIGHT! NOW SHE'S FOCUSING.
MEANWHILE, I'M GONNA TAKE THIS LITTLE GIRL...
TO THE LOST CHILDREN CENTER.
TP
TP
I WON'T BE GONE THAT LONG.

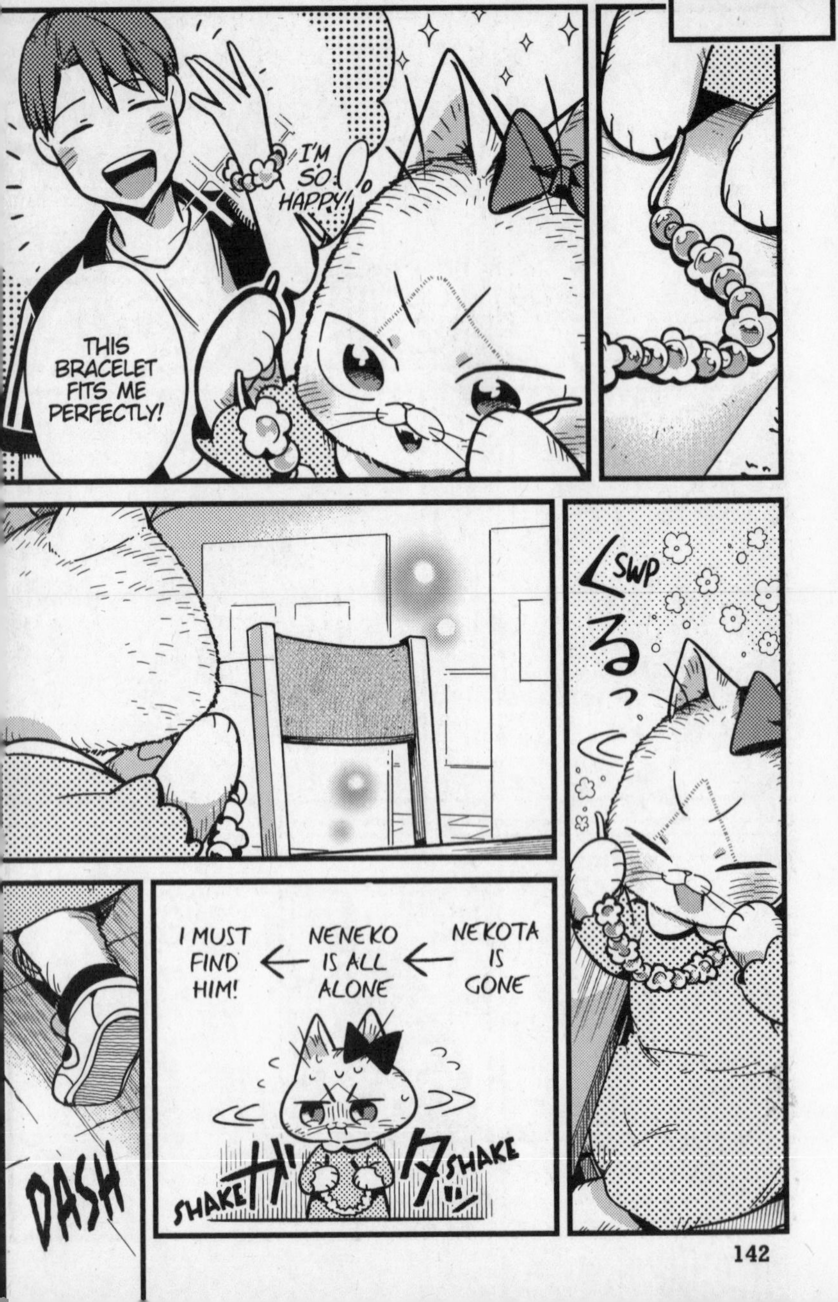
I'M SO HAPPY!
THIS BRACELET FITS ME PERFECTLY!
SWP
るっ
NEKOTA IS GONE
NENEKO IS ALL ALONE
I MUST FIND HIM!
SHAKE
SHAKE
DASH

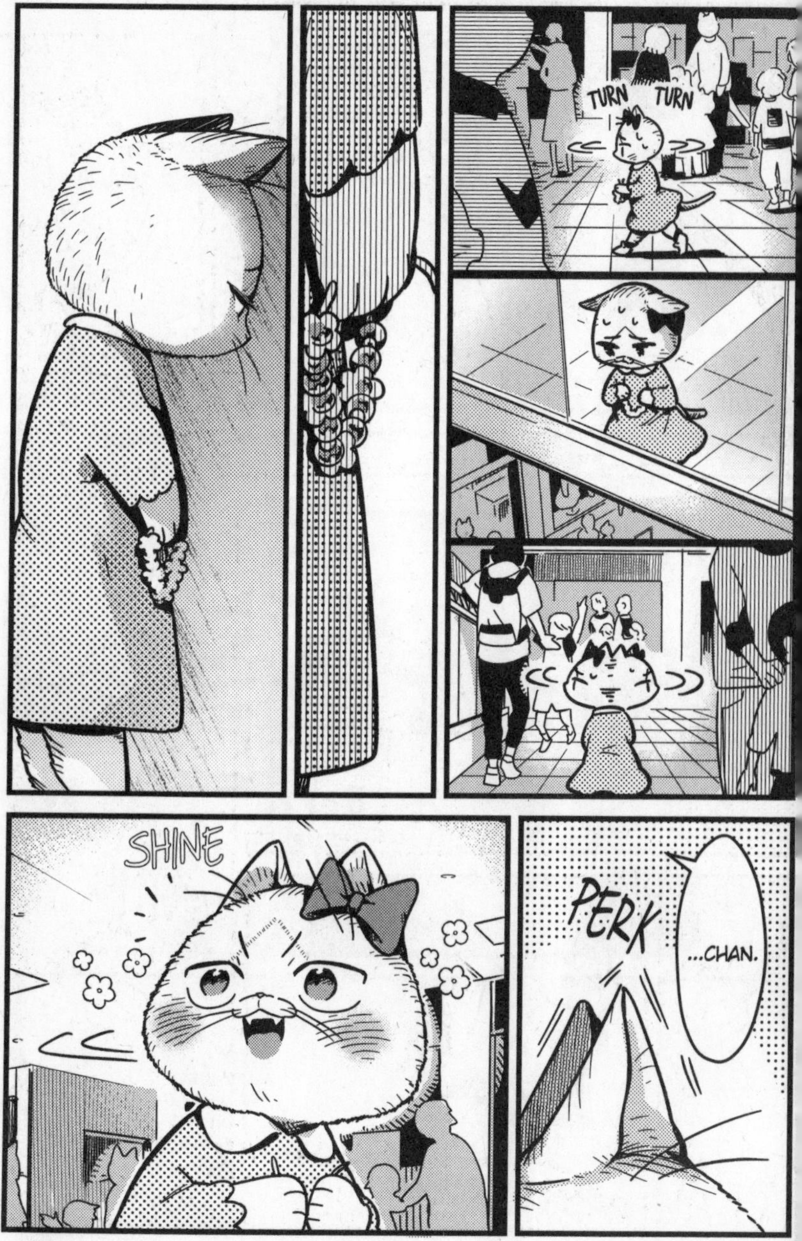
TURN
TURN
PERK
...CHAN.
SHINE

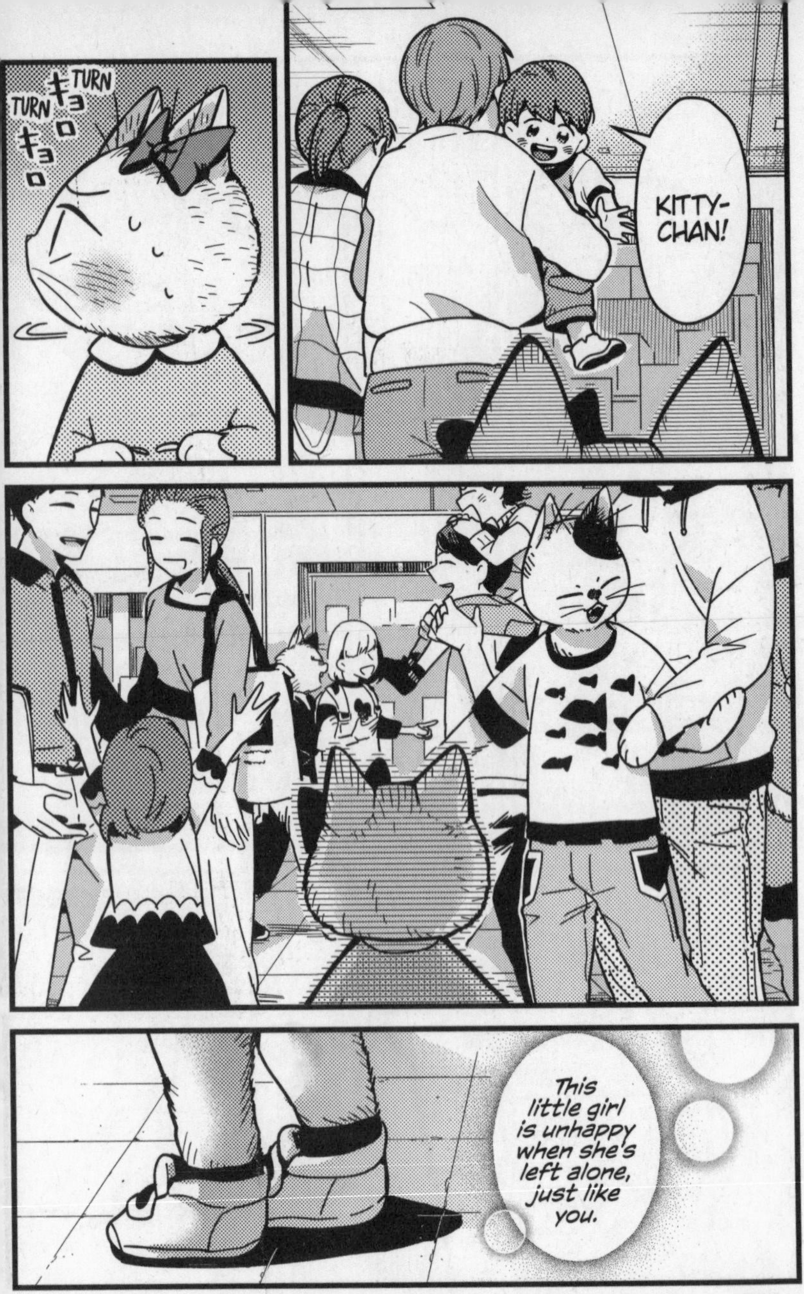
KITTY-CHAN!
TURN
キョロ
TURN
キョロ
This little girl is unhappy when she's left alone, just like you.

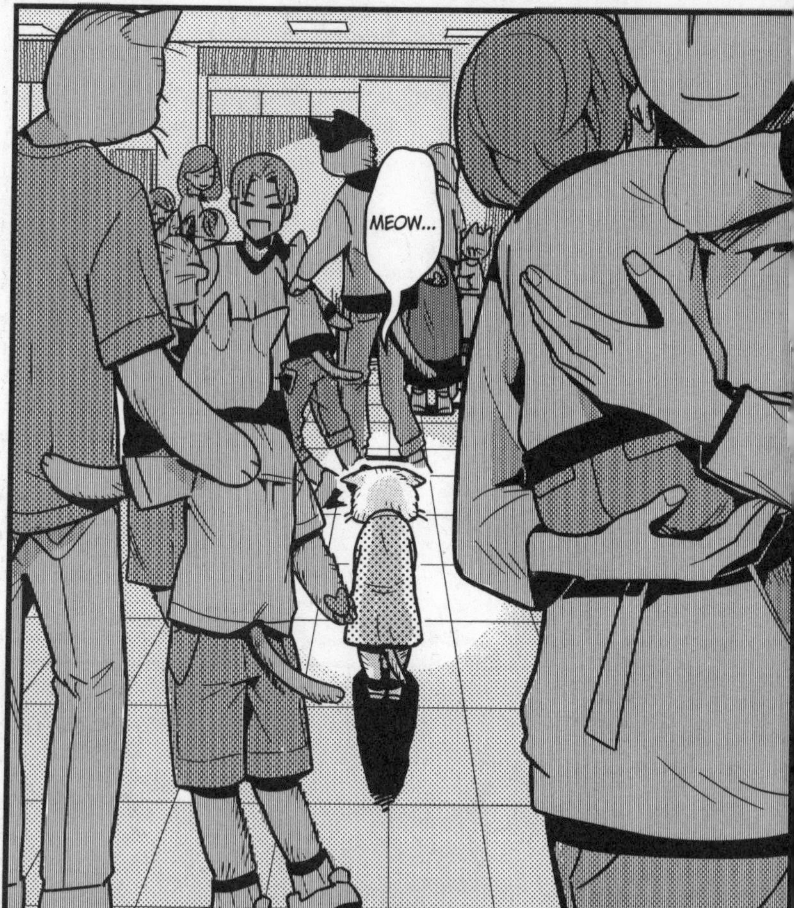
MEOW...
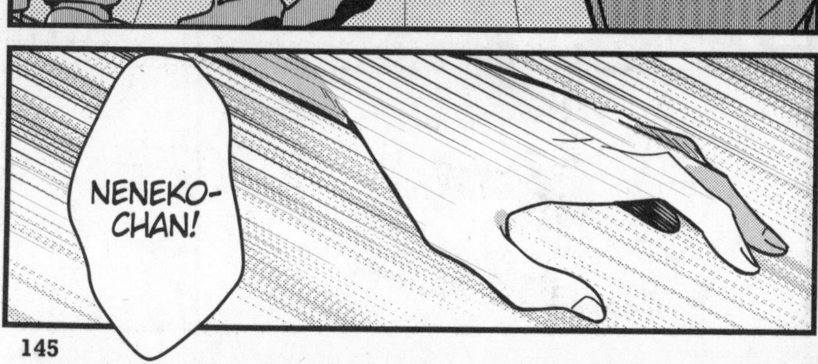
NENEKO-
CHAN!

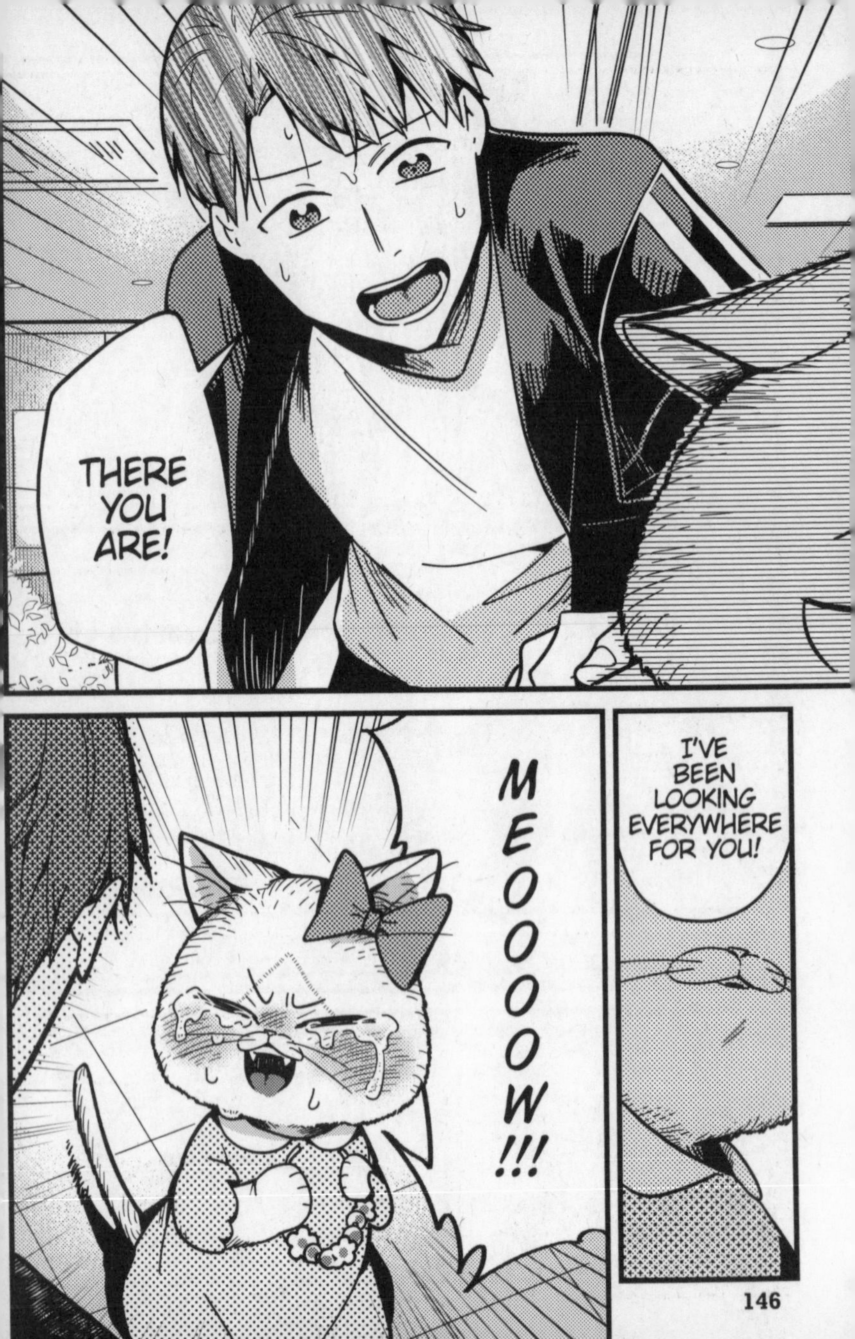
THERE YOU ARE!
I'VE BEEN LOOKING EVERYWHERE FOR YOU!
MEOOOOOW!!!

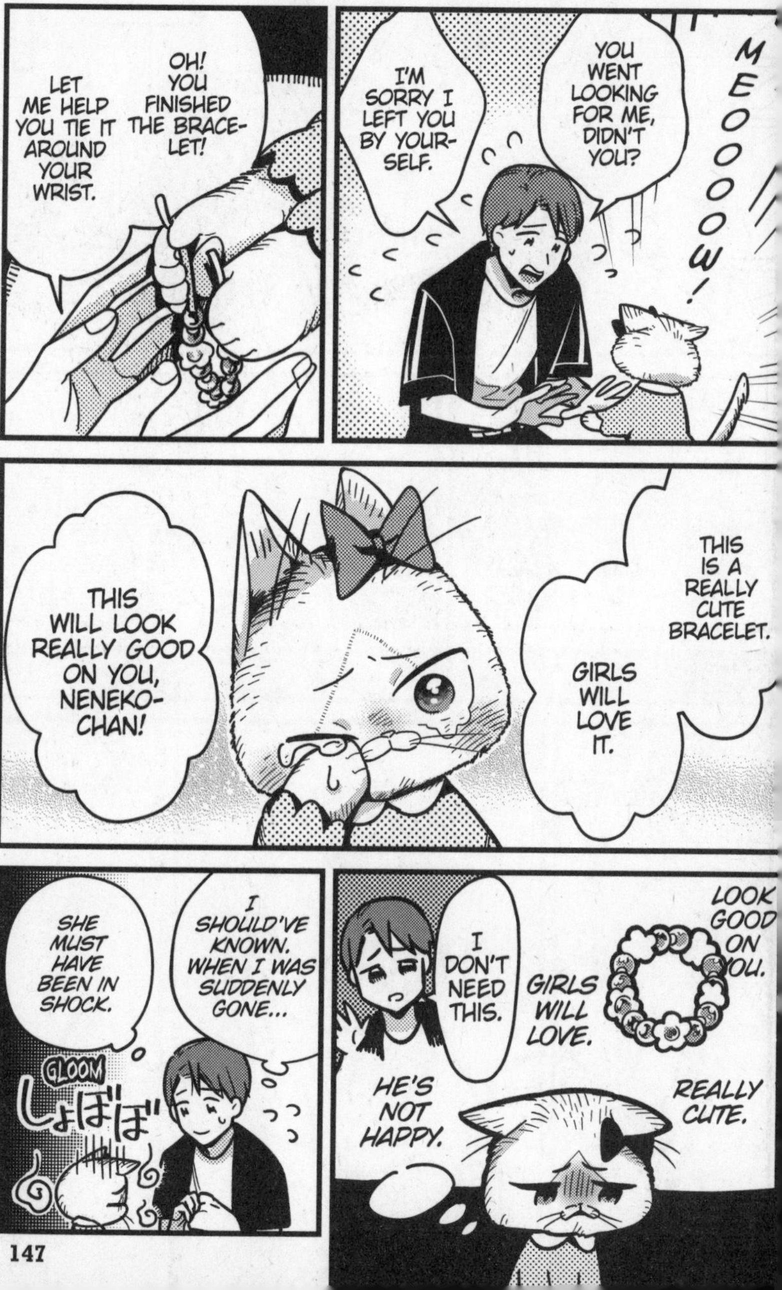
YOU WENT LOOKING FOR ME, DIDN'T YOU?
MEOOOOOOW!
I'M SORRY I LEFT YOU BY YOURSELF.
OH! YOU FINISHED THE BRACELET!
LET ME HELP YOU TIE IT AROUND YOUR WRIST.
THIS IS A REALLY CUTE BRACELET.
GIRLS WILL LOVE IT.
THIS WILL LOOK REALLY GOOD ON YOU, NENEKO-CHAN!
LOOK GOOD ON YOU.
REALLY CUTE.
GIRLS WILL LOVE.
I DON'T NEED THIS.
HE'S NOT HAPPY.
I SHOULD'VE KNOWN. WHEN I WAS SUDDENLY GONE...
SHE MUST HAVE BEEN IN SHOCK.
GLOOM
しょぼぼ

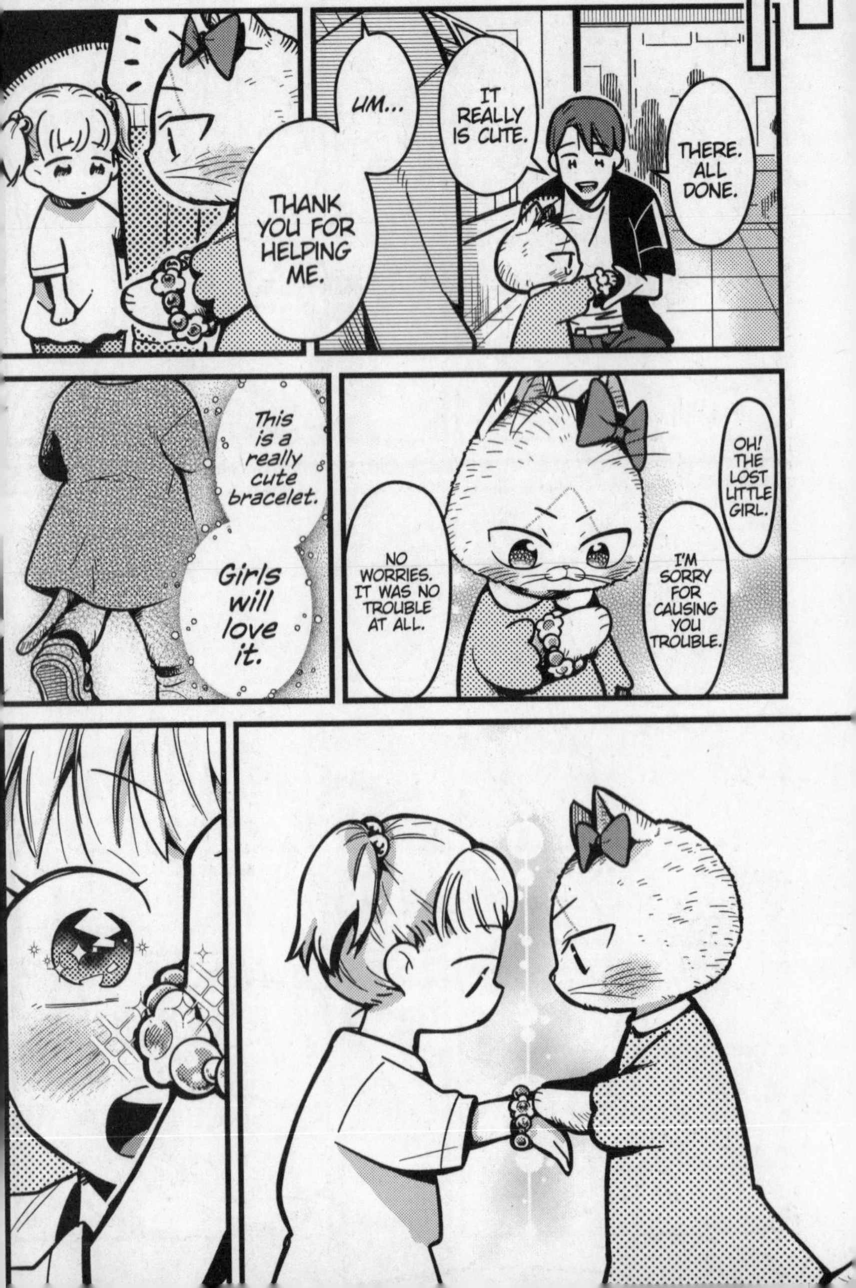
THERE. ALL DONE.
IT REALLY IS CUTE.
UM...
THANK YOU FOR HELPING ME.
OH! THE LOST LITTLE GIRL.
I'M SORRY FOR CAUSING YOU TROUBLE.
NO WORRIES. IT WAS NO TROUBLE AT ALL.
This is a really cute bracelet.
Girls will love it.

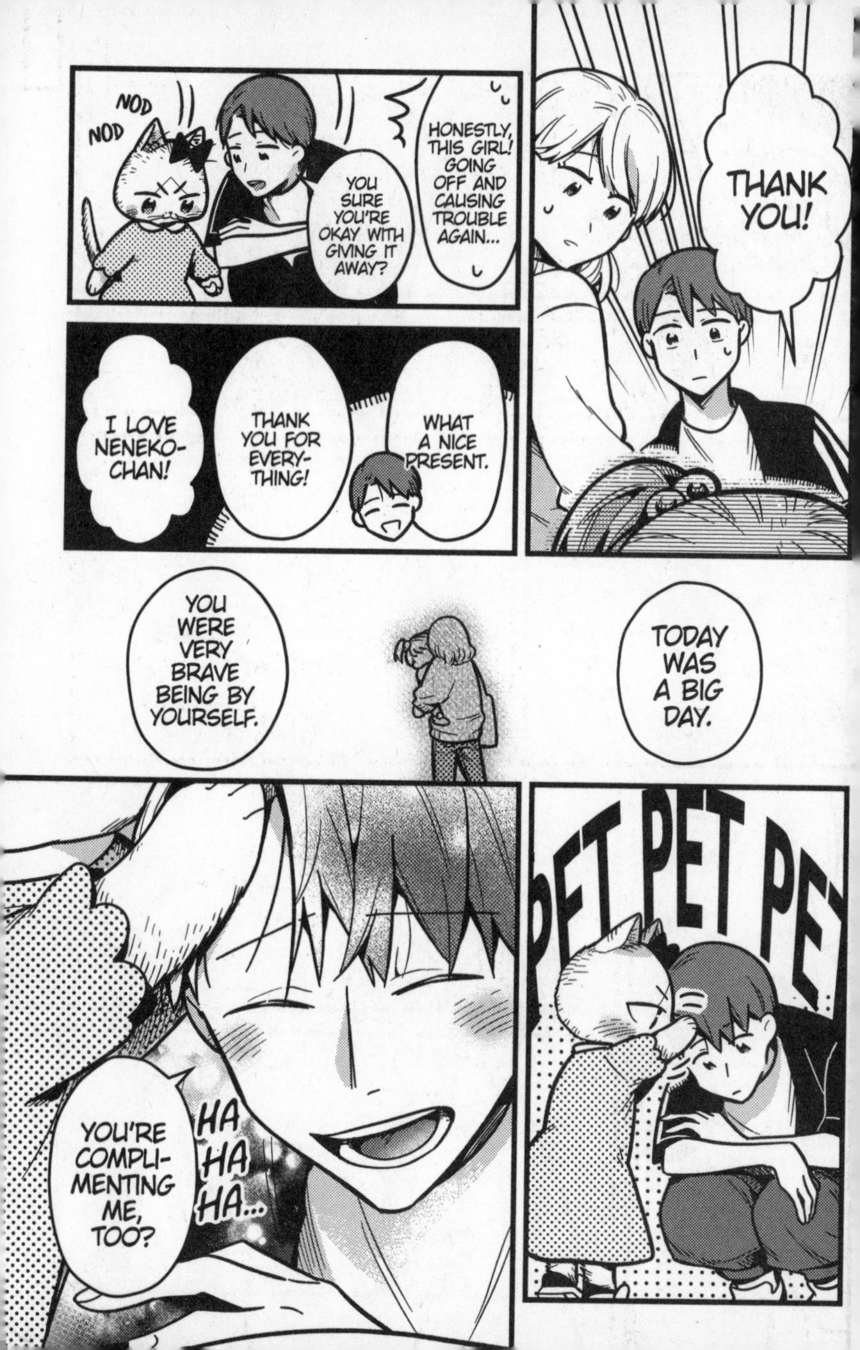
THANK YOU!
HONESTLY, THIS GIRL! GOING OFF AND CAUSING TROUBLE AGAIN...
YOU SURE YOU'RE OKAY WITH GIVING IT AWAY?
NOD NOD
WHAT A NICE PRESENT.
THANK YOU FOR EVERY-THING!
I LOVE NENEKO-CHAN!
TODAY WAS A BIG DAY.
YOU WERE VERY BRAVE BEING BY YOURSELF.
PET PET PET
HA HA HA...
YOU'RE COMPLI-MENTING ME, TOO?

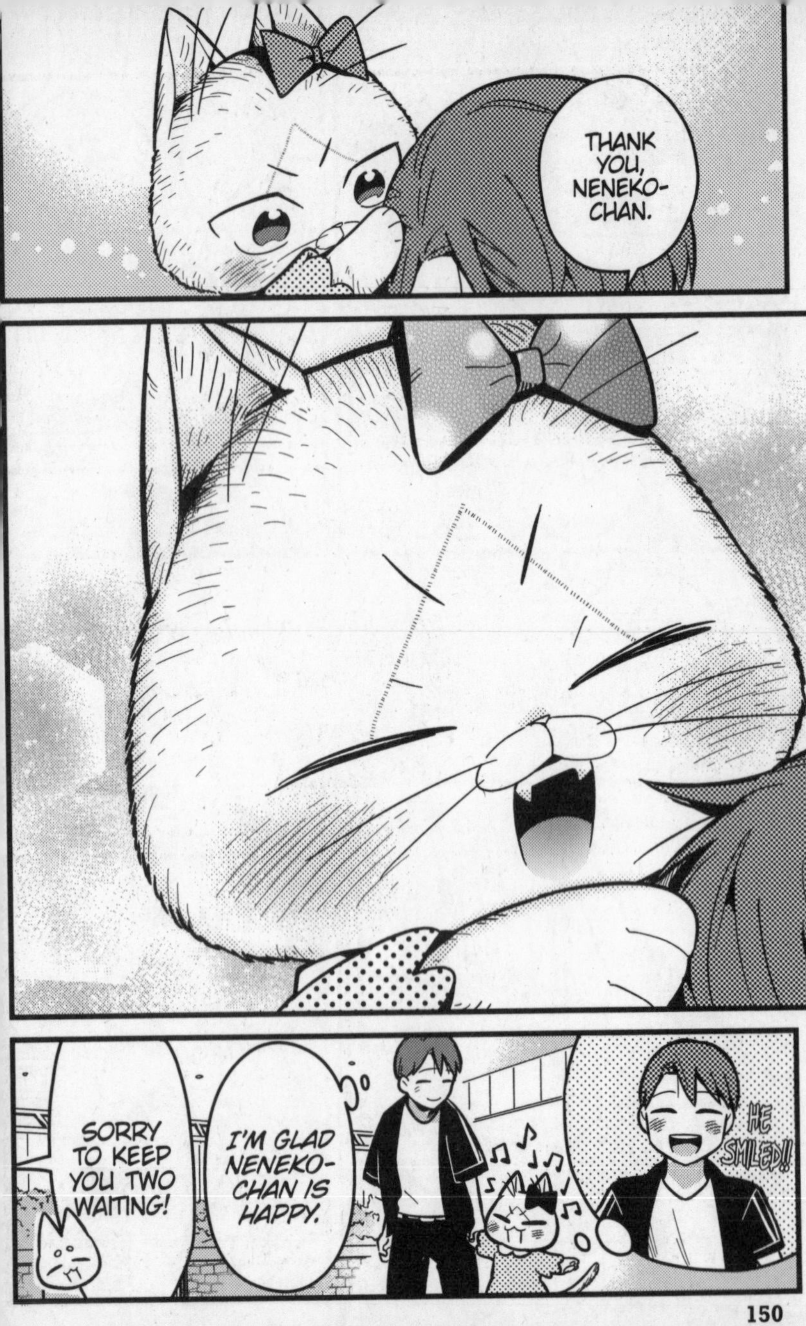
THANK YOU, NENEKO-CHAN.
HE SMILED!!
I'M GLAD NENEKO-CHAN IS HAPPY.
SORRY TO KEEP YOU TWO WAITING!

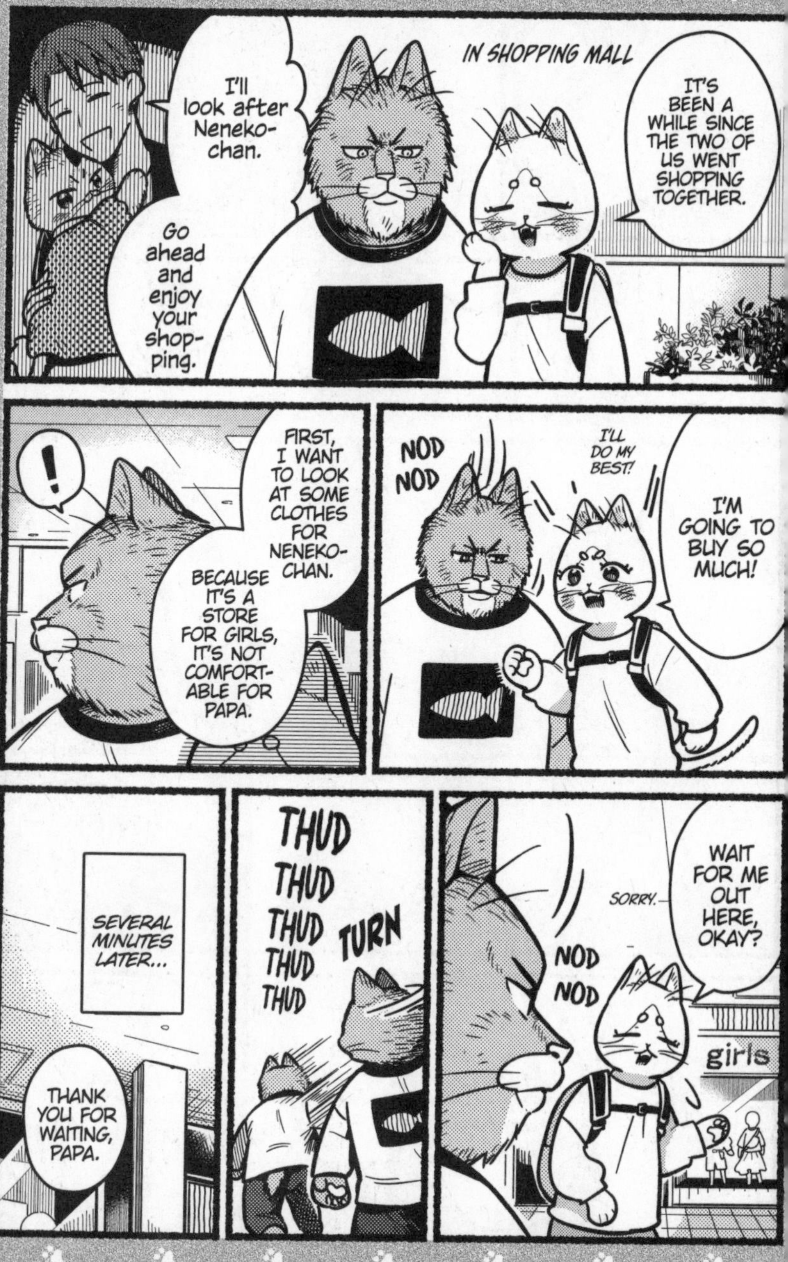
IN SHOPPING MALL
IT'S BEEN A WHILE SINCE THE TWO OF US WENT SHOPPING TOGETHER.
I'll look after Neneko-chan.
Go ahead and enjoy your shop-ping.
I'M GOING TO BUY SO MUCH!
I'LL DO MY BEST!
NOD NOD
FIRST, I WANT TO LOOK AT SOME CLOTHES FOR NENEKO-CHAN.
BECAUSE IT'S A STORE FOR GIRLS, IT'S NOT COMFORT-ABLE FOR PAPA.
!
WAIT FOR ME OUT HERE, OKAY?
SORRY.
NOD NOD
girls
THUD THUD THUD THUD THUD
TURN
SEVERAL MINUTES LATER...
THANK YOU FOR WAITING, PAPA.

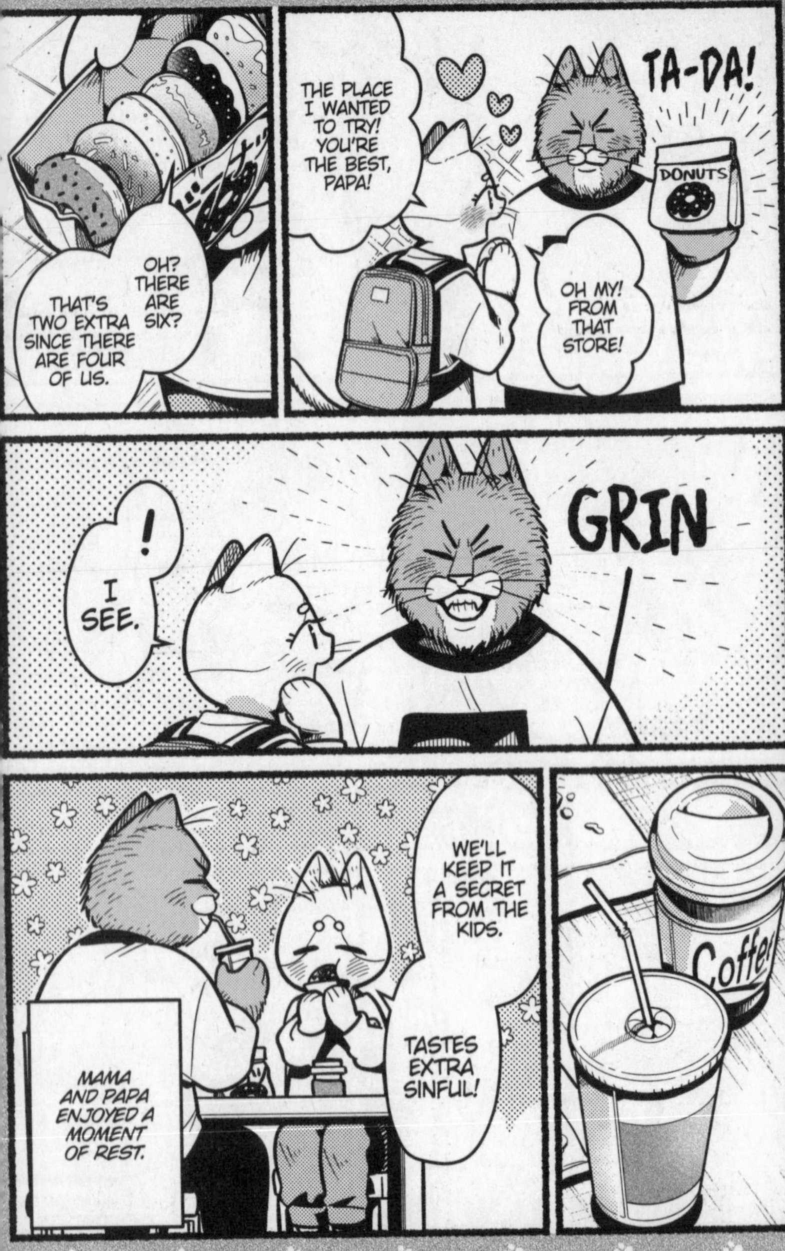
TA-DA!
DONUTS
OH MY! FROM THAT STORE!
THE PLACE I WANTED TO TRY! YOU'RE THE BEST, PAPA!
OH? THERE ARE SIX?
THAT'S TWO EXTRA SINCE THERE ARE FOUR OF US.
GRIN
! I SEE.
Coffe
WE'LL KEEP IT A SECRET FROM THE KIDS.
TASTES EXTRA SINFUL!
MAMA AND PAPA ENJOYED A MOMENT OF REST.

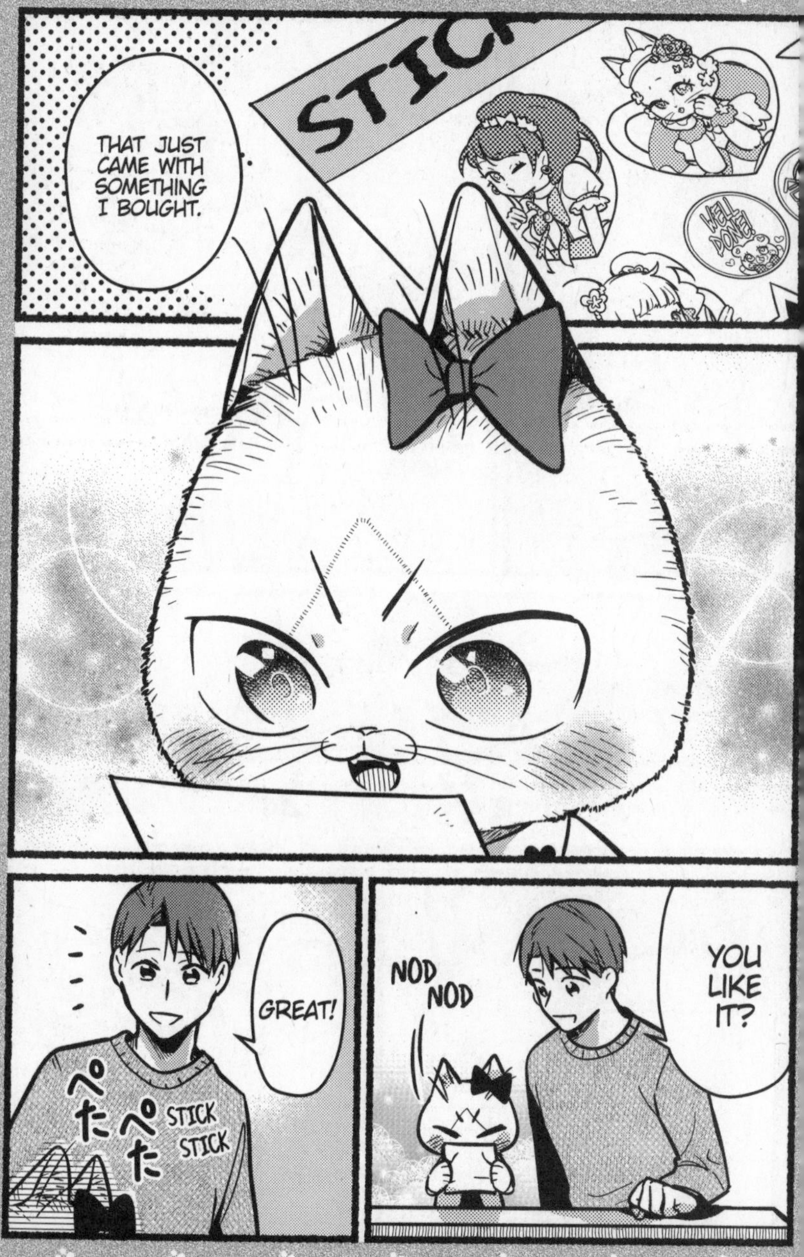
THAT JUST CAME WITH SOMETHING I BOUGHT.
WELL DONE!
YOU LIKE IT?
NOD NOD
GREAT!
ぺたぺた
STICK STICK

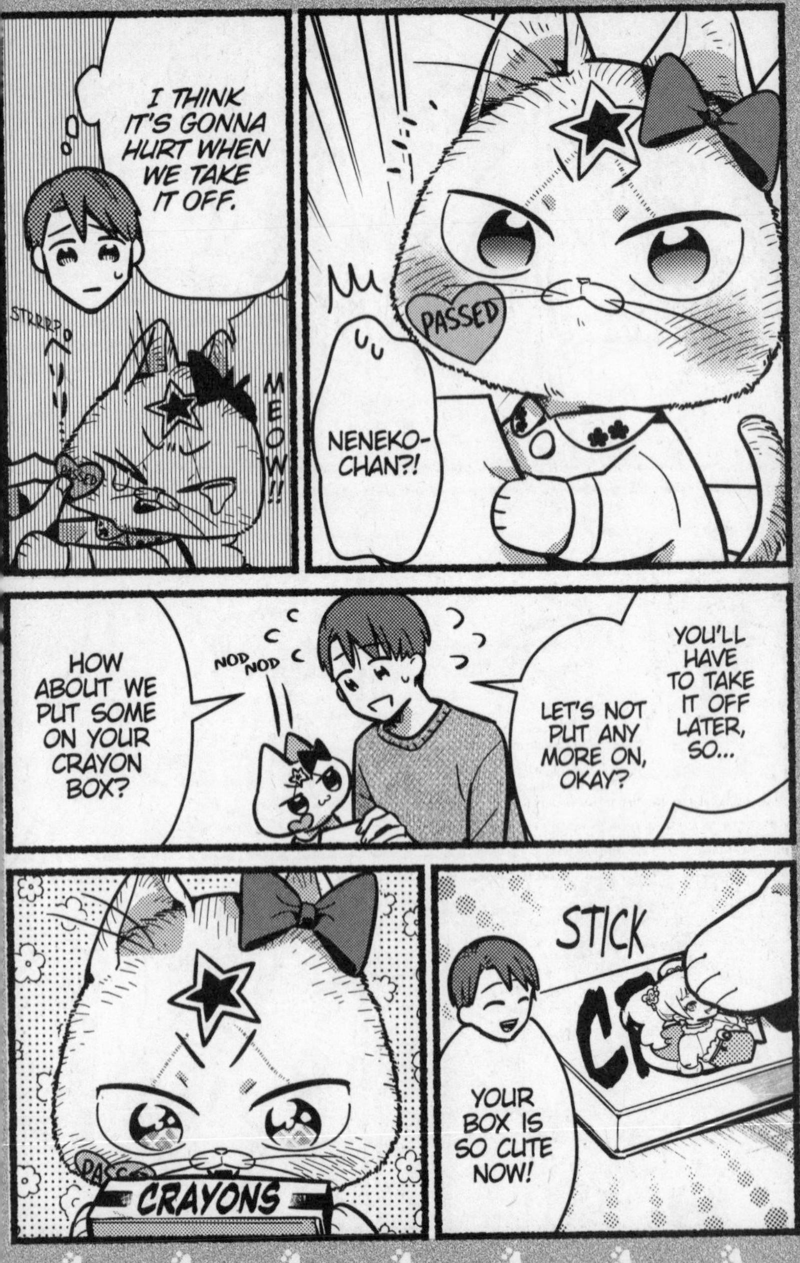
PASSED
NENEKO-CHAN?!
I THINK IT'S GONNA HURT WHEN WE TAKE IT OFF.
STRRRIP
PASSED
MEOW!!
YOU'LL HAVE TO TAKE IT OFF LATER, SO...
LET'S NOT PUT ANY MORE ON, OKAY?
NOD NOD
HOW ABOUT WE PUT SOME ON YOUR CRAYON BOX?
STICK
YOUR BOX IS SO CUTE NOW!
CRAYONS

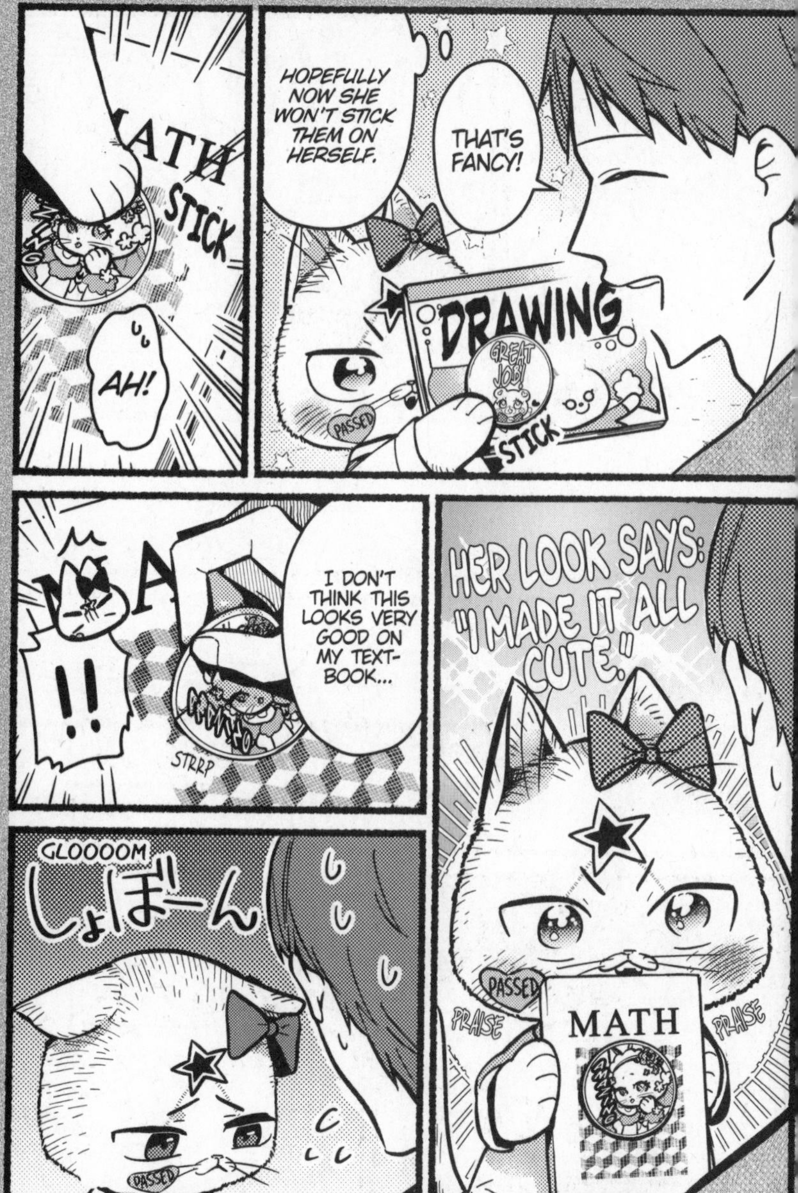
THAT'S FANCY!
HOPEFULLY NOW SHE WON'T STICK THEM ON HERSELF.
DRAWING
GREAT JOB!
PASSED
STICK
MATH
STICK
AH!
HER LOOK SAYS: "I MADE IT ALL CUTE."
PRAISE
PRAISE
MATH
PASSED
I DON'T THINK THIS LOOKS VERY GOOD ON MY TEXT-BOOK...
!!
STRRP
GLOOOOM
しょぼーん
PASSED

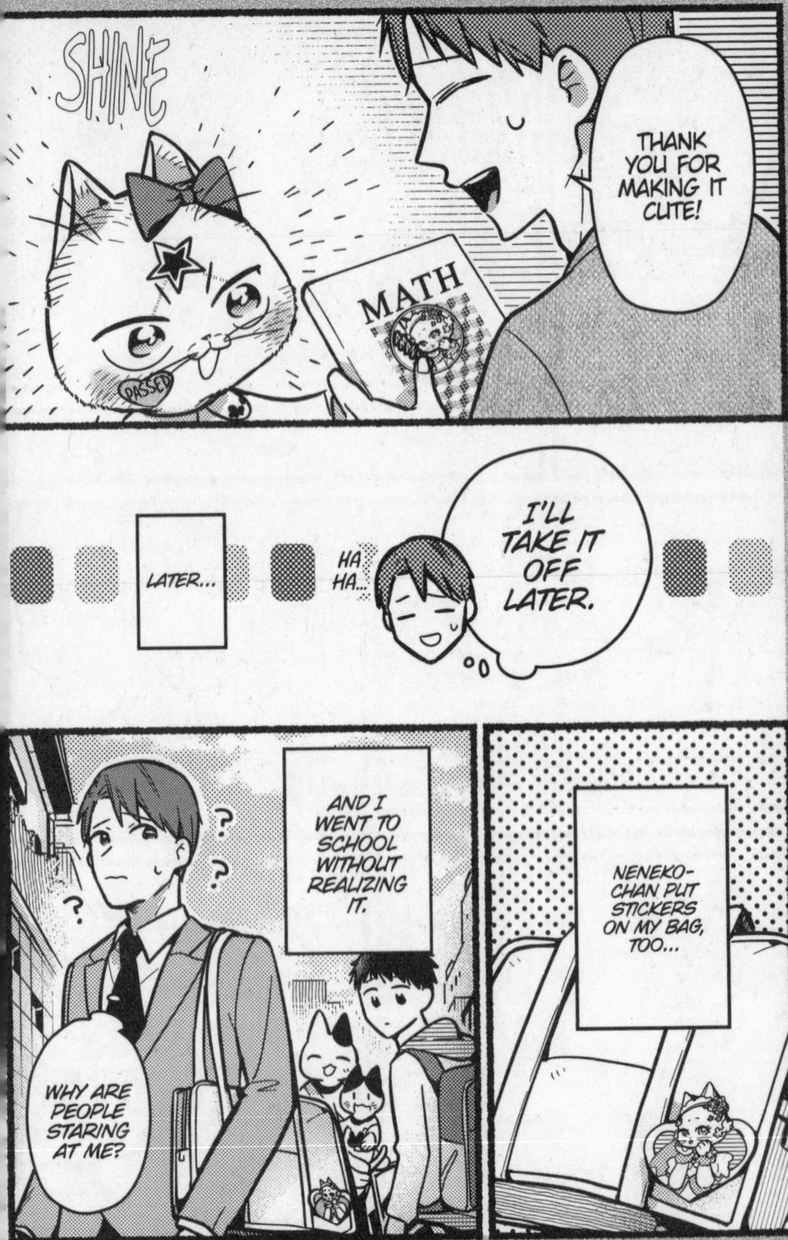
THANK YOU FOR MAKING IT CUTE!
SHINE
MATH
PASSED
I'LL TAKE IT OFF LATER.
HA HA...
LATER...
NENEKO-CHAN PUT STICKERS ON MY BAG, TOO...
AND I WENT TO SCHOOL WITHOUT REALIZING IT.
WHY ARE PEOPLE STARING AT ME?

Extra 12

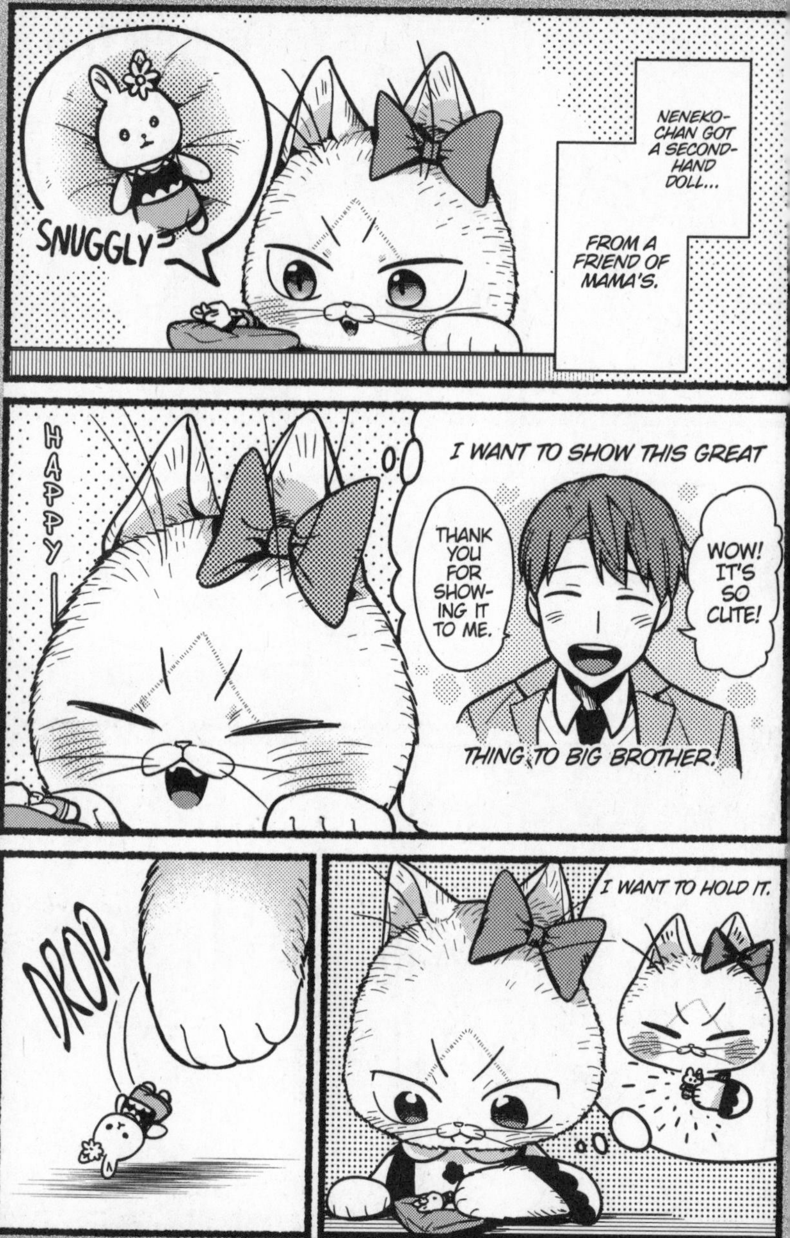
NENEKO-CHAN GOT A SECOND-HAND DOLL...
FROM A FRIEND OF MAMA'S.
SNUGGLY
I WANT TO SHOW THIS GREAT THING TO BIG BROTHER.
WOW! IT'S SO CUTE!
THANK YOU FOR SHOWING IT TO ME.
HAPPY
I WANT TO HOLD IT.
DROP

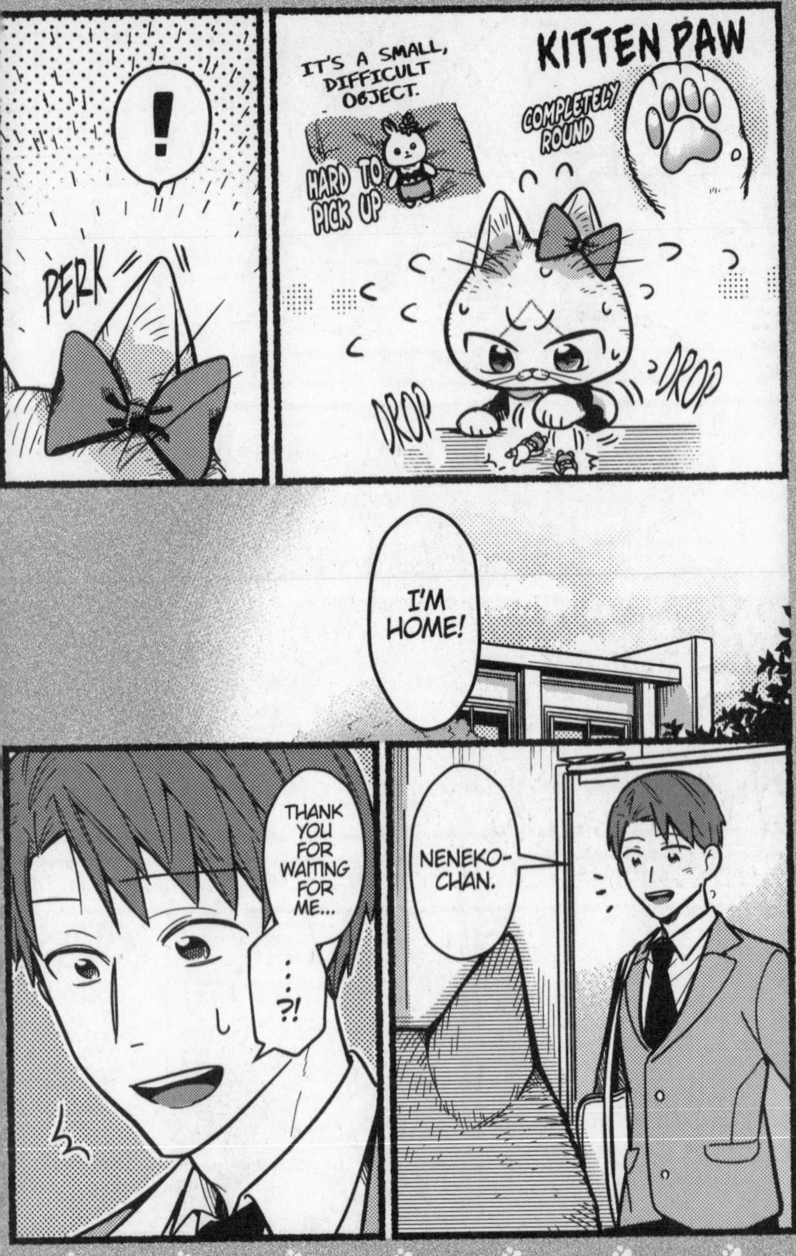
KITTEN PAW
COMPLETELY ROUND
IT'S A SMALL, DIFFICULT OBJECT.
HARD TO PICK UP
DROP
DROP
!
PERK
I'M HOME!
NENEKO-CHAN.
THANK YOU FOR WAITING FOR ME...
...?!

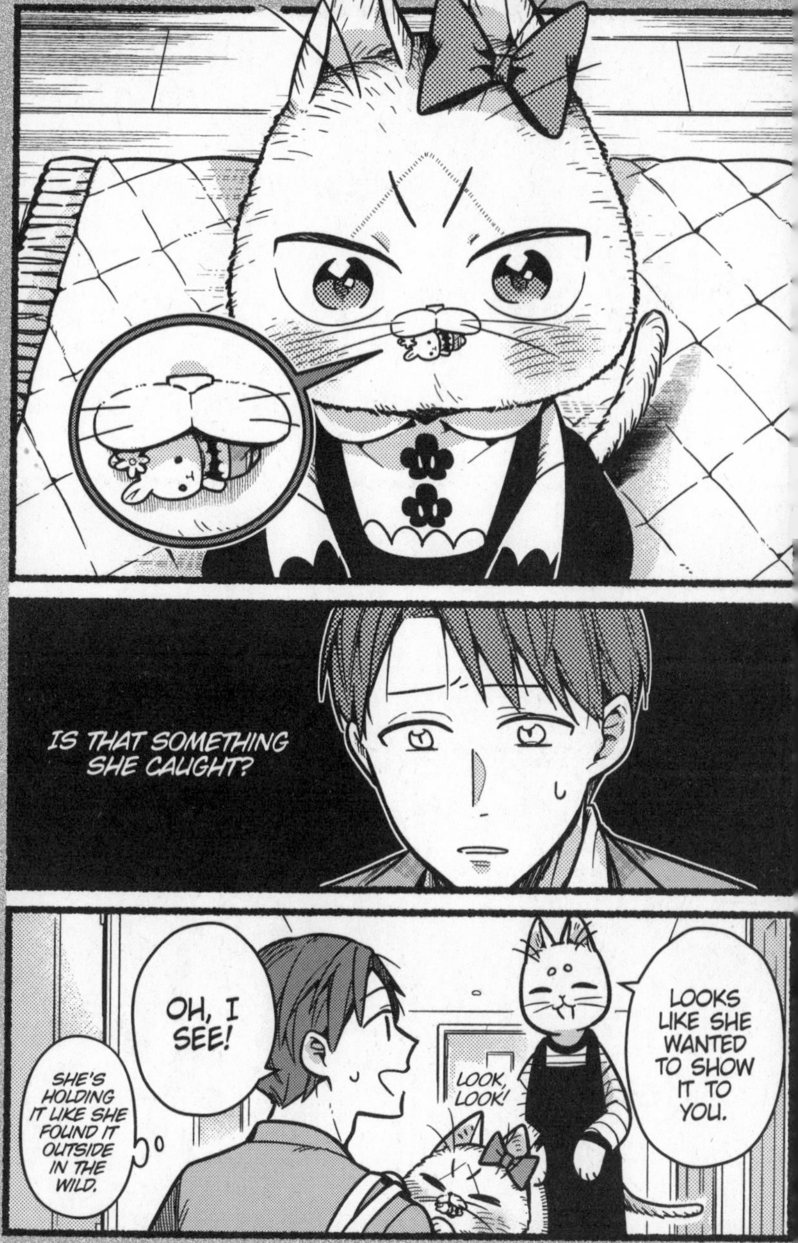
IS THAT SOMETHING SHE CAUGHT?
LOOKS LIKE SHE WANTED TO SHOW IT TO YOU.
LOOK, LOOK!
OH, I SEE!
SHE'S HOLDING IT LIKE SHE FOUND IT OUTSIDE IN THE WILD.

My Sister, the Cat

Snippet: Nekota and Neneko

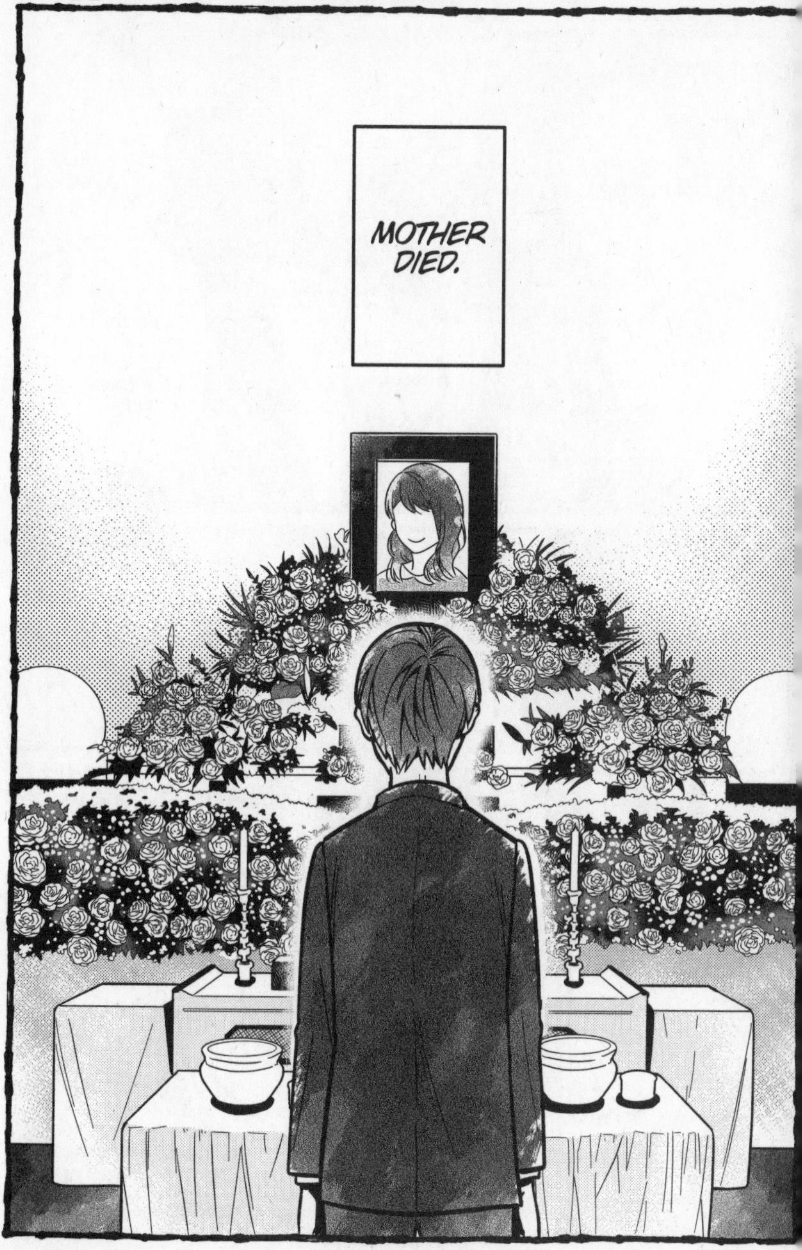
MOTHER DIED.

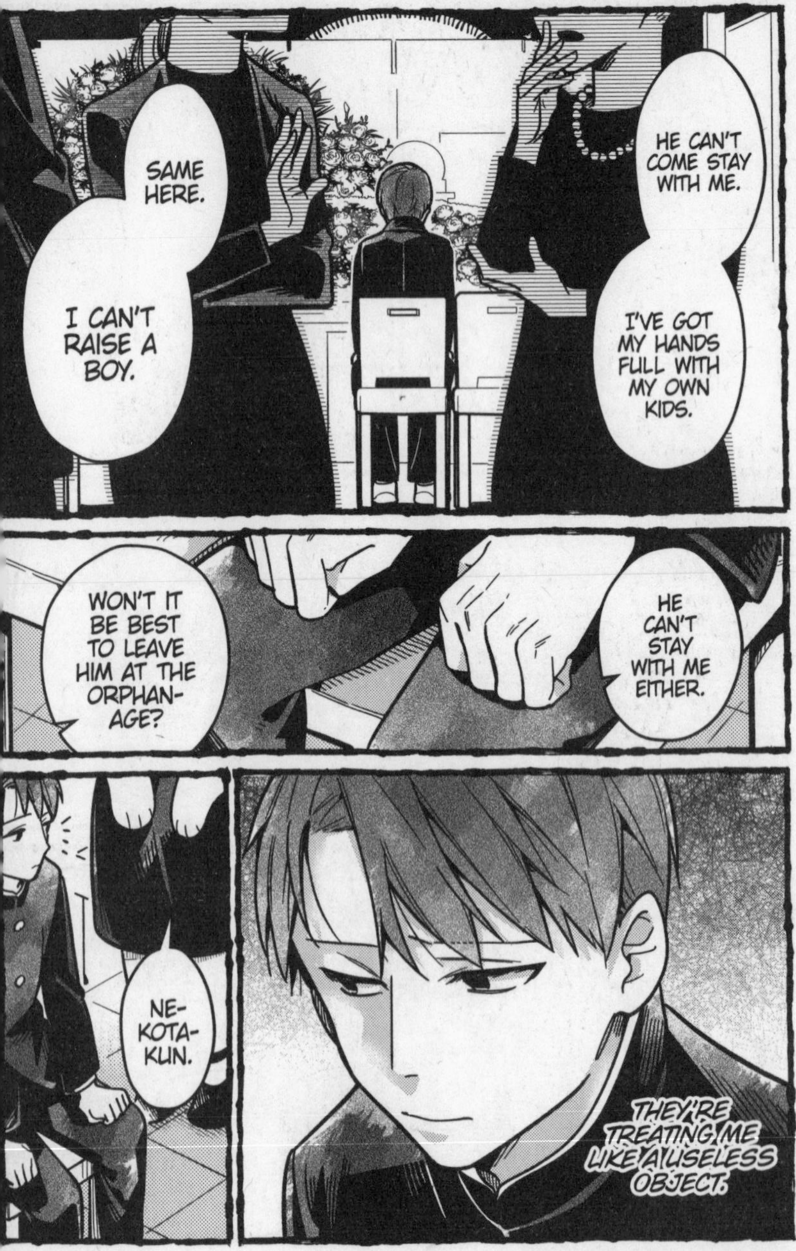
HE CAN'T COME STAY WITH ME.
I'VE GOT MY HANDS FULL WITH MY OWN KIDS.
SAME HERE.
I CAN'T RAISE A BOY.
HE CAN'T STAY WITH ME EITHER.
WON'T IT BE BEST TO LEAVE HIM AT THE ORPHAN-AGE?
THEY'RE TREATING ME LIKE A USELESS OBJECT.
NE-KOTA-KUN.

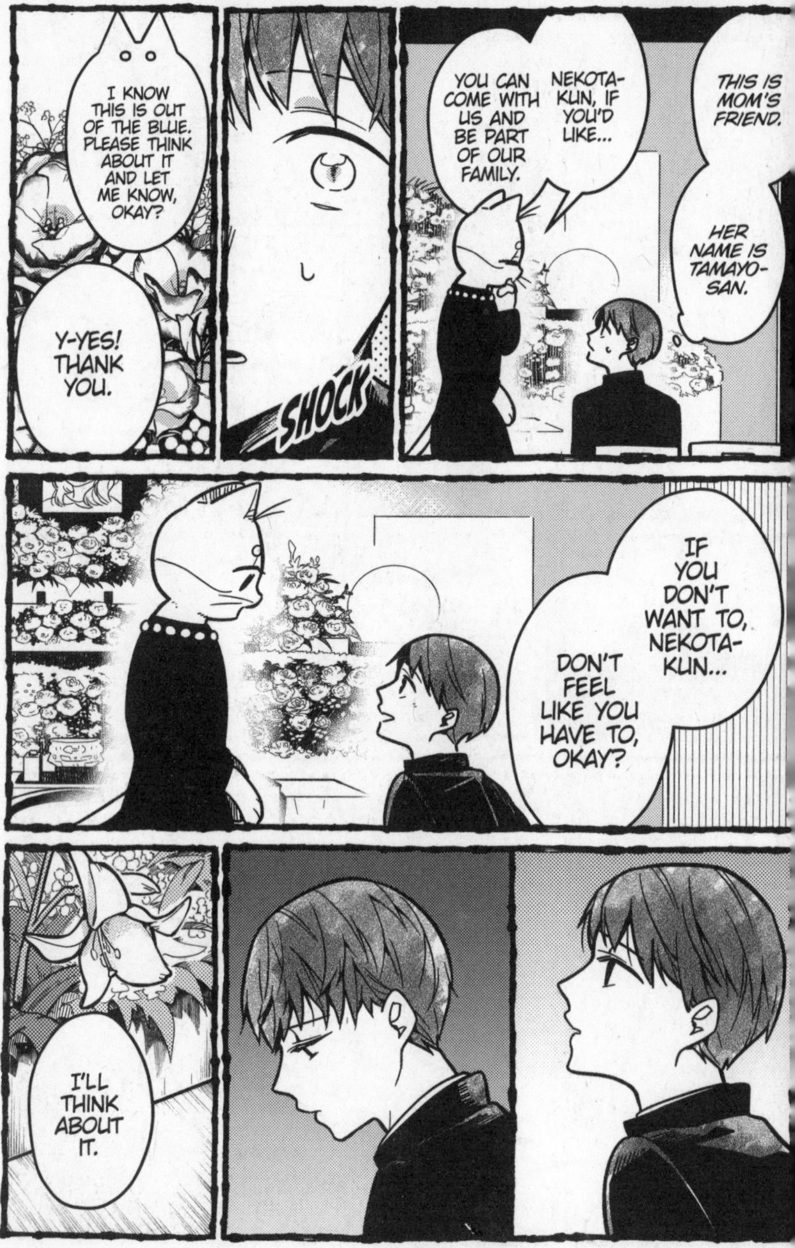
THIS IS MOM'S FRIEND.
HER NAME IS TAMAYO-SAN.
NEKOTA-KUN, IF YOU'D LIKE...
YOU CAN COME WITH US AND BE PART OF OUR FAMILY.
SHOCK
I KNOW THIS IS OUT OF THE BLUE. PLEASE THINK ABOUT IT AND LET ME KNOW, OKAY?
Y-YES! THANK YOU.
IF YOU DON'T WANT TO, NEKOTA-KUN...
DON'T FEEL LIKE YOU HAVE TO, OKAY?
I'LL THINK ABOUT IT.

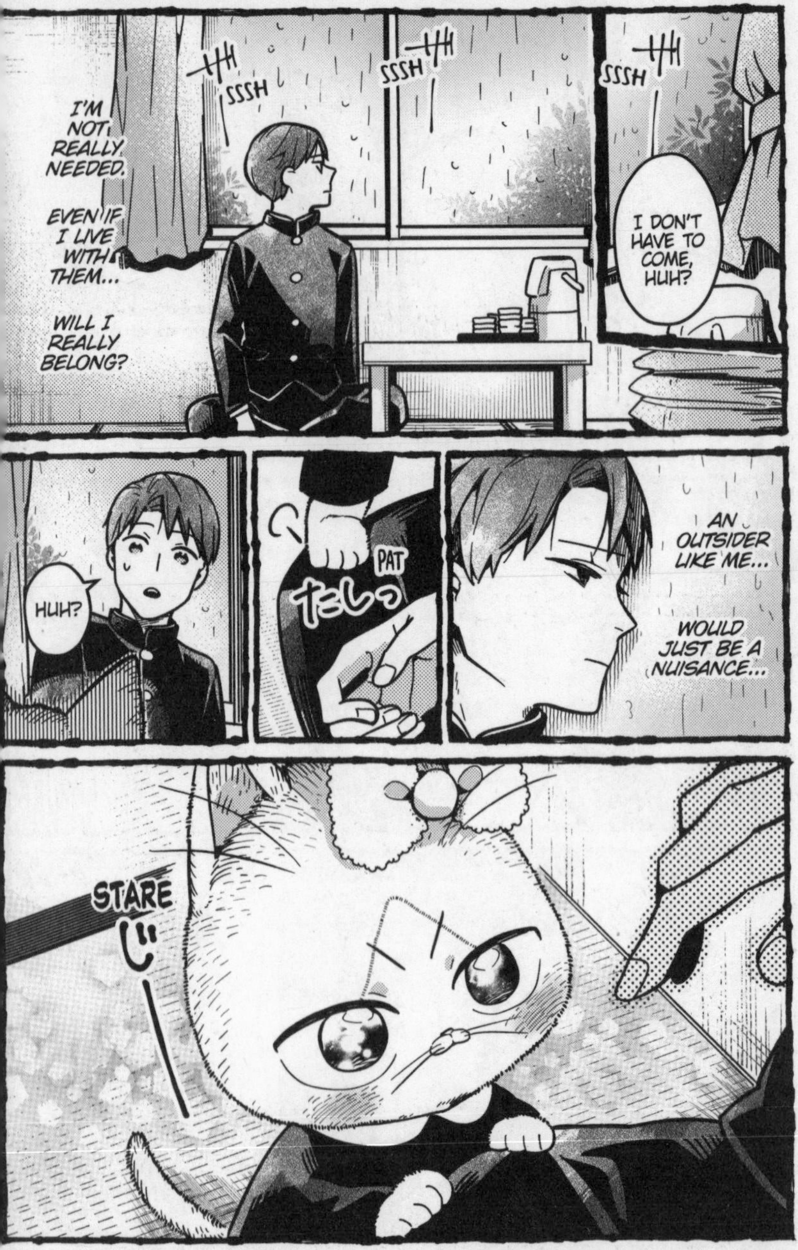
SSSH
I DON'T HAVE TO COME, HUH?
SSSH
SSSH
I'M NOT REALLY NEEDED.
EVEN IF I LIVE WITH THEM...
WILL I REALLY BELONG?
AN OUTSIDER LIKE ME...
WOULD JUST BE A NUISANCE...
PAT
たしっ
HUH?
STARE
じー

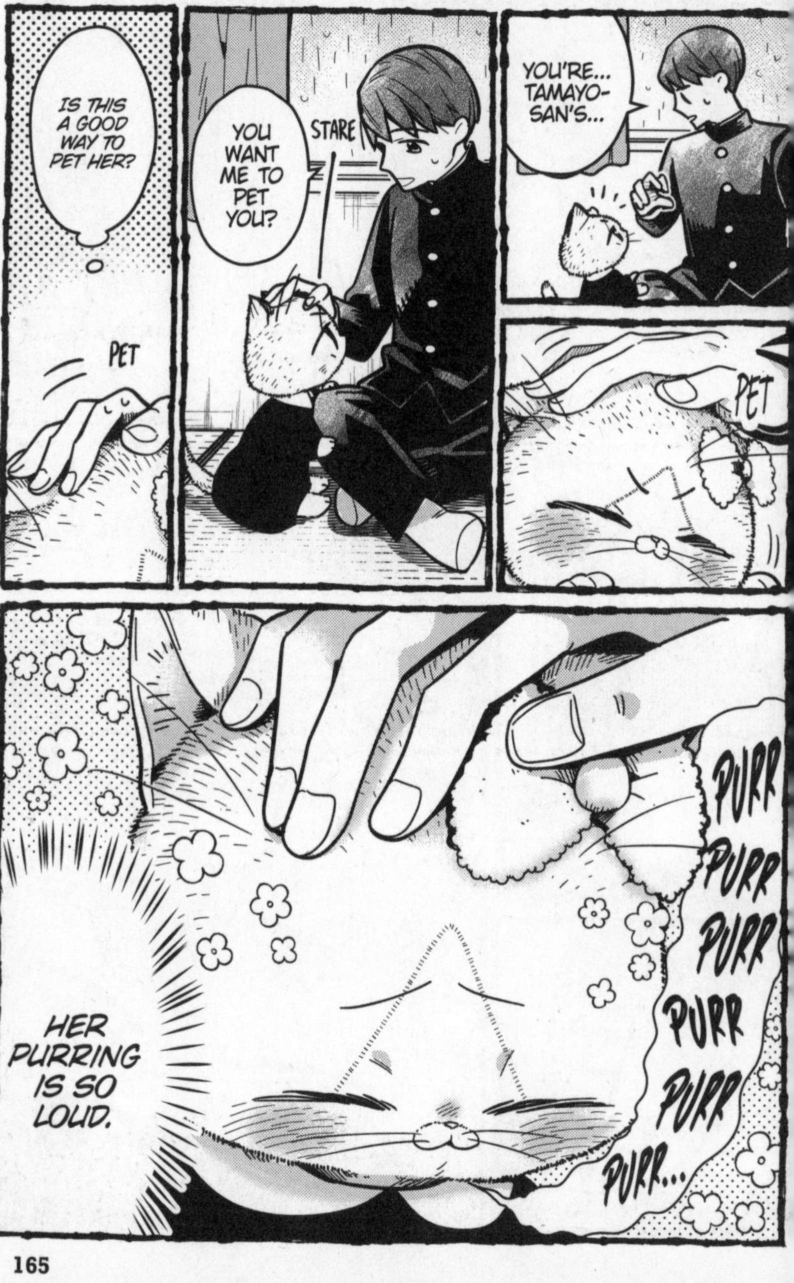
YOU'RE... TAMAYO-SAN'S...
PET
STARE
YOU WANT ME TO PET YOU?
IS THIS A GOOD WAY TO PET HER?
PET
PURR
PURR
PURR
PURR
PURR
PURR...
HER PURRING IS SO LOUD.

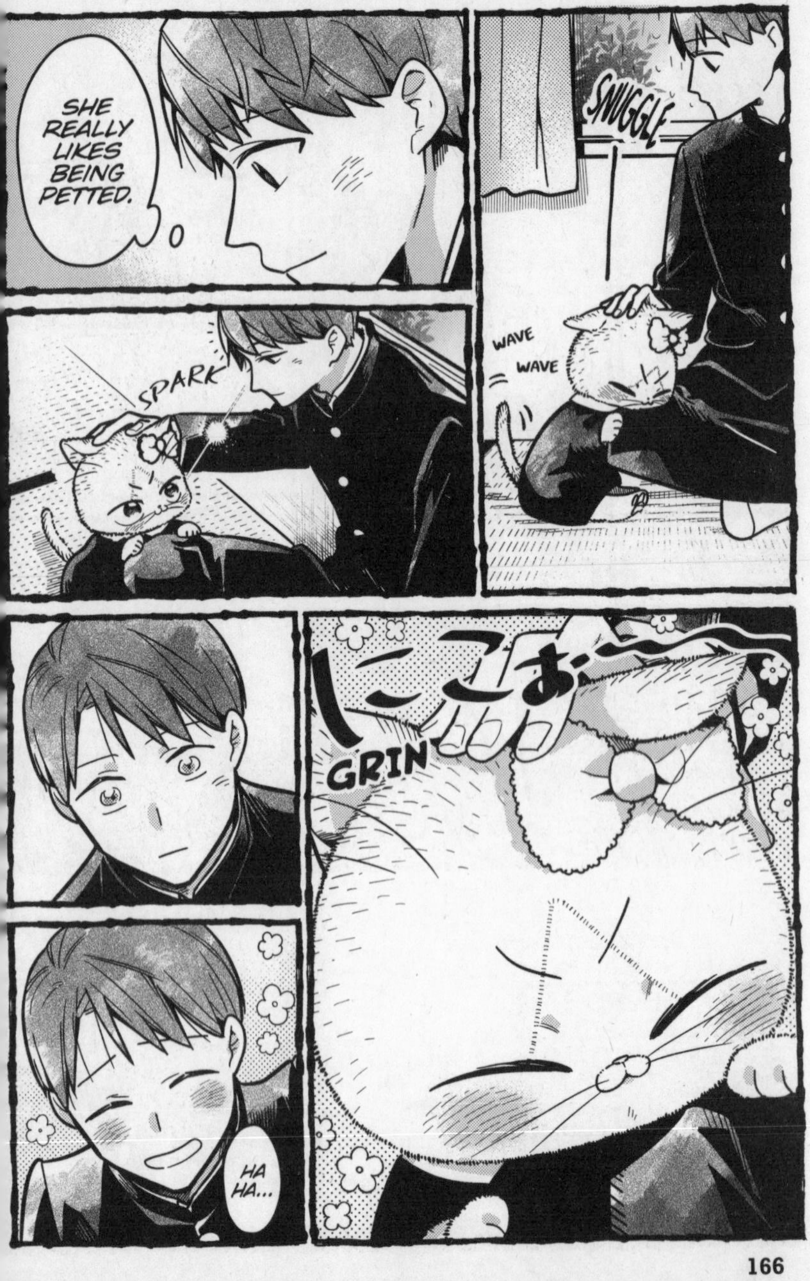
SNUGGLE
WAVE WAVE
SHE REALLY LIKES BEING PETTED.
SPARK
にこぉ~
GRIN
HA HA...

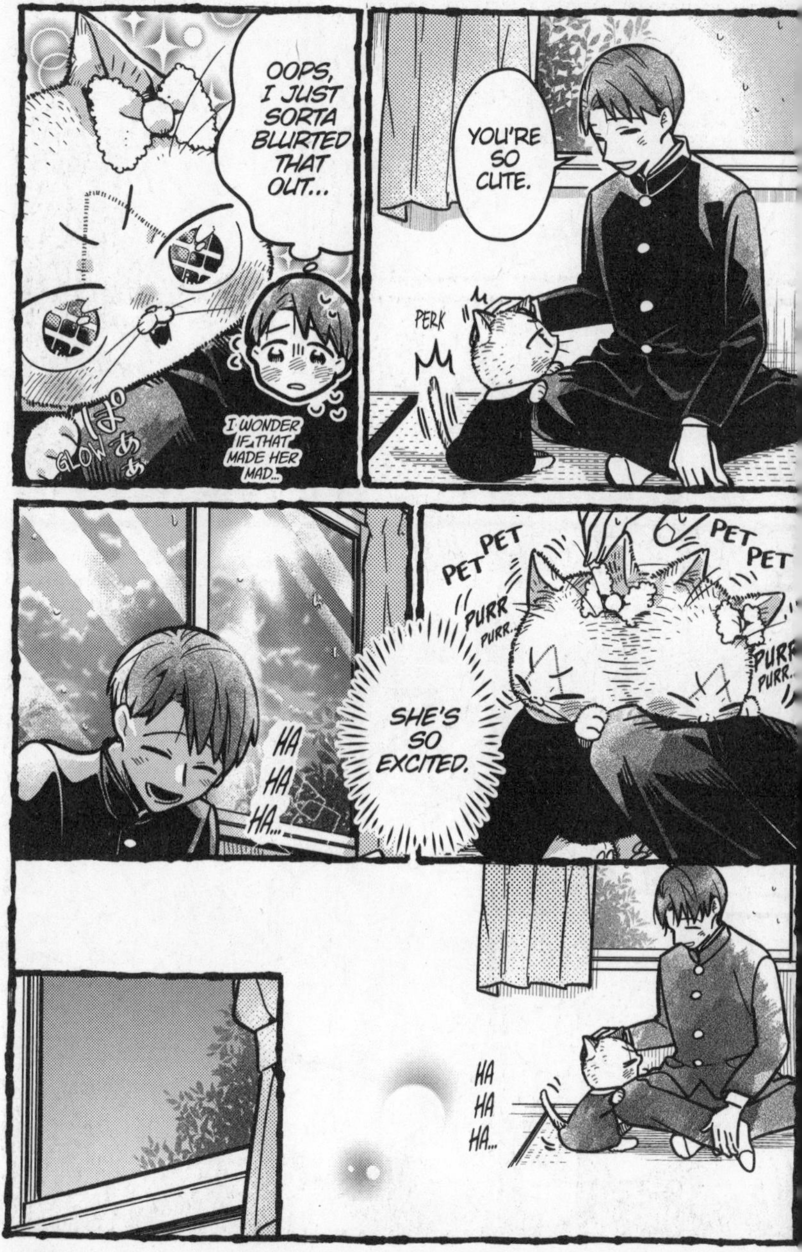
YOU'RE SO CUTE.
PERK
OOPS, I JUST SORTA BLURTED THAT OUT...
I WONDER IF THAT MADE HER MAD...
GLOW
PET PET
PET PET
PURR PURR..
PURR PURR..
SHE'S SO EXCITED.
HA HA HA...
HA HA HA...

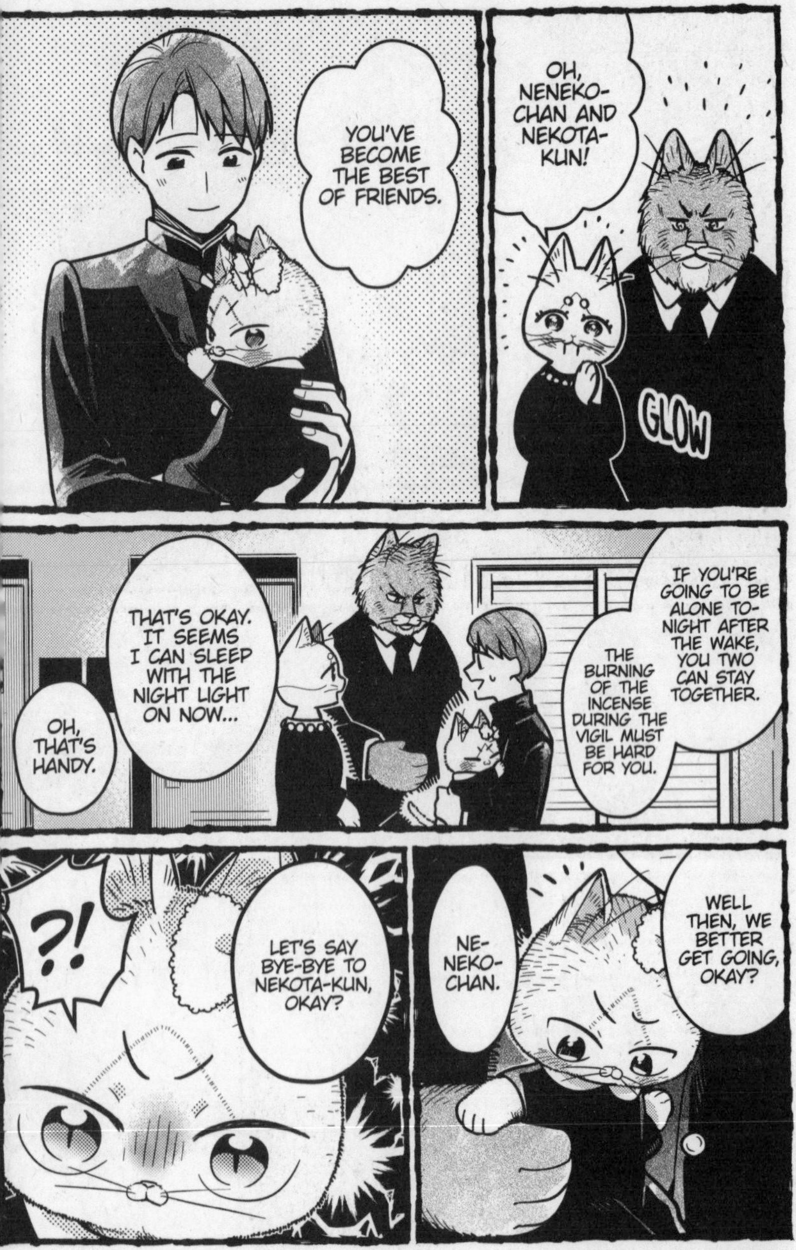
OH, NENEKO-CHAN AND NEKOTA-KUN!
GLOW
YOU'VE BECOME THE BEST OF FRIENDS.
IF YOU'RE GOING TO BE ALONE TONIGHT AFTER THE WAKE, YOU TWO CAN STAY TOGETHER.
THE BURNING OF THE INCENSE DURING THE VIGIL MUST BE HARD FOR YOU.
THAT'S OKAY. IT SEEMS I CAN SLEEP WITH THE NIGHT LIGHT ON NOW...
OH, THAT'S HANDY.
WELL THEN, WE BETTER GET GOING, OKAY?
NE-NEKO-CHAN.
LET'S SAY BYE-BYE TO NEKOTA-KUN, OKAY?
?!

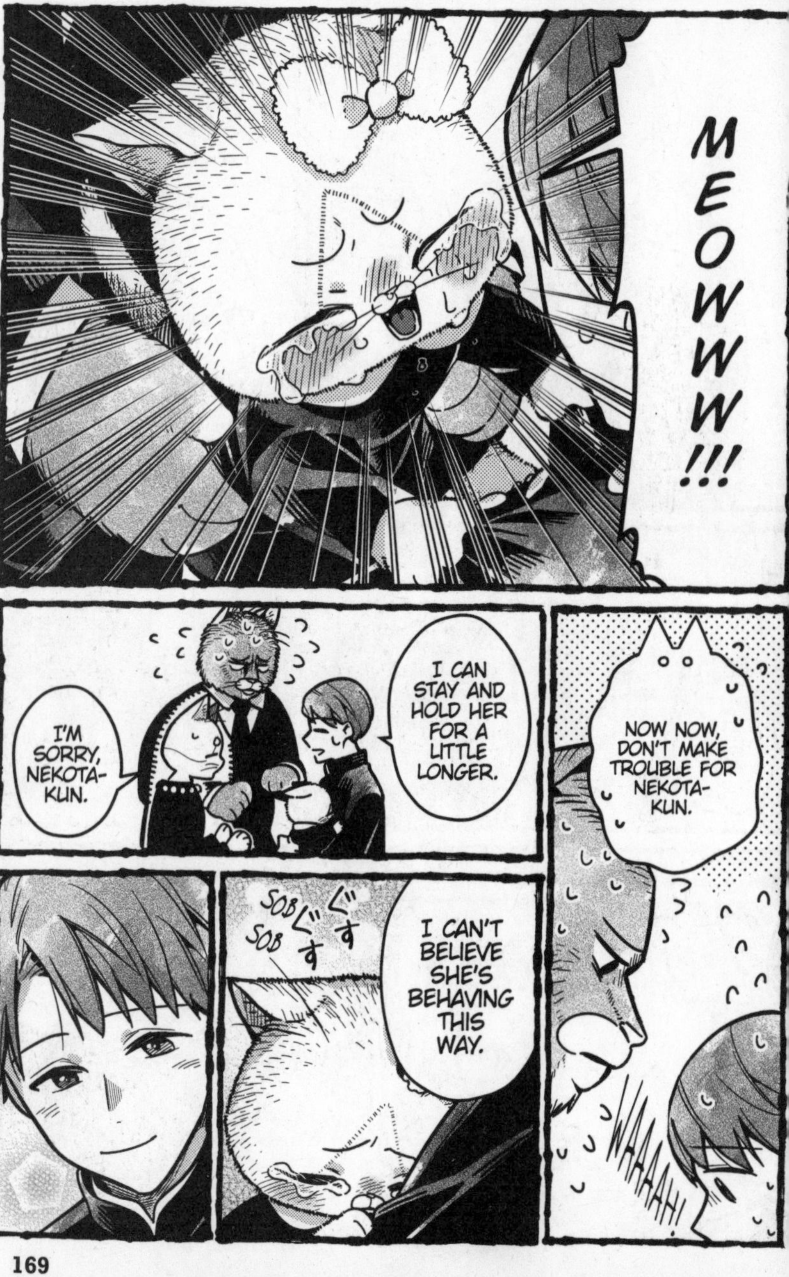
MEOWWW!!!
NOW NOW, DON'T MAKE TROUBLE FOR NEKOTA-KUN.
WAAAAH!
I CAN STAY AND HOLD HER FOR A LITTLE LONGER.
I'M SORRY, NEKOTA-KUN.
ぐすぐす
SOB SOB
I CAN'T BELIEVE SHE'S BEHAVING THIS WAY.

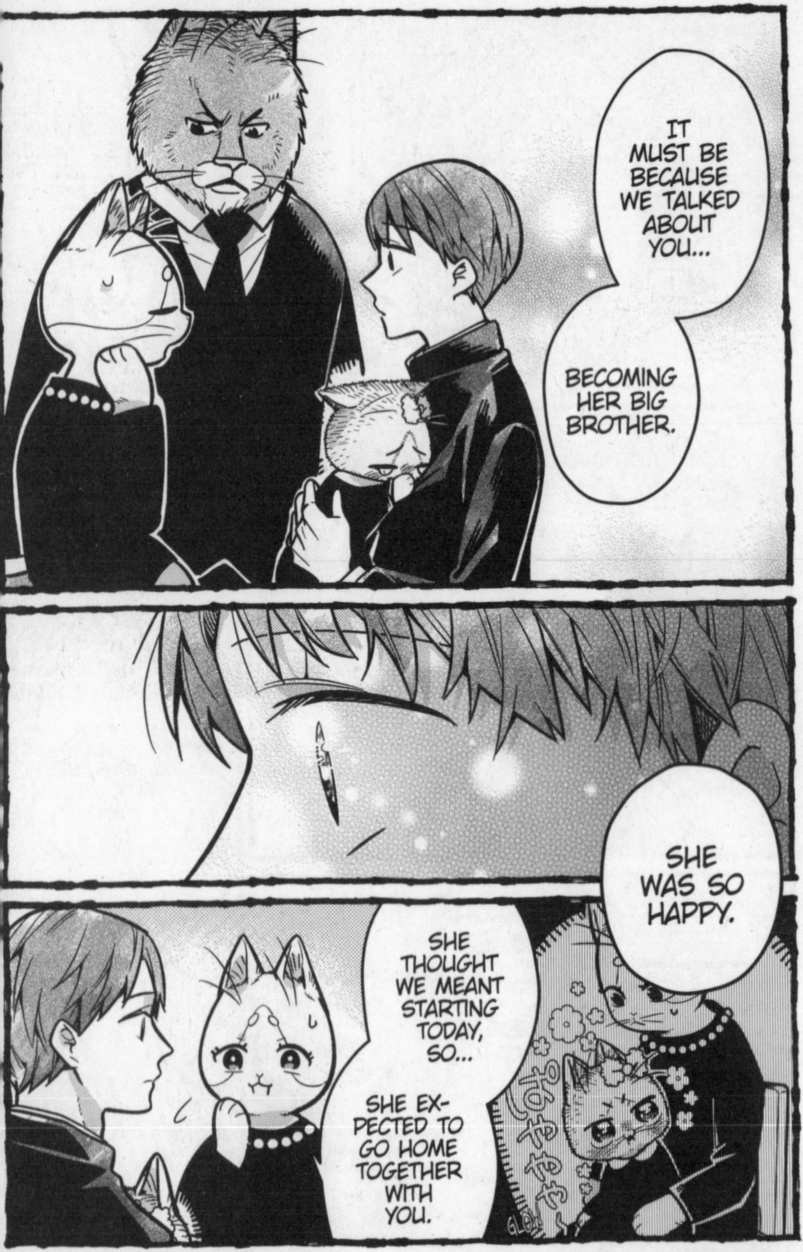
IT MUST BE BECAUSE WE TALKED ABOUT YOU...
BECOMING HER BIG BROTHER.
SHE WAS SO HAPPY.
SHE THOUGHT WE MEANT STARTING TODAY, SO...
SHE EX-PECTED TO GO HOME TOGETHER WITH YOU.
GLOW

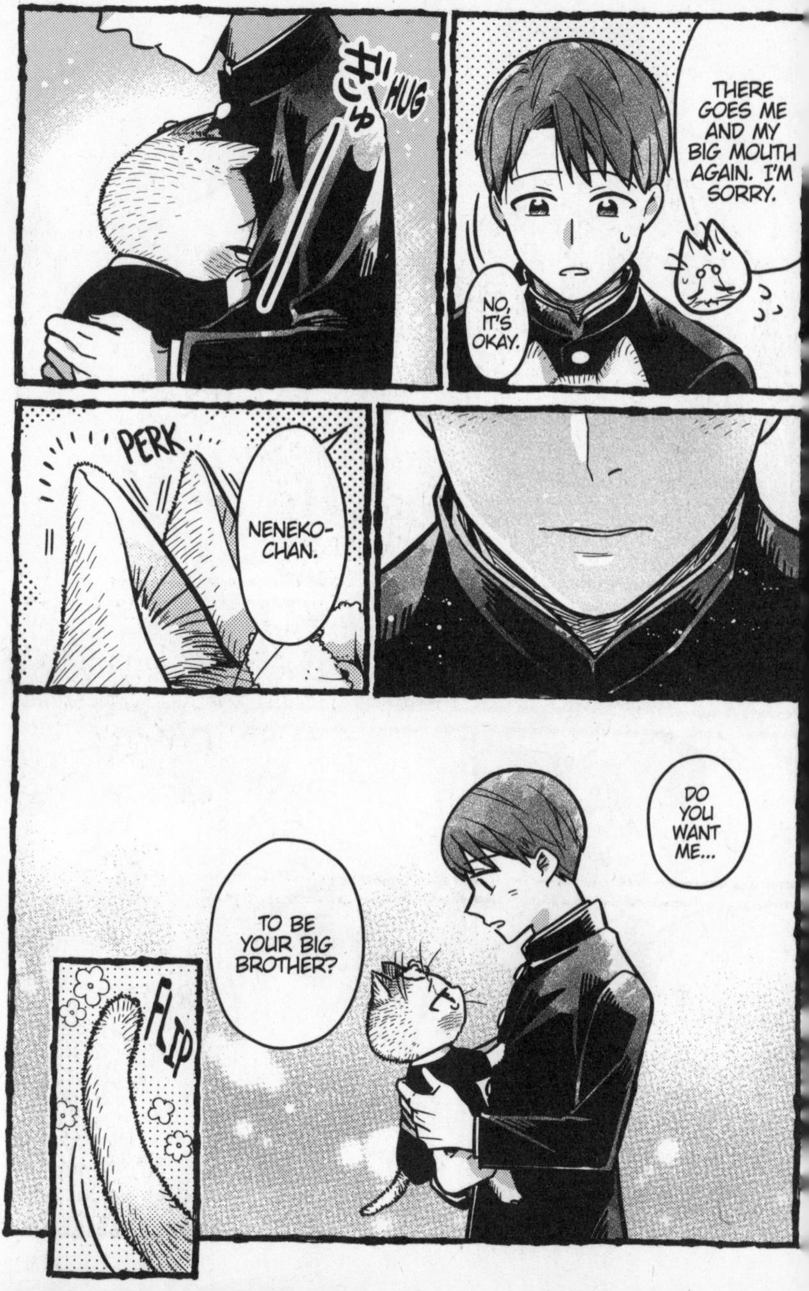
THERE GOES ME AND MY BIG MOUTH AGAIN. I'M SORRY.
NO, IT'S OKAY.
HUG
NENEKO-CHAN.
PERK
DO YOU WANT ME...
TO BE YOUR BIG BROTHER?
FLIP

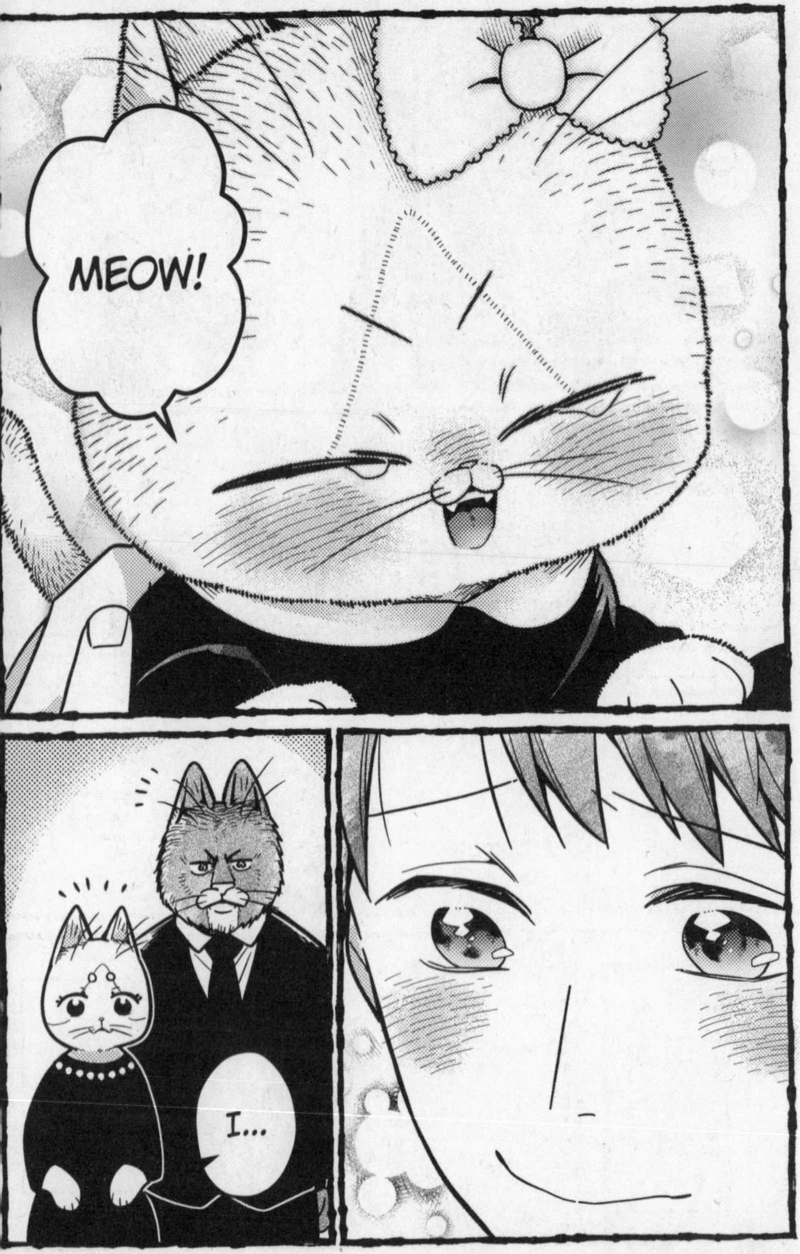
MEOW!
I...

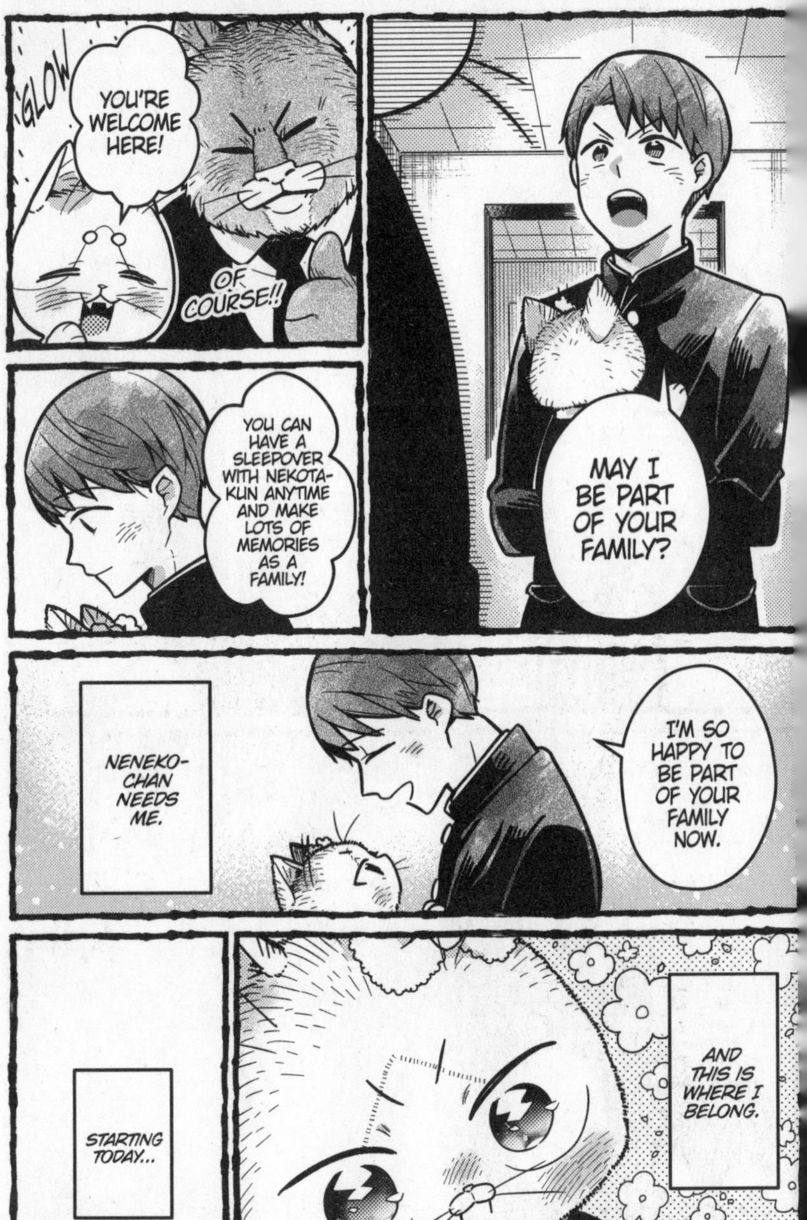
MAY I BE PART OF YOUR FAMILY?
YOU'RE WELCOME HERE!
GLOW
OF COURSE!!
YOU CAN HAVE A SLEEPOVER WITH NEKOTA-KUN ANYTIME AND MAKE LOTS OF MEMORIES AS A FAMILY!
I'M SO HAPPY TO BE PART OF YOUR FAMILY NOW.
NENEKO-CHAN NEEDS ME.
AND THIS IS WHERE I BELONG.
STARTING TODAY...

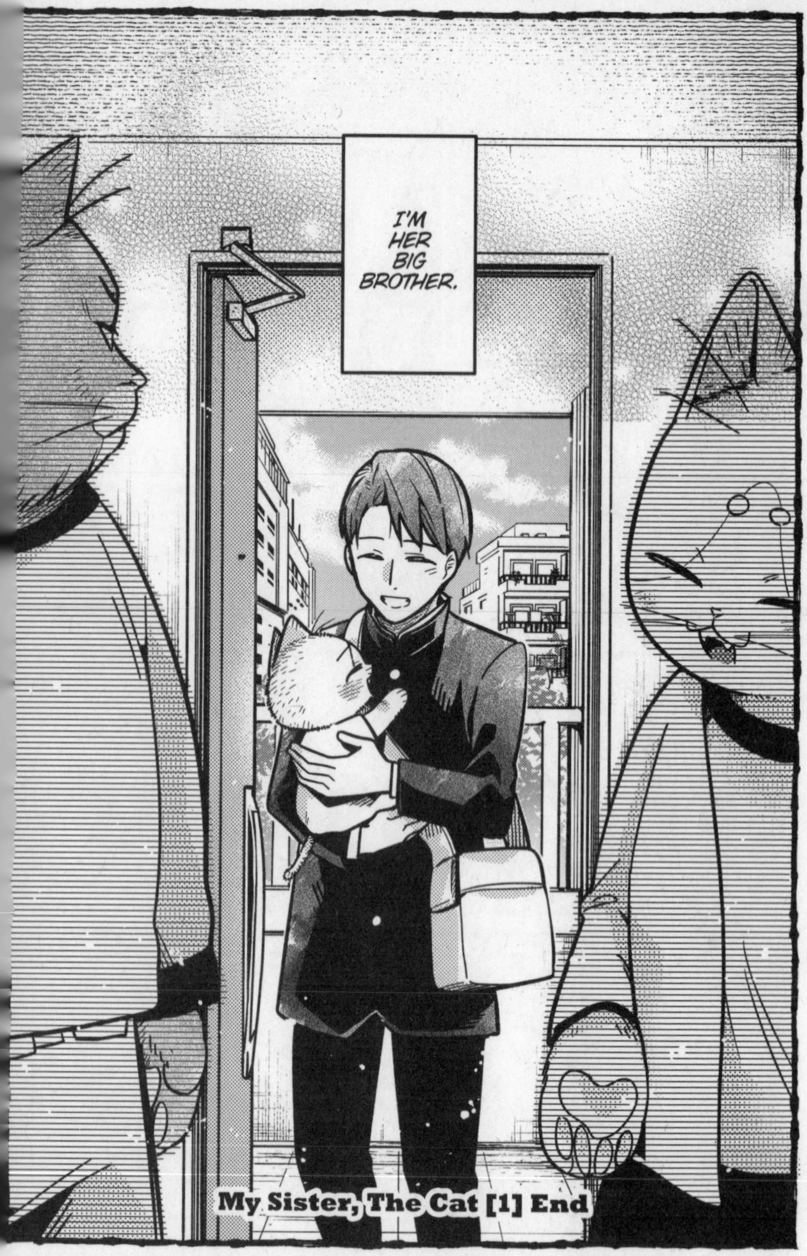
I'M HER BIG BROTHER.
My Sister, The Cat [1] End